The Borderlands of Southeast Asia: Geopolitics, Terrorism, and Globalization

Published by Books Express Publishing
Copyright © Books Express, 2011
ISBN 978-1-780399-22-5

Books Express publications are available from all good retail and online booksellers. For publishing proposals and direct ordering please contact us at: info@books-express.com

The Borderlands of Southeast Asia: Geopolitics, Terrorism, and Globalization

Edited by James Clad, Sean M. McDonald, and Bruce Vaughn

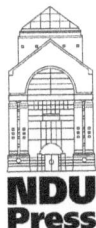

PUBLISHED FOR THE
CENTER FOR STRATEGIC RESEARCH
INSTITUTE FOR NATIONAL STRATEGIC STUDIES
BY NATIONAL DEFENSE UNIVERSITY PRESS
WASHINGTON, D.C.
2011

Contents

Illustrations

Introduction

As an academic field in its own right, the topic of border studies is experiencing a revival in university geography courses as well as in wider political commentary.

Of course, something about the postmodernist sensibility readily embraces the ambiguity, impermanence, transience, and twilight nature of bordered spaces among the planet's 192 territorially defined states. But we have another motivation in assembling this book, one rooted in contemporary rivalries sited in one of the world's most open regions.

Until recently, border studies in contemporary Southeast Asia appeared as an afterthought at best to the politics of interstate rivalry and national consolidation. The maps set out all agreed postcolonial lines. Meanwhile, the physical demarcation of these boundaries lagged. Large slices of territory, on land and at sea, eluded definition or delineation.

That comforting ambiguity has disappeared. Both evolving technologies and price levels enable rapid resource extraction in places, and in volumes, once scarcely imaginable. The old adage that God really does have a sense of humor ("after all, look where He/She put the oil") holds as true in Southeast Asia as in the Middle East.

The beginning of the 21st century's second decade is witnessing an intensifying diplomacy, both state-to-state and commercial, over offshore petroleum. In particular, the South China Sea has moved from being a rather arcane area of conflict studies to the status of a bellwether issue. Along with other contested areas in the western Pacific and south Asia, the problem increasingly defines China's regional relationships in Asia—and with powers outside the region, especially the United States.

Yet intraregional territorial differences also hobble multilateral diplomacy to counter Chinese claims. For the region's national governments, the window for submission and adjudication of maritime claims under the United Nations Convention on the Law of the Seas marks a legal checkpoint, but daily management of borders remains burdened by retrospective baggage.

The contributors to this book emphasize this mix of heritage and history as the primary leitmotif for contemporary border rivalries and dynamics. Whether the region's 11 states want it or not, their bordered identity is falling into ever sharper definition—if only because of pressure from extraregional states.

Chinese state and commercial power dovetails almost seamlessly with Beijing's formal territorial demands. Yet subregional rivalries and latent suspicions also remain firmly in place—as in those among Singapore, Indonesia, and Malaysia, or between Thailand and those states that encircle the kingdom. Tracing back to its history of tributary states, the Chinese colossus has fixed views about all states contiguous to its territory; in some Chinese dialects, Vietnam is still referred to as a "renegade province."

We chose to organize the chapters by country to elicit a broad range of thought and approach as much as for the specific areas or nation-states examined in each chapter. For both Southeast Asia and the outside world, the current era portends another unsettled period of border disputes and contentious territorial claims. Complex claims also have unsettled the Arctic and inland seas like the Caspian.

The precision we laud in global positioning and tracking systems has also wreaked havoc on the apparent certainties bequeathed by all the carefully surveyed (at least by 19th-century standards) boundaries left behind by the departing colonial powers. Of course, these new uncertainties about the place on the terrain of exact map coordinates can probably remain safely unsettled for a long time—but only so long as no resource discoveries emerge, which can lift the problem from obscurity to prominence in the political equivalent of a heartbeat.

Each chapter aims to provide new ways of looking at the reality and illusion of bordered Southeast Asia. We hope this volume marks the first of a series offering a similar variety of perspectives into the working of the Westphalian system in different parts of Asia—and the wider world.

We would like to thank the administration of Bentley University, which provided a generous amount of time, research, and publication support, and we remain grateful for the faith they have consistently shown in our efforts. We would also like to thank the United States–Indonesian Society for the travel research grant that enabled the authors to conduct field work in support of this project.

We would like to acknowledge the Institute for National Strategic Studies (INSS) at the National Defense University (NDU) for providing funding for this book's publication. We thank Lew Stern at INSS for initially recommending publication and Phillip Saunders at the Center for Strategic Research for reviewing and refining the manuscript; NDU Press, particularly Lisa Yambrick, for editing the manuscript and managing the publication process; and the Center for Strategic Conferencing, particularly Gerald Faber, for developing a targeted distribution strategy for the book.

Chapter 1

Delineation and Borders in Southeast Asia

James Clad

A comfortingly vague concept, *globalization*, became fashionable after the end of the Cold War. Obsessed by the dramatic immediacy of new global communication technologies, as well as by the annually doubling or trebling of passenger air miles flown and an increasingly prevalent human mobility in general, converts to the globalization creed lost their sense of proportion.

For starters, they assumed an irreversible global democratic agenda. In their uncritical lauding of ever freer trade, they also assumed an unending global readiness to lie supine before the crushing economies of scale that China and other emerging mega-manufacturers (India and Brazil sense their moment has also arrived) have consolidated in successive rounds of trade liberalization. Other trends also went "global"—terrorism, climate change, pollution, human trafficking, money laundering, and criminality.

Their most serious error stemmed from an implicit belief that national boundaries were destined somehow to fade away before the forces of globalization—an error leading to a conviction that we had already begun to inhabit a borderless world, a place where political boundaries had become passé and where people moved about without restraint ("the world is flat" was one refrain, meaning that everything was accessible to all).

During the last two decades, the academic literature focused on "agents of globalization"—whether ordinary travelers, smugglers, illegal migrants, petty traders, mainline exporters, or even terrorists bent on a specific job. In nearly all cases, the world became increasingly "globalized" as the expansion of Europe proceeded apace, though mobility through invasion or trading links predated that by several millennia. What changed the world was not mobility per se, but rather the arrival and gradual imposition on the rest of the world of a strange 17th-century matrix, a structure of economic, political, and social reality resting on thousands of kilometers of imaginary but rigidly enforced lines placed on and over both land and water.

One might argue that the pre-Westphalian world saw more globalization than later times. For the truth is, national borders can and do stop people in their tracks. Postmodernist writers correctly describe political borders as imaginary social constructs, but these abstractions shut out people as effectively as the toughest topography or stormiest sea. Even contemporary air transportation, which transcends all surface geography, has run into many post-9/11 restrictions. A wary world regulates air travel with new vigor, fueled by political reaction from the bordered world to the perceived *threat* of a borderless world.

Far from opening the truly borderless arena in which people may move at whim, the near future augurs even more readiness to monitor borders as governments react to public clamor for tighter controls. An extraordinary array of monitoring and interdiction technologies has emerged from private and government laboratories, increasingly inexpensive and readily available devices that can be easily installed in an afternoon on an open field or in airport departure lounges. Interdiction can and does occur from computers or closed-circuit television monitoring a "virtual border," boundaries wholly without identifying structures and frontiers policed by fused technologies—radar, sound sensors, night vision aids, unmanned aerial vehicles, motion sensors, and radio wave interruption devices.

While heightened concern about terrorism has prompted new border monitoring, the primal fear focuses on visions of unending waves of third-world migration—a vision that preoccupies the nations of Southeast Asia with rapidly growing economies, as governments devise new internal laws and root out illegally arriving economic migrants. Elsewhere, an emerging consensus in Organisation for Economic Co-operation and Development countries is that borders are the sole remaining barrier, lines that crucially obstruct, confine, protect, shelter, impede, *or* facilitate—but only as and when trade or tourism requires *permeable* boundaries.

Most of all, borders *define.* In Southeast Asia, they define the nascent but steadily more confident state-centered nationalism, heir to the departed, territorially defined European empires. China's increasingly assertive insistence upon its claim to the entirety of the South China Sea (SCS) hangs like a specter over the lines of maritime territory and exclusive economic zones created by the 1970s United Nations (UN) Law of the Sea. Southeast Asian countries zealously guard their common

Map 1–1. Southeast Asia

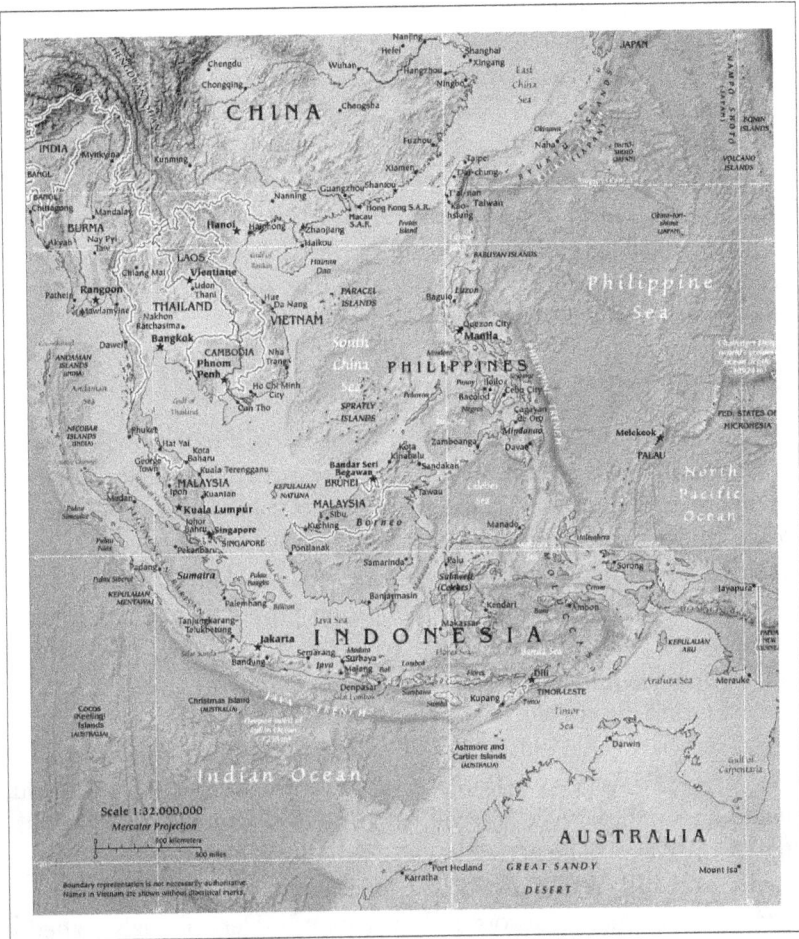

borders; where disagreement about borders prevails, the resulting tensions belie the smiling equanimity of the Association of Southeast Asian Nations (ASEAN), which projects the illusion of an economic community solidified by common purpose.

Therefore, to suggest that we now live beyond borders seems at variance with countervailing trends, both globally and regionally, that are making borders *more* durable, enforceable, and omnipresent. In global terms, entirely new sovereign borderlines have emerged in recent years (just the dissolution of Yugoslavia and the Soviet Union created 26 new sovereignties) where none existed before; regionally, East Timor emerged from the Indonesian archipelago, finding little welcome from a region suspicious of all drives for local autonomy.

As it happens, the last 60 years have witnessed the most rapid cumulative *lengthening* of international boundaries since the Treaty of Westphalia in 1648 legitimized the "inviolable international line" in European statecraft. After the 1960s, decolonization dramatically increased the length of all the world's sovereign borderlines; if we were to splice every current international boundary line end to end, the total mileage would reach to the Moon and beyond.

The Perfectly Surveyed State

Outside the West, the existence of fixed international borders originated in European colonialism. The dream of the perfectly surveyed territorial state found articulation in events such as the 1899 Hague Peace Convention. The idea that a world of bordered entities meant a world at peace found its way into a slew of pre–World War I border demarcation manuals; the first publication produced by the Carnegie Endowment for International Peace after its formation in 1910 was a border demarcation manual.

During the era of what might be called "direct administrative imperialism" between 1880 and 1914, colonial boundary commissioners and imperial surveyors tramped around the non-Western world, including Southeast Asia, a term that came into common use only during World War II. The perfectly surveyed state depended on what were known as the "three Ds": definition, delimitation, and demarcation.

The colonial surveyors and their joint border tribunals crafted a world that is still found on 21st-century political maps. The Royal Geographical Society in London contracted out the services of its surveyors, who cheerfully worked as surveyor-spies as they demarcated steamy or torrid frontiers, breathtaking alpine heights, or desert wastes. In Southeast Asia, borders dividing states almost always emerged from deals *between* the colonial powers. Only rarely did they arise from local accommodations to European territorial pressure—as happened in Thailand, which to this day is not reconciled to boundaries imposed on it by expansionist pressures from French Indochina and British Burma. (Bangkok's only fully settled boundary separates it from peninsular Malaysia.)

What type of boundaries emerged? The region's state frontiers often show some geographic logic, following topography or coastline. But boundary markers also march in rigid lines across challenging topography, dividing ethnicities and slicing through villages or river valleys. From a distance, outsiders accept these lines as normal, if only from force of map-reading habit. But the European legacy—a world of states *whose theoretical sovereignty runs without break right up to the limits of a bordered national territory*—has become just as fiercely defended a norm in Southeast Asia as it is elsewhere around the world.

Here we tread squarely on "mental geography" and people's "spatial positioning." Except for members of the region's commercially active ethnic minorities—most notably the Chinese but also other Asians and resident Western expatriates—Southeast Asia's resident populations now identify with parcels of land separated by lines originating in European turf disputes. *All* states are artifacts, of course. But Southeast Asia's expanding middle classes, urban dwellers, and governing elites unthinkingly carry these legacy lines in their heads whenever they view their surrounding world. In the West, we do the same, of course— but those lines are *our* constructs. Insofar as broad and unconscious acceptance of formal delineated boundaries is concerned, we can say that 60 years of Southeast Asian nation-building have perpetuated the mental dominion of Europe.

Boundaries are synonymous with identity. Postcolonial experience in Southeast Asia shows an intense insistence on maintaining the boundaries imposed by competing European states, sometimes almost as acts of whimsy. This mirrors the bedrock norms of African or Middle Eastern states. Beyond the lowly border guard, Southeast Asia's border protectors include scholars, journalists, diplomats, bureaucrats, and lawyers. Each invests the new nations' prestige by rejecting affronts to the territorial status quo. The same fear of an unraveling order prompts insistence on living with what has been bequeathed to the region.

When defending their national territorial positions, Southeast Asian governments rely on a variety of bequeathed tools from the vanished imperial age. Colonial border commission reports, centuries-old navigator notations, or dusty treaties between rival colonial powers buttress claim and counterclaim. For every accepted bilateral boundary, dozens of lines remain imprecise. And Southeast Asia faces a maritime border challenge from China, which bases its vague and contestable assertion of a right to tens of thousands of square kilometers of ocean on the continuing traversal of that ocean by Chinese people. "Since time immemorial, the South China Sea has been China's," Beijing proclaims. Even its name, China insists, proclaims ownership.

Though shrouded in arcane reasoning, these disputes have real-world immediacy. Miscalculation and national pride can spark, and have periodically ignited, armed hostilities—in the SCS as well as in other areas discussed in this book. Sharp encounters since the 1970s attest to this, the most recent standoff occurring between Cambodia and Thailand over sovereign ownership of an ancient Buddhist temple site—a lucrative source of revenue from tourism. Yet the more serious of these disagreements, especially those involving external claimants such as China, can quickly expand the dispute as outside states proclaim their own equities, as the United States has done in recent years regarding the SCS, where China's claims conflict with those of five other states.

By the beginning of the 21st century's second decade, successive U.S. administrations were signaling unease about unilateral moves to increase bargaining positions for resources and maritime passageways. In June 2008, Defense Secretary Robert Gates spoke of a "global commons" in the seas, the air, and cyberspace that needed to be respected. His audience, a gathering of defense officials in Singapore, knew exactly what he meant to convey to the Chinese authorities: that unilateral territorial ambitions in the East and in the South China Seas had elicited an American strategic watchfulness. Beyond this new articulation of respect for the global commons, American interests in Southeast Asia's border disputes remain anchored in traditional U.S. insistence on freedom of navigation or in bilateral security obligations to some regional states.

Dimensions to a Bordered Southeast Asia

The remaining pages of this chapter traverse a range of border security and borderland issues in an area stretching from India's Naga foothills near Burma to eastern Indonesian islands where the Malay realm either dissolves into Micronesia or approaches continental Australia. One such dimension concerns a nuanced memory of these borders' colonial origins. Another delves into activities both defined and enabled by the lawless frontiers and borderland nature of the region's many peripheral places that now appear as problems in national agendas, such as suppression of illicit trade or discouragement of unilateral action such as China's building many dams along the upstream Mekong River.

A more conventional approach to regional borders looks at successes, or the lack thereof, in solving, shelving, or otherwise defusing the long list of residual territorial disputes. This method includes mention by the contributors to this book of the ASEAN states' resource diplomacy or efforts to fashion legal regimes to exploit oil and natural gas in contested maritime areas. This approach reflects what might be called a "foreign ministry agenda" that speaks to dossiers and the legal dimensions of territorial adjudication. In 2001, for example, Malaysia and Indonesia agreed to refer a dispute over some islands near Borneo to the International Court of Justice in The Hague. In 2008, the court delivered a verdict giving each country some, but not all, of what it wanted.

In the SCS, the Southeast Asian states face a China that is inflexible, the correct adjective to describe Beijing's refusal to budge over a claim to assert its sovereignty over the entire SCS.

This enduring difficulty leads in turn to broader questions about the continuing importance of external powers to Southeast Asian security. The regional power equilibrium rests in part on maintaining an uneasy territorial status quo in places like the SCS where rival claimants agree to refrain, at least for the time being, from pressing their differences but refuse to settle them.

Beyond that, which foreign navies accept which maritime areas as international waters? What attitudes and comprehensive borderland and perimeter strategies lie behind Beijing's implacable claim, contested by five Southeast Asian states, to the entirety of the SCS?

Bordering an *Archipel*

In addition to considering physical geography, this book also traverses, explicitly or by implication, what we call Southeast Asia's *mental geography*. Some writers of a more romantic bent have written extensively about the region's "maritime soul." The French word *archipel* captures a sense and a depth of understanding that goes beyond the physical identification of the region primarily as an "archipelago." Irrefutably, the sea defines the reach and temperament of Southeast Asia. "*Tanah Air Kita*," as the Indonesians say, "Our beloved land/water." The Malays add "*Kepulaua*," an abstract noun that can best be translated as "island-ness."

Across the 3,000 miles stretching from the Kra Peninsula and north Sumatra to Ambon and the Spice Islands, only the deep interior of Borneo and the peninsular mainland's river valleys that drain once-forested upland hills can affect indifference to the sea. Right down to the present era, the region's seas acted as natural obstacle *and* highway, as barrier *and* open door. They shaped outlook and mental horizon. They channeled and inhibited movement. Proximity to the sea meant mobility and elastic political identity. Only mainland Southeast Asian and Javanese upland empires developed many deep hierarchies and formal continuities. And even then, cities and surrounding agricultural domains developed languages and concepts entirely at home with owing a gradated allegiance to two, three, or even four nearby kings. Coextensive, territorially defined, and impersonal "sovereignty" came to Southeast Asia as a strange, alien concept.

The colonial era brought enormous material change, but the most important colonial legacy lies in its "geography of the mind." Colonial-era archaeology rediscovered indigenous empires from the distant past that subject peoples later invoked and employed as a national history to contest control of areas delineated by those scientifically surveyed colonial borders.

Though originally drawn in distant European capitals, these borderlines as noted now determine spatial location for nearly all the region's 700 million people. Only a tiny number of "sea gypsies" still roam what are now the islands of Indonesia, Malaysia, and the Philippines. And while hill tribes in Southeast Asia's mainland once crossed colonial borders obliviously and with impunity, today they cannot avoid the pull of modernity and an enforced "bordered" identity. As Burma's long conflicts reveal, mainland hill minorities must accommodate the territorially defined national authority, and they do so from a position of gathering weakness and exposed isolation.

Although Asia experienced roughly 400 years of European intrusion, colonial powers directly governed their subject territories (or ruled indirectly, as in British Malaya) for a very short time. This era of direct administrative imperialism had a big agenda. It included a liberal plan for enlightened rule and administrative order. This same era saw the creation of many boundary commissions and the convening of border determination conferences involving contending European empires.

For local peoples, most of the resulting borderlines arrived as if out of the sky. Indigenous rulers saw them as an outright imposition, a fait accompli, or both. The local kingdoms and sultanates mostly had succumbed to direct European rule by the turn of the last century—notably the Acehnese, Balinese, Burmese, and Makassar states. Only the Thai kingdom preserved some independence; adroit manipulation of competing foreigners may be said to characterize Thai diplomacy even to this day.

All of this occurred quite rapidly in historical terms, between the 1880s and the end of the 20th century's first decade. Like any intruder intent on profit, European traders and the joint stock companies chartered by European sovereigns to advance their interests did everything they could to avoid the cost of direct rule. Only rarely, as in 18th-century Java, did Europeans seize direct and formal power—and even then the Dutch preserved in febrile form the indigenous Solo and Yogyakarta dynasties. Even as Europeans became more overtly the deciding powers in the region, surveyed boundaries usually had to wait.

Most often, intra-European wars and rivalries forced territorial delimitations. The growing list of colonial tasks, from antipiracy patrols to orderly customs collection, forced more collaboration with neighboring colonial powers. This collaboration in turn required administrative order and rationality.

Bit by bit, colonial administrators determined, divided, and demarcated the subject lands for purposes of both control and exclusion. In doing so, they gave their subject peoples a profoundly different conception of space, order, and authority. Princeton University emeritus anthropologist Clifford Geertz has written about differences between foreign and indigenous conceptions of sovereignty in Southeast Asia. In an influential essay, he likened Javanese conceptions of political power to a candle whose light and warmth becomes progressively weaker as one moves away from the flame. By contrast, and especially after the 17th century, European colonizers thought in terms of a distinct territorial entity whose sovereign writ runs *without interruption or diminution* right up to a treaty-defined, latitudinal/longitudinal limit.

British diplomatic dispatches narrating dealings with Burmese kings and Dutch accounts of negotiating with the Mataram kingdom in central Java show this mental disconnect. Territorial segmentation in Southeast Asia happened in a historical hurry, with subject peoples slow to realize the irrevocable changes brought by the surveyor's skills and cadastral surveys.

Still, in the 19th century, frontier ambiguities yielded one by one to the formal, abstract, and rigid logic of longitude and latitude. Often coupled to multipurpose geographical expeditions, border demarcation teams arrived before, or after, periods of intra-European tension. Many pieces were in play. For example, Anglo-French colonial rivalry in Africa saw a French expansionary dynamic going in an east-west direction from Sahel and Central African toeholds. This directional push famously met Britain's north-south thrusting, from Egypt to southern Africa, at Falusha, along the Nile in what is now central Sudan.

Governments in London and Paris perceived these competitive plays *in aggregation.* So did Germany, Russia, and such lesser colonial states as the Netherlands. So driven by the same dynamic and alert to news from Africa and elsewhere, British agents in Southeast Asia pushed east and north from positions in Burma and Malaya against Siam (Thailand). The French pushed west against the Thais from their toehold in Annan (Cambodia) and Vietnam.

Though Thailand survived as a constrained but genuinely independent country, it emerged bruised and shorn of lands that it saw (and at some level still sees) as rightfully its own. Thailand's ongoing reluctance to formalize unambiguously those same frontiers thus becomes more understandable, if no less infuriating, to its neighbors.

Other contenders lost ground entirely. The Philippines passed to the United States in 1898 after what some historians view as a barely disguised aggressive war against Spain. Other lagging European powers found themselves relegated to marginality, as Portugal yielded ground to the British in Macao and the Netherlands East Indies took more ground in Timor. As the 19th century wore on, the Dutch and British traded ports for other ports—Malacca for Bengkulu on Sumatra's west coast, and islands near Singapore to tidy up navigation channels and deal with administrative anomalies.

By the late 1890s, Southeast Asia's colonial map had taken the shape it has today. True, reluctant independence pushed Singapore away from the rest of the former Federated Malay States. British sovereignty in north Borneo, the lines of which were settled in the 19th century with the Dutch, passed in the 1960s to two entities, Sabah and Sarawak, which in turn joined in somewhat reluctant federation with the peninsular Malay sultanates and with Penang.

By the 19th century, the Sultan of Brunei had yielded to British "advisors" who sought to preserve the fiction of their wards' political independence but really governed in their stead. But doing so enabled the separate survival, in its own right, of the Sultanate—unlike the situation in the Malay Peninsula. Brunei never lost its formal independence, but neither did its royal descendents forget the glory days when Brunei controlled Borneo's entire northern coastline.

Forcible changes to the colonial map have not fared well. Jakarta's solution to the question of East Timor was a 1975 invasion and the benighted territory's forcible incorporation as Indonesia's 27th province. Yet this imposed arrangement collapsed in 1999, yielding a weak, poorly managed but sovereign East Timor 3 years later.

French Indochina after 1952 dissolved into its three constituent parts, Cambodia, Laos, and Vietnam. The ruling junta of Burma now calls the country Myanmar. But the country's demarcated territory, despite Thai ambivalence, remains as it was during British rule. Rangoon has had to settle for some territorial changes to win a border agreement with China, not least because 19th-century European land delineations gave no considerations to what was then the Chinese Empire.

Frontier Life

The European experience left another legacy. The perfectly surveyed state was also expected to be an administratively competent entity. Borders connote firm management. For policemen, borders connote control. For government exchequers, borders connote revenue, whether customs duties or import levies. For armies and navies, the formal guardians of national security, borders connote a barrier, a place where security forces can interdict threats. There are other dimensions. For innkeepers, borders offer enforced resting spots. For transporters, they offer transit and repackaging opportunities. For nomadic seafarers and itinerant hill tribesmen, borders on administrators' maps in distant capitals had negligible impact on their lives. But the prospect of enforced borders with guards, barriers, fences, and other paraphernalia was quite another matter.

Arguably the region's most absurd border slices straight down the middle of New Guinea. It separates Indonesian Papua on the west and Papua New Guinea to the east. Those affronted by border barriers can only wish for the same indifference Dani tribesmen display to occasional border markers in New Guinea's dense mountain forest or lowland mangrove jungles. Dayak or Iban tribes also remain oblivious to the international boundary separating Sarawak from Indonesia's three provinces in Borneo, the world's second largest island.

What are now the region's "firmly fixed" frontiers could have looked very different. During World War II, for example, Japan apportioned both Malaya and Sumatra to the Imperial Navy. Java passed under Japanese army control. Had the war ended differently, we might have seen a perfectly natural Malay linguistic and cultural area on both sides of the Strait of Malacca contained by boundaries enclosing a sovereign political union. The Japanese high command discussed this prospect as the war entered its last phases.

The idea of transcending European lines had a strong hold on Indonesian president Soekarno. In the early 1960s, he aspired to a grand union of Malay peoples in *Maphilindo*, an acronym formed from the names of the three archipelagic states left behind by the Dutch, British, and Americans. Lest this seem far-fetched, nationalists like Soekarno sought to bring independence to Indonesia, a name coined by a 19th-century Dutch anthropologist. They identified this as their national homeland, territorially coextensive with the Dutch East Indies.

Each year, 50,000 vessels use the strait that now separates three sovereign states. The Strait of Malacca channels two-thirds of the world's entire freighted oil and half of its liquid natural gas tankers. Apart from energy supply vessel transit, the strait funnels about a third of the world's annual freighted tonnage between the Indian and Pacific Oceans.

Most foreign navies, including those of the United States and most Western countries, regard the strait as international waters. Countries adjoining or contiguous to the region's straits and other marine passageways measure territorial waters at right angles out to a notional median line that follows opposing shoreline contours. This enormous expansion of national sovereignty into the world's oceans followed 1970s conventions developing a new Law of the Sea (LOS), which further complicated the region's territorial contentions.

Multilateral responses to specific but overlapping territorial tasks have had mixed results. Malaysia, Indonesia, and Singapore formed a tripartite commission to regulate and manage the Strait of Malacca. They pledged best efforts to suppress the persistent piracy bedeviling parts of the strait, especially the Phillips Channel near Singapore and areas of the Sumatra coast.

In the 1980s, executives with the marine insurer Lloyds of London sent the author some aerial photographs that revealed incidents of piracy as they were occurring in broad daylight in the Strait of Malacca. Each photo vividly proved that Indonesia's antipiracy enforcers and the pirates they ostensibly sought to suppress had become one and the same group. At the time, official patrol craft flying Indonesian and other flags routinely extorted money from small vessels. Some also connived in attacks by specially fitted speedboats on far larger ships nearing Singapore.

The contrast between official and pragmatic jurisdiction in areas like this remains just as stark today. Away from global shipping lanes, the lines become even more blurred. In lesser waterways or in the Sulu Sea or Lombok Strait (a deep channel used by submarines and the largest oil carriers), fishermen or petty traders ply a sideline in piracy.

Brazen displays of piracy last received sustained global attention when ethnic Chinese migrants from Vietnam in the late 1970s ran into Thai pirates. These moonlighting fishermen routinely killed and robbed the passengers, then sank the victims' barely seaworthy vessels. This seems old history, but sea travel continues to be risky for Filipinos, Thais, Indonesians, and Malaysians, who can still suffer attack or extortion away from foreign or their own media attention. In their countries, the official reaction too often approaches indifference.

As on water, so also on land: Southeast Asia's peripheral areas usually touch the frontier adjoining official borders. Often depicted as noble ethnic groups rebelling against cruel central governments, insurgent hill tribes in Laos and Burma often fund these insurrections against the government by trafficking in tropical timber and endangered animal species.

But that is just the start of it. Trafficking along the borderlands involves both profit-sharing in and protection for ethnic Chinese business networks trading in commodities such as women for sale to gender-imbalanced marriage markets in China or children heading for destinations in Thailand that specialize in pedophilia. Not least are weapons and drugs. Some borderlands are fearsome indeed.

The corollary to border creation supposedly comes in border management and control. But administrative competence only reaches

Southeast Asia's border control in airports and other destinations for well-heeled tourists. Middle-class and foreign business patronage usually brings a degree of respectful monitoring by the authorities at the region's entry airports. But overcrowded bus and long-distance ferry journeys remain the option of necessity, not choice, for local people. For them, their own or their neighboring country's border formalities can be a harrowing experience.

The chapters of this book provide fuller explanations and descriptions of these brief vignettes. The literature of borderlands has grown rapidly in the last 15 years, reflecting rising interest in seemingly unstoppable migration from Mexico and other places into the United States. Meanwhile, scholars in Europe follow the European Union's (EU's) expansion, focusing on migratory consequences and analyzing a frontier shifting eastward as new EU members (Hungary, Romania, and Bulgaria) join the group. Wariness toward North African migration also focuses European scholars on borders and borderlands.

By comparison, Southeast Asian scholars have only recently begun to take the topic seriously. This is odd. Behind the plentiful ASEAN communiqués is an implicit assumption—that each member state really does monitor its borders to contain or prevent avian influenza, transit by Islamic terrorists, or cross-border pollution. Border studies should become first-order topics for political studies in Southeast Asia, as no stronger disconnect exists than that between weak state capacity (exemplified by lax border control) and the aura of modernity that Southeast Asia would prefer to project.

Tracking the "Disputes Trend"

When assessing successful attempts to stabilize or solve inherited territorial disputes through regional diplomacy, the glass—as the saying has it—really is half-full or half-empty. Southeast Asian states can truly point to many achievements that now reduce the impact of territorial disputes on bilateral ties and regional security. On the other hand, however, this work has only dealt with second-order problems.

The major disagreement, and even a few of the lesser ones, stubbornly resists solution. Two first-order problems are evident—the first is overt, and the other is a latent problem that could turn the world upside down if attitudes changed.

Elephants in the Parlor

The region's overt territorial problem arises from the stark contrast between various second-order ASEAN country claims on parts of the SCS and China's vast claim on the *entirety* of that body of water.

From this claim, Beijing has not budged an inch. Although they have settled their proximate land borderlines, neither China nor Vietnam can agree on how to reconcile competing claims to the Paracel Islands. Vietnam and four other ASEAN states have overlapping, albeit partial, claims to other SCS areas and the Spratly archipelago; all these collide with an implacable claim by China to *everything*, a claim based in part on historical association by Chinese navigators and traders.

This deadlock has important consequences. Beijing tries to divide ASEAN diplomatic cohesion by holding out joint SCS development prospects. It did so successfully with the Philippines in 2004, though Manila has tried to backtrack since then. Beijing takes a dim view of signs that ASEAN countries are trying to harmonize their diplomacy.

As Daojiong Zha and Mark Valenzia wrote in 2001, the SCS problem is an order of magnitude much greater than the other problems. China's steady encroachment upon a Philippine shoal aptly named "Mischief Reef" led to its outright occupation by Beijing in 1995, a move that "set off a chain reaction among Southeast Asian countries . . . [and by] the U.S., Japan, Australia, New Zealand and even the European Union."[1] By mid-2010, China's unilateral claim to the entirety of the SCS, including subsurface features and airspace, had risen to a higher profile, as claimant states filed territorial claims under a deadline set out in the UN Law of the Sea treaty.

China's actions, Zha and Valenzia continue, scarcely "contribute to fostering a favorable external environment for China's economic modernization program . . . [while] maintaining a presence in the Spratlys demarcates a 'strategic territory' (*zhanlue jiangyu*) permitting China to influence use of international sea-lanes."

For the U.S. and allied navies, the SCS matters most of all in a framework prizing freedom of navigation above everything else. Various external powers also registered reservations about extending LOS "archipelagic principles" in Southeast Asia. The principle holds that archipelagic states may claim as national territory all waters encompassed by baselines drawn between each of its farthest flung islands. The Philippines and Indonesia understandably have embraced the principle.

Hence, the second, scarcely discussed, latent problem that could shake the status quo. In different and inimical hands, Indonesian sovereignty could be turned into an instrument seeking to deny transit through its claimed *national* territory to foreign shipping, including naval vessels. Submarines prefer Indonesia's deep internal channel, the Lombok Strait, over the Strait of Malacca.

To be sure, most if not all navies extend routine courtesies to Jakarta for many acts of transit. But an overt effort to prevent passage would precipitate a serious crisis if forces sought to enforce the prohibition. Nothing would more readily be seen as "strategic denial," detested in American strategic thinking ever since the young republic sent a demarche to European states rejecting efforts to lock Yankee traders out of the China trade way back in 1791.

The Positive Side of the Ledger

The positive side of the regional diplomacy ledger merits praise. Since the late 1970s, bilateral disagreements over territory have greatly diminished. The record of settling upon final land and maritime frontiers has been good for both mainland and maritime Southeast Asia.

Many territorial understandings went back to the European era. For example, the 1939 Brevie Line settled—for French colonial bureaucrats, at any rate—ownership by Vietnam or Cambodia of many offshore islands in the Gulf of Thailand. The two countries settled the matter in 1985—but that left multilateral disputes about possession and sovereignty in the Gulf of Thailand still unresolved.

In another example, the 1990 Laos-Vietnam border settlement resulted in demarcation of a line that was very close to but not identical with 1945 borders set down by the French between Laos, Vietnam (then known as Tonkin), and Cambodia (at the time called Annam), respectively.

The appearance of LOS diplomacy has added new complications to the region's already heavy legacy of territorial delineation problems. Price spikes drove mineral and hydrocarbon exploitation in the 1970s and are doing so again in the current decade. The need for legal regimes to attract resource extraction investment gave new urgency to seeking bilateral agreements about the division, or at least use, of seas so narrow that new LOS rules often left no area of open ocean or international waterway outside the reach of one or another nation's sovereignty.

The 1990s witnessed progress in *bilateral* diplomacy toward both final territorial determinations and development regimes that at least would freeze the question of which country had sole sovereignty in which region. Various self-described "codes of conduct" also emerged to govern the way states might behave in disputed areas, even in the SCS, where China's claims dwarf those of the five ASEAN states.

Even the difficult frontier between China and Vietnam, site of a short but bloody war in 1979, seemed to be approaching resolution as sustained talks during the 1990s yielded the Land Border Treaty signed in December 1999. On the maritime side, a Sino-Vietnamese working group met 17 times before both countries reached the December 2000 Agreement on the Delimitation of the Territorial Seas, Exclusive Economic Zones, and Continental Shelves in the Gulf of Tonkin. Their final maritime boundary agreement went into full force in June 2004. Meanwhile, Indonesia and Malaysia, and even Singapore and Malaysia, also moved to determine exact borderlines. So did the Indochinese states, all working bilaterally to lock up definitive and mutually accepted lines on the political map.

On the debit side of the diplomacy ledger, the 1990s did little to reconcile Indonesian maritime claims vis-à-vis Vietnamese ones, despite a generally cordial bilateral relationship for many years.

In addition, new land border problems surfaced in Hanoi's relations with Cambodia while Manila continued to avoid burying its 1962 claim to what has become the Malaysian state of Sabah. Fortunately, neither of these situations, nor the occasional bluster between and among Singapore, Malaysia, and Indonesia, has the potential to seriously destabilize regional security.

For example, East Timor's refusal to accept a maritime border agreed to prior to its independence by Australia and Indonesia simply delays deepwater investment by footloose foreign energy firms— which, in the end, costs East Timor dearly in lost opportunity time. Not even occasional gunfire between Thai and Burmese (along a border Bangkok leaves deliberately vague) tips the regional consensus in favor of the present order.

As Ramses Amer and Nguyen Hong Tao noted,[2] "Full normalization of bilateral relations [between China and Vietnam] took place without resolving the border issues." The article detailed the settling by Vietnam of five land and maritime disputes with Malaysia, Thailand,

China, and Indonesia between 1992 and 2004, contributing along the way "to the development of international law such as application of the *uti possidetis* principle, the 'equitable principle,' the application of single lines for maritime delimitation, [and new approaches to] the effect of islands in maritime delimitation."

Nor should we see progress as solely a one-on-one effort. A few multilateral initiatives among ASEAN countries have also emerged. One is a trilateral effort by Malaysia, Thailand, and Vietnam to settle on a regime to develop an area of overlapping claims in the Gulf of Thailand. This would mirror bilateral deals in the same area by Malaysia and Thailand, Cambodia and Vietnam, and Thailand and Cambodia.

Southeast Asia "On the Map"

In Southeast Asia, as elsewhere, borders form the world's basic building blocks. Without them, the international order as currently defined would vanish in an instant. Everything durable in a contemporary social and political sense—money, law, loyalty, and patriotism—can be traced to them. These lines accompanied Western world supremacy, and they shore it up today. Boundaries, like money, law, or property, arise from human abstractions; they are mental constructs applied to a fluid physical world. Nowhere is this plainer than in Southeast Asia.

This chapter has offered some perspectives on how the grid of lines set upon and over Southeast Asia acts to determine social and political realities from mundane daily life to the highest statecraft. Over the years, a once-easy ambiguity about place and identity has yielded to a mapped order imposed at the onset of the last century by colonial rulers using the extreme precision of longitude and latitude and, in many places, not much else.

We might recall that land delineation attempts go back to Sumerian surveys in around 3000 BCE. Political maps depicting territory survive from Mayan, Aztec, Roman, Chinese, Indian (Mauryan and Gupta empires), Incan, Celtic, and other realms. But these took a view of "borders" as "borderlands" with generous provision for permeable frontiers, indistinct zones, and transitory areas. Precision lines are quite another thing. Even in Europe, the technology and skill to create them did not arrive until little more than a century ago.

Rivers and mountain ridgelines usually sufficed to delineate the frontier points where, as the Victorian phrase went, "empires meet." Local peoples in Asia watched with vague suspicion as colonial surveyors clambered over stumps or paddled upriver with heavy surveying equipment. Europeans surveyed Southeast Asia to determine, with a greater degree of precision than ever before, exactly what they owned and what they might still covet.

We think of these times as far-off days, consigned to a past as distant as the racist discourse of imperialism. We forget that we live within a seam of lines determined by that just-departed era. We think we see our world today as a seamless arena where universal forces are at play. Until September 2001, at least, the spirit of our times had posited a world of global flows, global forces, and global movements—of people, capital, ideas, talent, goods, and services. We forgot that this flow might also include terrorists, criminals, and smugglers.

Since the drawing of those Southeast Asian lines, so many empires have fragmented—British, French, Dutch, Spanish, Portuguese, Austrian, Ottoman, and Russian. The paths taken during the last half of the last century steadily added more sovereign states, each with often troublesome borders. In the face of mounting evidence of comprehensive "state failure," we have no answers—except redoubling our effort to breathe life into postcolonial structures stubbornly resisting any self-sustaining identity, allegiance, or authority.

Some scholars, even in Southeast Asia, have suggested breaking down the lines still further in an elusive search for earlier constituent parts. We heard talk of this when some saw Indonesia close to breaking up after President Suharto's grip slackened in the late 1990s. Yet the Soviet Union's or Yugoslavia's dissolution shows what can happen when another scramble begins for one's own state and one's own borders. As moderate thinkers realized, *any* new boundaries will have to rest on distinctions just as whimsical as those on which the current lines are based. There is no perfect, irreducible territorial unit.

Why does a line that is as straight as a ruler cut through the east-west orientation of all the valleys in New Guinea? The line slices the big island into Papua New Guinea on the east and West Papua (formerly Dutch New Guinea) on the west. How did this piece of geographic genius happen? Some accounts suggest it occurred at a European boundaries conference as inebriated diplomats pondered the British, German, and Dutch spheres of influence in Southeast Asia over cigars and brandy. For their purposes, the abstract lines put down by these distant imperialists dealt with a problem seemingly remote from all immediate consequence, as the rugged island's topography runs east and west, while the line runs north to south, straight as an arrow.

Some bizarre lines bring unexpected benefits. The demilitarized zone dividing North and South Korea seems an unmitigated insult, a corridor of latent death. Yet the heavily mined and fortified zone cutting across the Korean Peninsula gives sanctuary to unique wildlife. When Korea reunifies, ecotourism can flourish there.

The ebb and flow across the world of all these lines, some more senseless than others, have not rewarded every nationality hungry for boundaries and a flag. Neither Turkey, nor Persia, nor Britain could find a way after World War I to accept a Kurdish yearning for a bordered national territory. Nothing has changed since then. Or consider how, just before the same war in 1913, some Chinese envoys traveling to Sinha in British India evaded British pressure to accept a sovereign Tibetan entity. That incident has left the Tibetans in a limbo from which they may never escape.

Yet a closer look at the intended result of Tibetan self-determination brings us no closer to clarity. What *is* "territorial 'Tibet'" anyway? At least five sets of persuasive boundaries exist. Real success can come only from the international community. And its recognition can only come when and if Beijing's central power has receded into insignificance—not an imminent prospect. Still, one can always hope. In the meantime, even the Dalai Lama has not yet decided quite what his national homeland area should encompass. There is no hurry for him to do so.

Southeast Asia should count itself lucky to escape most border conflicts. In 1997, armies mobilized and tensions rose as Ecuador and Peru fought a short war over a tract of Amazonian jungle. The cause for this foolishness? Fee-grubbing surveyors over 100 years ago whose mismatched and confusing survey maps have prompted claims and counterclaims ever since.

Indeed, despite the SCS, Asia's most contentious boundaries lie elsewhere. Routine dueling went on for years between Indian and Pakistani units positioned at the frigid Aksai Chin glacier, 17,000 feet in elevation. Chinese and Indian army scouts still glare at one other in other Himalayan passes 1,000 miles east of Aksai Chin.

In the study of boundaries, political geographers can sometimes retreat into a cubbyhole, fretting about such chicken-and-egg questions as, "What comes first, boundaries or identity?" In truth, the evidence has already come in: Like other people becoming *citizens*, Southeast Asians find themselves "spatially compartmentalized within a fixed territory," to use one geographer's phrase. As a result, Southeast Asians are developing steadily more identifiable national identities. The lead book here remains Thongchai Winichakul's *Siam Mapped*, a tour de force in its field that shows how foreign geographic concepts, including territoriality and sovereignty, became identified with "Thai-ness."[3]

Finally, to return to this chapter's beginning assertion: Is globalization a hoax? Strictly speaking, the idea of a borderless world collides with a durable reality of fixed and obstructive frontiers. Indeed, more of these lines exist today—all necessarily artificial—than ever, thereby posing more arbitrary impediments to human movement than ever. Even when some borders fade or disappear altogether, others will emerge. Lines have failed to lock in functioning sovereignties in Africa, Asia, and the south Pacific, but no one has anything better to offer.

It seems safe to speculate that this century's remaining years will see changes in technology enabling a more aggressive monitoring of boundaries. Cross-border terrorism and criminality will engender new forms of interdiction. For Southeast Asia, only a return to the fluidity of the *archipel* will reduce or eliminate these intruding, obstructive lines. But that is not about to happen soon.

Notes

[1] "Mischief Reef: Geopolitics and Implications," *Journal of Contemporary Asian Studies* 31, no. 1 (2001).

[2] "The Management of Vietnam's Border Disputes: What Impact on its Sovereignty and Regional Integration?" *Contemporary Southeast Asia* 27, no. 3 (2005).

[3] Thongchai Winichakul, *Siam Mapped* (Madison: University of Wisconsin Press, 1995).

Chapter 2

Archaeology, National Histories, and National Borders in Southeast Asia

Michael Wood

This chapter will examine how archaeology, the study of the material culture of past societies, has been used to define and critique national histories and borders in Southeast Asia. Archaeologists have reconstructed broad cultures identified as using similar artifacts and embracing common worldviews. These cultures (or "civilizations") do not usually correspond with modern nation-states (or with ancient polities, for that matter). This is especially the case in Southeast Asia, a region long part of larger cultural units and open to border-crossing influences (the very concept of a border in fact having little resonance in the region until recent times). Southeast Asia has been described as a "crossroads," and the description is not inaccurate.

The first section of the chapter will describe how Southeast Asia has historically been open to outside inputs; Hindu and Buddhist architecture, Chinese models of governance and trade, Chinese immigrant groups, the Islamic religion, and Western economic penetration and colonial rule have all marked the culture of the region. By 1900, virtually the entire area had come under some form of colonial control. Colonial authorities defined clear borders for their possessions, replacing earlier forms of state organization. A final foreign intervention came in the form of imperial Japan, which overthrew the European colonial order. Japanese victory paved the way for the emergence of independent Southeast Asian nation-states, which had the task of defining national borders and asserting common national histories.

The second part of the chapter will show how these tasks were facilitated by the earlier experience of colonial rule. Treaties between European powers defined borders between colonies, which largely remained intact after independence. Ancient symbols were presented as emblematic of a Southeast Asian past that glorified outside influence at the expense of local genius. Indonesia and Cambodia kept much of the history unearthed by Dutch and French scholars and used it for purposes of nationbuilding. "National history" glorified such ancient civilizations as the Majapahit and Angkor and often linked present-day struggles to past triumphs. Thus, in freeing themselves from Dutch control and constructing a unified nation-state, Indonesians were simply building on the earlier work of Gajah Mada, the great 14th-century ruler of Majapahit. Cambodians were reminded that if their ancestors could build Angkor, they could do anything. Although partially constructed by rulers foreign to the region who, at least in the case of Cambodia, denigrated local achievements, national histories have been used by modern nation-states as a way to stress the uniqueness of their local cultures and to bolster national unity.

Not all Southeast Asians were satisfied with pasts handed to them by colonial rulers. Also troubling was that national histories often marginalized large segments (if not sometimes the majority) of a country's population and instead glorified distant cultures that had little if any current resonance. This situation was particularly notable in Indonesia, where the Java-centric national history was felt by many to have downplayed the contributions of Muslims. The third part of this chapter looks at how some Indonesians have turned to archaeology in order to reconstruct a national history that emphasizes links to the Islamic world. Such a history might in fact also act as a reminder that Southeast Asia has always been at the center of larger currents, while at the same time having a strong tradition of autonomous development. The chapter concludes with some comments on whether such archaeological research, intended to reorient Indonesia toward the Islamic world, might also in fact strengthen a national identity or even a regional Southeast Asian one, rather than, as some have suggested, pave the way for some form of pan-Islamic caliphate.

Southeast Asia as a Crossroads

Southeast Asia has seldom been victim to land invasion, as was often the case in continental Eurasia. Much more common was the arrival by sea of outsiders from China, India, the Middle East, and eventually Europe. Foreign visitors were chiefly motivated by trade rather than the desire to conquer, even though almost the entire region eventually lost its independence. The Indian Ocean long functioned as a major trade corridor. Links to China, India, and the Middle East/ Mediterranean world date to around the time of Christ. Trade networks also served as a conduit for ideas and religious beliefs, including Hinduism, Buddhism, Islam, and Christianity.

The Influence of India

When Western scholars first began to study the archaeology of Southeast Asia, they were struck by an apparent Indian cultural influence. Sustained Indian contact or perhaps even some form of colonization best explained the impressive Hindu monuments found in the region. The *kshatriya* theory of a Southeast Asia settled by Indian warriors was supplemented by the Brahmin theory, which involved Hindu religious practitioners bringing high culture to the region. Brahmins were held to have strengthened local rulers by performing magical rituals, creating mythological symbols, and providing prestigious iconography. A few argued that Indian civilization was brought to Southeast Asia through the arrival of the *vaisya* caste of traders and craftsmen.[1] However, these models of Indian colonization or passively accepted "Indianization" are no longer tenable.[2] The scenario of an expanding Indian high civilization encountering a stone-age Southeast Asia with any local innovations such as metallurgy as late or derivative developments no longer stands up. Recent archaeological research has established that rice cultivation developed in the major valleys of mainland Southeast Asia between 2500 and 500 BCE. From 500 BCE until around 800 CE, agricultural intensification and centralization occurred, along with technological innovations in the use of bronze and iron. There was more local demand for prestige items from India, which helped enhance the status of local rulers, and that stimulated trade. The initial Indian impact acted as a catalyst; the Indian presence played a more direct and positive role with time and eventually resulted in the adoption of writing systems, political philosophy, and the Hindu and Buddhist religions. This helped nurture complexity in Southeast Asian societies; local chiefs attracted more retainers and employed craftsmen while mobilizing the local population in order to construct irrigation systems and temple complexes.[3] Whatever the exact dynamics of how India influenced Southeast Asian culture, it seems clear that imported concepts were accepted only as far as they complemented and reinforced local traditions.

Islamization

A similar process may have brought Islam to Southeast Asia. Muslims, making up about one-half of the population of the region, presently reside in a "Muslim zone" consisting of Indonesia, Malaysia, Singapore, and Brunei, as well as the southern parts of the Philippines, Thailand, and Cambodia. There is no evidence of large-scale Muslim invasions or even immigration into the region. Instead, Islam developed in Southeast Asia as the result of peaceful interaction between Muslim visitors and the local population. Muslims came to Southeast Asia for trading purposes, from perhaps as early as the 7th century, as part of a well-established process of globalization focused on the Indian Ocean.[4] (The wreck of a 9th-century Indian or Arab ship recently discovered between Sumatra and Borneo attests to the existence of these early trade routes.[5]) With trade came religious change. Anthony Reid relates the Islamization of parts of Southeast Asia during this "age of commerce" (1450–1689) to the integration of the region into larger cultural and commercial systems.[6] But as Reid's timeframe indicates, this was far from an overnight process. In fact, Muslims may have been visiting Southeast Asia for centuries before local inhabitants took a real interest in this new religion. Traders lived in separate communities and only slowly began to integrate themselves into the larger Southeast Asian society. Muslims often married into local ruling dynasties or held the important position of harbormaster, in charge of settling disputes among merchants. A shared religion also allowed access to trade and credit networks that transcended the region. By the late 13th century, some Southeast Asian rulers began to see advantages in converting to Islam, and Islamic polities become evident. Muslim states apparently first emerged in northern Sumatra, where such travelers as Marco Polo and Ibn Battuta noted their presence and early grave markers of Islamic rulers have been found. Fourteenth-century grave markers also have been found in Brunei and the Philippines. The 15th century saw the rise of a series of Islamic states in Malaysia and Java, although especially in the case of the latter, the process of Islamization was to take many centuries. The 16th century saw the penetration of the Moluccas; such Islamic polities as Ternate and Tidore were soon to encounter the aggressive Christian powers of Portugal and Spain.

It has been argued that the Islamization of island Southeast Asia is an ongoing process, or has not in fact occurred at all. Southeast

Asian Islam is held to be quite distinct from that of the Arab Middle East, which is held to be normative. Thus, Clifford Geertz chose to entitle his anthropological study of a small East Java town *The Religion of Java*, implying the existence of a unique Javanese worldview clearly distinguishable from Islam.[7] Earlier Dutch analyses, which for political reasons downplayed Islam's hold over the population, made a similar assertion: that Islam was somehow foreign to the natural culture of the archipelago. The real civilization of Indonesia, it was argued, had been an Indic one. When the Islamic presence in Indonesia was acknowledged, it was held to be a corruption of the "true faith" of the Middle East.[8] Geertz himself is apparently cited by some Indonesian Muslims as "scientific proof" that the nation's believers have strayed from Islamic norms.[9] But, as Mark Woodward points out, it is a mistake to identify a text-based version of Islam not only as normative, but also as the sole barometer by which one can measure what is and what is not Islamic.[10] Ignoring some of the more "ritualistic" and "mystical" elements of Islam in general and Islam as it is practiced in Java in particular, Geertz identifies a "real religion" as emphasizing texts; he has difficulty understanding the rationale for "chanting" of the Koran by non–Arabic speakers. But from a traditional Javanese perspective, it is quite problematic to claim that people are not pious simply because they cannot read Arabic.[11] Marshall Hodgson noted that when Javanese Islam is seen from the perspective of Islam as a whole, it exhibits many similarities to that of South Asia and the Middle East.[12]

That is not to say that Southeast Asian Islam does not have a unique character. Many local customs survived the process of religious change. The Islamic rulers of Java adopted earlier Hindu-Buddhist/Javanese models of governance, as can be seen in their use of Majapahit regalia and the fabrication of genealogies linking their houses to the Majapahit dynasty. Local belief may even have facilitated the acceptance of the Islamic religion; the *wali songo*, a semilegendary group alleged to have brought Islam to Java, are held to have drawn on Java's rich cultural traditions in order to convert the population. Sunan Kalijaga, for example, was said to have brought the *wayang* puppet play to the region and used it to explain Islamic doctrine and history, despite that fact that at present the most popular subjects for the *wayang* are two Hindu epics, the *Ramayana* and the *Mahabarata*. Sufism has long been held as instrumental in making Islam attractive to local sentiment. Anthony

Johns sees the Mongol invasions of the Middle East in the 13th century as scattering many mystical practitioners across Asia, some of whom eventually arrived in Southeast Asia via the established trade routes.[13] Sufism's stress on mystical experience of the divine as well as ideas about secret wisdom reserved for the initiated may have appealed to a Hindu-Buddhist society built around semisacred rulers. It offered continuity; Islam need not have overturned all that had come before it. Islam was accepted in Southeast Asia because it fit in with local norms. Even the *pesantren* system of Islamic boarding schools, a crucial element in Islamic society in Indonesia to the present day, may have had Hindu-Buddhist antecedents.[14]

The Chinese Footprint

The extent of Chinese influence in Southeast Asia varied considerably. Vietnam was a Chinese province until it won its independence in the 10th century. Subsequent Chinese military interventions were not uncommon, the latest occurring in 1979. Many Chinese cultural traits were adopted by Vietnam: the Confucian examination system, the institution of emperor, and styles of dress and architecture. These deep connections between China and Vietnam have led to the suggestion that the latter country should be more properly seen as part of a greater Chinese sphere (along with Korea and Japan) rather than as part of Southeast Asia.[15] Archaeology has been used to emphasize the uniqueness of Vietnamese cultural achievement and to stress that its development was not wholly dependent on outside impetus. This is particularly the case in regard to the Dong Son culture of the first millennium BCE.[16] Named after a site in northern Vietnam, the culture was held by European scholars to have originated in China. Postindependence Vietnamese archaeologists instead identified it as a Vietnamese culture that had emerged before the establishment of Han imperial hegemony.[17] However, the famous bronze kettle drums, emblematic of this advanced culture, were in fact produced in northern Thailand as well as in the Chinese provinces of Guangxi and Yunnan; it is hard to say how "Vietnamese" the objects are. And while Vietnam does historically have much in common with southern China (and vice versa), its distinctiveness rests less on its bronze age culture than on the fact that it continued to have strong contacts with the rest of Southeast Asia, even during the centuries of Chinese control. In any event, the Vietnamese felt confident enough to establish their own system of rule, although one modeled after that of imperial China.[18]

Evidence for a Chinese presence in island Southeast Asia before 1000 CE is scant, consisting of a small amount of pottery found in southern Sumatra and the accounts of Buddhist pilgrims.[19] Direct Chinese control did not take place outside of Vietnam. Instead, the Chinese tried to impose a form of tributary control. Southeast Asian rulers would make occasional visits to the Chinese capital bearing gifts. They would pledge allegiance to China and agree to not act in a manner detrimental to Chinese interests. In turn, they would be offered Chinese protection and would be allowed access to Chinese trade networks. Srivijaya and Malacca both developed into thriving commercial centers under the umbrella of Chinese security. China seldom actually intervened militarily and the engagement of its merchants in the region was sporadic.[20]

A major exception to this pattern involved the voyages of Admiral Zheng He. In the early 15th century, the Ming dynasty sent out a series of huge fleets of up to 300 ships, which traveled as far as the coast of Africa and made many stops in Southeast Asia.[21] The fleets were meant to display Chinese power and to gather intelligence; the writings of the admiral's secretary Ma Huan have survived to this day.[22] Tribute was collected; Chinese gifts were left in return (the tributary system was a form of trade, but to the Chinese, commerce was to take place between equals, and as can be seen in the writings of Ma Huan, the Southeast Asians were deemed inferior). The voyages of Zheng He have been seen by historians as a great "might have been" (they took place mere decades before those of Columbus); they were shut down by the imperial authorities, perhaps because it was felt that they were too expensive and that China had little to learn from the outside world. But while Chinese ships did not reach the New World, contacts with Southeast Asia continued. The voyages may even have aided the spread of Islam; Zheng He was both a eunuch and a Muslim, and there is apparently a relationship between the Chinese presence and Islamic activity in northern Java in the 15th century.[23] An elaborate Chinese pagoda has been built in Zheng He's memory in Semarang, a seaport in northern Java. The shrine attracts Javanese Muslim pilgrims and is only a short distance from Demak and Kudus, the sites of the two oldest mosques in Indonesia. The cross-cultural popularity of this temple could be seen as emblematic of Southeast Asia's status as a crossroads; a foreign visitor, representing an imperial power, remains a figure of devotion to a broad spectrum of local people. It is perhaps not surprising that Zheng He, long forgotten in China proper, is also celebrated in Singapore, where he is seen as an example not just of connections to China but also of an innate openness to trade and the outside world.

The Chinese of Semarang cannot be traced directly to these 15th-century voyages, but certainly by this time a Chinese immigrant presence was observable; it was to expand substantially in subsequent years. In the 18th century, powerful Chinese commercial communities were present in Spanish Manila and Dutch Batavia (Jakarta). (The latter community was the target of a Dutch pogrom in 1740, the survivors going on to take part in the dynastic struggles then convulsing Java.) Chinese workers were encouraged to settle in British-controlled Malaya and in Siam in the 19th century. The Chinese authorities had an ambiguous attitude toward these overseas populations; the issue of whether they remained Chinese citizens or had in fact lost this status was a complicated one that in some cases was not really resolved until the 20th century.[24] Local reaction was sometimes hostile; ethnic Chinese populations, who in many cases no longer spoke Chinese or used Chinese names, were subject to violence in Indonesia as late as 1998. Anti-Chinese actions were often fueled by the perception that the Chinese held an unfair economic advantage and were also perhaps more loyal to China than to their native country. While Chinese populations generally did better in Thailand and the Philippines, the government in Malaysia enforced discriminatory measures in order to bolster the status of the Malay majority. The justification given was that the Chinese were in a sense merely visitors who should not profit at the expense of the "indigenous Malays."

Voyages on the scale of those made by Zheng He were never attempted again. Ironically, Chinese immigrants to Southeast Asia were encouraged to settle by other imperial powers. From the beginning, Europeans acted somewhat differently than earlier visitors. The Portuguese had apparently heard of the great wealth and vast trade opportunities associated with Malacca, a port controlling the waterways between Sumatra and the Malay Peninsula. Rather than try to integrate themselves into the existing commercial routes connected to Malacca, they simply seized the city in 1511. This was part of a larger campaign to capture and maintain a network of fortified posts stretching into the eastern parts of Indonesia in order to establish a monopoly on the spice trade. The Portuguese had the secondary motivation of wishing to spread the influence of their religion into regions that had not previously had much exposure to Christianity.

The European Impact

In the long run, the ambitions of the Portuguese were not fulfilled. Trade simply moved away to other ports. The Portuguese by the end of the 16th century had to come to terms with the local trading system and in some cases hired out their ships to local commercial interests (similarly, Portuguese mercenaries operated frequently in mainland Southeast Asia). Although some local rulers did convert to Christianity in the Moluccas, no Christian kingdoms survived for more than a few years. But some of the population of eastern Indonesia remains Catholic to this day. The influence of Portuguese on the languages of Southeast Asia might also be seen as significant. In addition to its use in East Timor (Portugal's last actual Southeast Asian possession), Portuguese has given many words to Malay, the language that for years competed with Portuguese and eventually surpassed it as the common tongue of the commercial ports of the region.[25]

If the Portuguese impact on the region was ephemeral, the same cannot be said of the other European powers. In 1602, the separate Dutch trading companies operating in the region joined together to form the *Vereenigde Oost-Indische Compagnie* (VOC, or United East Indies Company). A joint stock company operating under a charter from the Dutch government, it was given a monopoly over all trade in the Indian Ocean basin and was granted the rights of a sovereign state. Although in theory a board of directors in the Netherlands was in charge, in reality the governor of the VOC, from 1619 resident in Batavia, exercised almost total freedom of action, due to difficulties in communications. The company's plan was to establish a monopoly over the spice trade by forcing local rulers into restrictive treaties, barring any outside European or Asian competition, and actually going as far as destroying spice-producing plants and exterminating the inhabitants of several islands in the Moluccas in order to drive up commodity prices.[26]

This strategy was, in the end, a failure. Because of the vast distances involved, supply and demand could never really be controlled. The company was plagued by inefficiency, corruption, and low-quality personnel who were often more interested in their private smuggling activities than in the organization's financial well-being. The VOC declared bankruptcy in 1799, its Indonesian assets being taken over by the Dutch government. These holdings were considerable; by the end of the 18th century, the VOC controlled all of the island of Java, having forced local rulers into the position of powerless vassals. This was the final result of a series of wars during which the Dutch intervened militarily to support various Javanese dynastic factions. The Dutch were initially motivated to do so by a desire to ensure their own supply of rice and timber; they had little interest in either the trade or the politics of Java itself. Later, as Java sank into chaos, they found they could get concessions from Javanese eager for their military aid.[27] The net effect was that the Dutch government inherited territories in Java, Sulawesi, and Sumatra, which were later expanded upon until by 1910, all of present-day Indonesia was under colonial control. In addition to facilitating the colonial takeover of Indonesia, VOC activities also had an effect on the whole region, in that attempts to establish a spice monopoly, while ultimately unsuccessful, did largely drive Southeast Asians out of long-distance trade. With the loss of economic clout, perhaps the loss of political power was inevitable.[28]

By the mid-1500s, all of Luzon and the Visayas had been incorporated into the vast holdings of the Spanish Empire (Mindanao, populated by Muslim converts, resisted the Spanish advance, as it later did the authority of the United States and the Republic of the Philippines). In many ways, the Spanish ruled the Philippines in a manner similar to how they administered Latin America. At the top of the hierarchy was the colonial governor. Spanish soldiers and officials, many of the latter Catholic priests, collected taxes, dispensed justice, and kept order. Christianity spread rapidly through the local population; the Philippines are presently the only majority-Christian country in East or Southeast Asia. Until the 19th century, the majority of religious practitioners were foreigners, although low-level monks and nuns, along with lay workers, often had indigenous origins. The economy of the Philippines was based on large estates and peasant labor producing surpluses of rice. Cash crops such as sugar were not an important element of the economy until the late 18th century; much of the latter activity was developed by American and British investors as well as by indigenous Filipino entrepreneurs. Before this time, international commerce was conducted on a much more basic level. Chinese merchants in Manila would trade Southeast Asian and Chinese products for silver brought to the Philippines from the mines of Mexico. Once a year, a "treasure ship" would return to Acapulco with the commodities purchased through these transactions. There was no large-scale Spanish immigration to the islands, although intermarriage was quite common. A *mestizo* elite eventually emerged, although real political power was always reserved for colonial officials sent from Spain. However, local elites adopted not just the religion of the Spanish, but also their language and in many ways their culture. Wealthy Filipinos received an education in Spain, and it was this Spanish-trained elite who in the final decades of the 19th century agitated against continued Spanish rule. They demanded the independence of the Filipino nation, something that they were actually in the process of constructing from the country's diverse ethnic groups, at the same time as the rest of Southeast Asia was only just falling under full colonial rule.

The advances of the French and British in securing colonial possessions in Southeast Asia took place somewhat later, in the 19th century. Political control followed military action, which was prompted by the desire to protect European economic interests. These differed in many ways from earlier Dutch commercial interests. Of prime importance were resources connected to European industrialization and urbanization: oil, tin, rubber, palm oil, copra, coffee, tea, as well as rice and tropical fruit to feed Europe's expanding population. Colonial possessions were also to act as markets for European goods. Southeast Asians were important yet largely passive participants in these new economic arrangements: peasant farmers, small-scale traders, low-level functionaries, workers in the transportation sector. Southeast Asia did not industrialize; it was a component of an industrial transformation taking place elsewhere. Some Western theorists even advanced the concept of dual economies within the boundaries of colonial Southeast Asia: a modern one based on industrial capitalism run by and for Europeans, and a precapitalist one based on the village, where money was less important than traditional culture. European administrators tried to preserve in isolation traditional Southeast Asian ways of life. Administration and commerce were to be left to Europeans, and in the case of the latter, also to immigrant minority groups, the Chinese, Indians, and Arabs. With the British in Malaya, even "modern" agricultural products, such as rubber, were to be harvested by imported laborers. Although French activities in Vietnam can be viewed as a partial exception, there was little interest on the part of European colonial administrators in imposing Christianity on Southeast Asians. Such sentiments were probably not motivated by European sympathy toward local religious customs; "fanaticism" (as Europeans labeled any religious manifestation with political or protonationalistic undertones) was always ruthlessly crushed. Instead, the working principle was that religion was integral to an inferior local worldview, but if practiced peacefully it would be left alone. In devising the Dutch response to armed resistance in Aceh, Dutch Islamic scholar and government official Christian Snouck Hurgronje went so far as to divide society into "good Muslims," associated with local chiefs to whom religion was a matter of faith, and "bad Muslims," many of whom had come under the influence of foreign Islamic scholars who resisted Dutch rule.[29] Consequently, the Dutch, along with the British, were very concerned over the increasing numbers of pilgrims, who because of improved transportation were able to visit Mecca for the annual *hajj*.[30] Such suspicions about, and sometimes open contempt toward, local custom was not, however, universal. Similarly, some Southeast Asians did break out of the constraints of the dualistic model, were able to function to a certain extent within European society, and did acquire a European education. It is these Southeast Asians who would eventually develop national identities that could replace the colonial models developed by the Europeans.

It may be easy to exaggerate the impact of Western colonialism on Southeast Asia. Thailand was never colonized, although its national sovereignty was certainly compromised. It had to allow Western economic penetration and had to cultivate British diplomatic support in order to avoid direct foreign control. Thailand acted as a buffer zone between French and British spheres of influence while giving up its traditional hegemony in Cambodia and Laos. The Americans, who after defeating the Spanish turned the Philippines into a protectorate, had a marked impact on local culture. Systems of administration and education were set up, and the independent Republic of the Philippines inherited an American style of government and politics. To this day, a large number of Filipinos speak English while retaining Spanish surnames (the saying "the Philippines spent 300 years in a Spanish convent and 50 years in Hollywood" does perhaps have an element of truth to it). But it is difficult to separate the American transformation of the Philippines from larger currents of globalization; if the office towers of Manila look like those of Los Angeles, they also look like those of Tokyo, or of Jakarta, for that matter. Whereas previous observers have stressed the crucial importance of a Western presence, the consensus among many scholars today is that the character of the region is the result of an "autonomous history."[31] Western colonialism was important (perhaps more important than some Southeast Asian nationalists wish to acknowledge) as were the previous contacts with India, China, and the Islamic world, but the region's inhabitants always understood, adopted, and adapted to outside influences through the prism of local custom and belief. Southeast Asian ways proved remarkably strong in the face of foreign political, economic, cultural, and even military interventions.[32] This process was apparent in the newly independent nation-states of Southeast Asia; national histories had to reflect unique national identities, while acknowledging age-old connections to the wider world.

Archaeology, Modern Borders, National Histories

Independent states had the task of building new identities and histories; new regimes drew on a mythic past to build a future. Each nation-state tried to emphasize its singular character. This task often involved the acceptance of colonial-era differences; older transnational identities were discarded. Colonial borders remained largely intact. The British possessions of the Malay Peninsula and Borneo eventually coalesced into the independent countries of Malaysia, Singapore, and Brunei; the French colonies became Cambodia, Laos, and (after 1975) a unified Vietnam. The Philippines, Burma, and Thailand remained intact, despite regional rebellions, based at least in part on religion or ethnicity. After the 1962 "Act of Free Union," Indonesia was eventually able to claim possession of the entirety of the Dutch East Indies and even for a time (1975–1999) incorporate the former Portuguese colony of East Timor. The continued success of the imagined borders of colonial Southeast Asia might seem surprising in light of how radical a break with the past the modern nation-state system constituted. Benedict Anderson points out that prior to the rise of the colonial system, Southeast Asia was organized in a much different way, whereby power decreased in both a symbolic and an actual manner the farther a subject was from the royal palace. Southeast Asian states could be pictured as a series of "concentric circles of power."[33] Countries such as Cambodia and Thailand were not separated by fixed borders. Instead, indistinct borderlands marked the space where the area of influence of one royal court blended into that of its neighbor. Also surprising was the lack of any attempt to redefine Southeast Asia in terms of more "natural" cultural zones. Breaking down national borders in favor of bigger regional groupings was always advanced in terms of political alliances or vague cultural affinities (for example, *Malphindo*, an abortive scheme to merge Malaysia, the Philippines, and Indonesia into a loose federation). The Association of Southeast Asian Nations (ASEAN) was devised as a defensive measure aimed at an expansive North Vietnam, rather than as a coming together of nations sharing the same basic identity. While Singapore might stress connections with China in terms of trade, or even put forward a type of "neo-Confucianism" as a good developmental model, no one has ever suggested that all Southeast Asian Chinese band together as a single entity. Blueprints for a transregional Islamic caliphate have remained the province of marginal extremist groups; no politician has ever campaigned on such a platform.

Majapahit

One of the only real exceptions to the idea that the borders of Southeast Asia, as unfortunately defined by Western colonialism, should remain unchanged comes from Indonesia, where secular nationalists associated with Sukarno appeared to occasionally question the national borders inherited from the Dutch. They did so with reference to the empire of Majapahit. According to some readings of the *Nagarakertagama*, an epic 14th-century poem that described the activities of the monarch Hayam Wuruk, Majapahit may have included much of the territory of present-day Indonesia.[34] Controversy remains as to whether place names mentioned in the *Nagarakertagama* were actually part of a coherent empire or were simply loosely held tributaries. Dutch scholar C.C. Berg even argued, to largely negative reactions from Indonesian nationalists, that the "glory of Majapahit" was largely a fiction and that the text should be read as a magical exercise intended to bolster the prestige of an otherwise modest Javanese ruler.[35] But for Indonesian nationalists, Majapahit provided firm borders with which to define an independent state. In fact, nationalist writer Muhammad Yamin went further and claimed that Majapahit included all of the Dutch East Indies, the British possessions of Malaya and Borneo, and Portuguese Timor, as well as parts of the Philippines, Cambodia, and even northern Australia. He consequently demanded in the immediate run-up to the declaration of Indonesian independence in 1945 that all of island Southeast Asia be incorporated into the new nation, regardless of its current status. This "Greater Indonesia" idea was dropped on the insistence of such leaders as Muhammad Hatta, who recognized that it would in fact retard the granting of independence.[36] Little was heard of the concept later, although some observers interpreted the Indonesian *Konfrontasi* (Confrontation) campaign against the formation of an independent Malaysia as evidence of Indonesian expansion or even Javanese imperialism.

The campaign to take possession of the western part of New Guinea could be seen as simply making all of the Dutch East Indies independent. The invasion and eventual annexation of East Timor were apparently motivated more by immediate Cold War worries about the emergence of a potentially hostile, possibly communist neighbor than by the desire to rework colonial borders. The event is somewhat comparable to the 1979 invasion of Cambodia by Vietnam, an action prompted by Khmer Rouge attacks rather than part of a long-held desire to create a "Greater Vietnam." Of course, some had identified North Vietnam as a "Southeast Asian Prussia" gleefully tumbling "dominoes" as it annexed South Vietnam and brought Laos and Cambodia into its sphere of influence. South Vietnam had existed as an independent state from 1954 until its collapse under North Vietnamese military attack in April 1975. Its viability and legitimacy as an independent state have been questioned, but it is a fact that most of northern and southern Vietnam has long been a single political and cultural entity. Attempts to separate from larger states in Burma, the Philippines, and Thailand by distinct ethnic groups have all been failures. While the British territories of Malaya and Borneo were eventually turned into three separate states, their borders with neighbors have been little changed.

Borobudur

Similarly, independent Southeast Asia kept much of the history developed by colonial scholars. Archaeology as a discipline practiced in Indonesia dates back to the 18th century. The Dutch colonial administration set up museums and organizations to study the material remains of the Indonesian past. Before independence, the Dutch also began to train a few Indonesians in archaeological excavation and restoration techniques. The Dutch and the Indonesians who followed them generally concentrated on researching the archipelago's pre-Islamic past, whether prehistoric or classical (Buddhist and/or Hindu in orientation).

Emblematic of this interest was the attention paid to the study and restoration of the 9th-century Buddhist site of Borobudur, located in central Java. Originally revealed to the outside world by Lieutenant Governor Sir Thomas Raffles during the British occupation of Java, it was cleared, studied, and rebuilt by Dutch archaeologists.[37] It became and remains to this day one of Indonesia's top tourist draws. Borobudur was a powerful symbol for the Republic of Indonesia; Sukarno made a point of showing the site to foreign dignitaries, while the New Order Suharto regime, with help from the United Nations Educational, Scientific, and Cultural Organization, embarked on a massive restoration project. Almost every museum in Indonesia contains a scale model reproduction of Borobudur. The monument has become almost an icon, grouped with the *wayang* puppet play and *gamelan* music into a vague classical/Javanese past from which all Indonesians are to draw inspiration. Majapahit was also subject to a similar process of cultural endowment. After Dutch historians discovered the Majapahit of the *Nagarakertagama*, Dutch archaeologists such as Henri Maclaine-Pont excavated and restored the Majapahit capital of Trowulan. This site remains an important source of Indonesian national pride; the Suharto government spent a great deal of effort on reconstructing its gates, temples, and sacred pools, and augmenting it with modern museum facilities.

In contrast, less attention has been paid to the material remains of Indonesia's Islamic past. Dutch scholars never developed the passion for Islamic antiquities that they had for those of ancient Hindu Java. In fact, the Archaeological Service of the East Indies was specifically mandated to restore Hindu antiquities. Such attitudes remained strong among outside researchers. Timothy E. Behrend notes that works by Claire Holt and F.A. Wagner leave the impression that "monumental building, or any significant building of any sort, ended in Java with the 15th-century temples Suku and Cetha on Gunung Lawa." He also notes that even foreign experts in Indonesian Islam are more familiar with Borobudur than with Islamic grave complexes.[38]

The situation is not much different among Indonesian researchers. The *Hasil Pemugaran dan Temuan Benda Cagar Budaya* ("The Results of the Restoration and Discovery of Cultural Heritage") describes research and conservation work done on Indonesian archaeological sites from 1969 to 1994.[39] This report, while not comprehensive, gives a good representation of the type of archaeological work carried out in the country during the New Order. The only Islamic site of note that was the focus of actual excavation work appears to be the mosque and palace complex at the West Java port of Banten. Certainly, there is no Islamic equivalent of the work on Trowulan or Borobudur.

Such attitudes are reflected in what Anthony Reid has described as the "nationalist orthodoxy."[40] This national past stressed a "golden age" during which Indonesia was a prosperous, unitary state, whose territory stretched across the archipelago. This time of power, justice, and order was associated with Buddhist Srivijaya (centered in Sumatra during the 7th to 10th centuries) and especially Majapahit. Subsequent Islamic kingdoms and the role of Islam in national development were downgraded in importance. Islam, it was even implied, might have been one of the factors that had allowed Indonesia to succumb to Dutch aggression. Little attention was paid to links with the worldwide Islamic community. The argument was made that Indonesia had a unique identity that set it apart from the larger currents of Islamic history. Indonesia's national history was developed by such figures as Sukarno and Muhammad Yamin as part of the independence struggle.[41] It drew at least partially on the work of Dutch historians and archaeologists, who had reconstructed Majapahit as a powerful empire in line with the description provided by the *Nagarakertagama*.[42] This orthodoxy continued after Indonesia won its independence. National history was reflected in textbooks, monuments, museums, and historical research.[43]

Angkor

Ancient Cambodia, like Java, was home to a sophisticated, Indian-influenced civilization based on wet rice cultivation that has left behind many impressive ruins. The empire of Angkor, which flourished from around 800 to 1400 CE, for a time dominated present-day southern Laos, eastern Thailand, all of Cambodia, and southern Vietnam.[44] Angkor Wat, a massive temple complex in the interior of Cambodia, has been consciously used as a symbol by every modern Cambodian regime. Political leaders, including Prince Norodom Sihanouk and Khmer Rouge leader Pol Pot, saw this Khmer society as an inspiration, if not a possible model, for modern Cambodia. Yet as late as the 19th century, Angkor was largely forgotten by Cambodians themselves; no one really knew why the monument had been built or by whom.[45] In 1959, David J. Steinberg wrote that for most Cambodians, history was "the subjective experiences of their ancestors rather than the more or less factual record of events usual in the West."[46] The ruling Cambodian dynasty claimed direct descent from ancient Khmer sovereigns; this was a source of some national pride. But at the same time, many Cambodians rejected the Khmer as the builders of Angkor; popular memory and belief contained a different tradition involving a now-vanished group of ancients.[47] Cambodians could neither name Angkor's rulers nor decipher its inscriptions.[48]

It was not this poorly remembered Angkor that inspired the likes of Sihanouk and Pol Pot, but one more recently discovered and popularized by the French colonial authorities. For Sihanouk, "The past was a *recently discovered* talisman, which offered an assurance that Cambodia and its population might have a more glorious future than seemed possible in the uncertain and troubled present."[49] The French naturalist Henri Mouhot had been shown the ruins of Angkor in 1860; starting in the 1870s, French scholars deciphered numerous ancient Khmer and Sanskrit inscriptions. Hong Lysa has noted that the recovery of ancient Southeast Asian civilizations like Angkor was very much a part of the colonial enterprise. Colonial states were interested in proving a noble ancestry for the space they now occupied and in demonstrating their own superiority in recovering the physical remains of such a past. The French contrasted ancient splendors with a weak Cambodian society that, as far as the French were concerned, had lost its capacity for greatness. In any event, any greatness it had enjoyed had been the product of "Indianization" rather than native talents. An outside force had transformed Cambodia a millennium earlier, and another one, the French, would do so again.[50] The grandeur of Angkor's rulers made the apparent impotence of Cambodia's kings, who were handpicked by the French, even more obvious. These contradictions later proved a catalyst for all varieties of Cambodian nationalism.[51]

The resurrected symbol of Angkor was used by all Cambodian regimes. Cambodians responded to the mixed messages put out by the colonial authorities by relating the past to the present and by identifying with Angkor.[52] Educated Cambodians, while proud of their country's past, were ashamed of its present condition.[53] Sihanouk may have shared some of their doubts, although in visiting the Cambodian countryside he often identified the peasantry, the "little people," with the builders of the great Khmer temples.[54] Benedict Anderson mentions November 1968 celebrations commemorating the 15th anniversary of Cambodian independence from the French. For this event Sihanouk had a garish wooden replica of the central tower of Angkor Wat displayed in the national sports stadium in Phnom Penh. This model acted as an immediately recognizable logo, linking current political achievements to an impressive medieval empire.[55]

The Khmer Rouge also glorified Angkor. In a September 1977 radio address, Pol Pot stated that "we all know the Angkor of past times. Angkor was built during the slave period. It was all slaves who built it under the exploiting classes, for the enjoyment of the king. If our people were capable of building Angkor we can do anything."[56] Despite the fact that Angkor might be seen as a symbol of royalist exploitation, Pol Pot far from condemned this period of Cambodian history; in many ways, the Khmer Rouge looked back to the height of the Khmer Empire as Cambodia's golden age and even tried in a sense to resurrect this period. If the French had revived the memory of Angkor, perhaps Pol Pot wished to rebuild, at a terrible cost, its reality. Foreign scholarship had once erroneously noted that the ancient Khmer, through elaborate irrigation systems, had been able to cultivate rice intensively on a year-round basis. This historical misinterpretation was to have tragic results. The Khmer Rouge regime was convinced that they could duplicate the agricultural productivity of ancient times. Through a doubling of rice production, Cambodia could finance an industrial expansion.[57] When these results inevitably failed to be achieved, the leadership blamed not themselves and their shaky grasp of past and present realities, but rather the treason of the Cambodian people. Under the Khmer Rouge, ill-fed laborers in work camps were forced to build "an ill-conceived irrigation system meant to propel Cambodia into a rich future by copying the methods of the past."[58] The Khmer Rouge leadership tried to show that their rule was directly descended from that of Angkor and combined their belief in the innate greatness of the Khmer people with a violent hostility toward outside powers, which were routinely blamed for economic and political disasters. Despite no longer seeing Angkor as proof that Cambodia really had no need for the outside world, the Vietnamese-sponsored regime that succeeded the Khmer Rouge still stressed the importance of the ancient empire in school texts and worked to restore the site.[59] Today, the site continues to draw tourists and remains emblematic of Cambodia.

Alternate Histories in Waiting

Not all were satisfied with these new national histories. A version of the past not just approved by foreigners but in fact partially constructed by them was problematic for many Indonesian Muslims. National history tended to isolate Indonesia from larger Islamic currents; it also tended to ignore connections with the rest of Southeast Asia, India, China, and Europe (the Dutch were seen as either largely irrelevant to Indonesia's story or cartoon villains). The emphasis on Majapahit clearly marks national history as Java-centric. Although millions of Indonesians practice Buddhism and Hinduism, the ancient versions of these religions have little resonance today; this is especially the case with the larger Muslim population. A history that underlines Indonesia's past Islamic character (and possible Islamic future) might be more compatible with contemporary tastes. Majapahit was organized according to a rigid hierarchy and ruled by a semi-divine king, which made it particularly popular with New Order ruler Suharto. The New Order could be seen (and perhaps saw itself) as a "New Majapahit" fulfilling Gajah Mada's goal of unifying the nation and protecting it from outside threats, while ensuring the prosperity of a grateful population. In this view of history, Suharto was an incarnation of Gajah Mada, and the suppression of the Indonesian Communist Party in 1965 was a restoration of the nation to its natural state of passive obedience to directives issued from a Javanese *kraton* (royal palace).

Archaeology might actually be a good place to start in constructing "counter-histories," despite the fact that the discipline usually requires government support. Some Indonesian archaeologists have focused on the nation's Islamic past. Of particular note are Uka Tjandrasasmita and Hasan Muarif Ambary. Tjandrasasmita was long the head of the Islamic section of the Indonesian Archaeological Service.[60] Ambary received his training under the direction of French scholar Denys Lombard of the *annales* school of Fernand Braudel. He has published many works on Islam and archaeology as well as studies on Srivijaya and Banten.[61]

Both these scholars have put forward reconstructions of the Indonesian past that differ somewhat from a nationalist orthodoxy that sees the modern, unitary Republic of Indonesia as the direct descendant of Majapahit. From this viewpoint the most important event in pre-modern Indonesian history was Gajah Mada's taking of the *palapa* oath in which he refused to rest until the archipelago had been unified. Such events as the arrival of the Islamic religion (which is practiced by at least 85 percent of Indonesians today, although not of course by Gajah Mada) are considered less important. Islamic (and non-Javanese) rulers such as Aceh's Iskander Muda are also less celebrated. Although many Islamic figures, such as Diponegoro, Iman Bonjol, and Teuku Umar, are celebrated for battling the Dutch (as are Christian and Hindu Indonesians), Gajah Mada, his patron Hayam Wuruk, and Majapahit's last monarch Brawijaya are really the only personages who are venerated simply for their efforts in forming the nation. Other heroes contribute in a purely negative fashion, not by building a nation but rather by opposing colonial domination. The only possible exception to this pattern may be the *wali songo*. However, while they are celebrated on a popular level, they find little place in official nationalist narratives.[62]

In contrast, Tjandrasasmita and Ambary are concerned with the arrival and development of Islam in Indonesia as an historical phenomenon. In doing so, they continue in the tradition of a series of seminars held in 1963 in Medan, in 1978 and 1980 in Aceh, and in 1986 in Palembang that attempted to shift the focus of Indonesian historical research from Majapahit to the place of Islam in Indonesia.[63] Many of the papers presented at these seminars debated when and where the Islamic religion first arrived in the archipelago. The notion is entertained that Islam arrived in Sumatra relatively early, perhaps within a century after the death of Mohammad, and directly from the Arab Middle East. This is in contrast to the general consensus of Western scholars that Islam arrived in Southeast Asia via India and was not really visible until the end of the 13th century. These alternate scenarios regarding Islam's birth in Indonesia draw on different sources of data than Western researchers, who had relied on gravestone inscriptions and the accounts of European and Arab travelers, such as Marco Polo, Tome Pires, and Ibn Battuta.[64] Evidence for the early establishment of Islamic kingdoms includes Malay manuscripts, archaeological remains from northern Sumatra, and references in Chinese texts to Arab migrants to the region.

Uka Tjandrasasmita included some of this evidence in a presentation at one of these seminars as well as in an English-language article he produced for a book intended for foreign visitors to Indonesia, but in general he treats it with some skepticism. He notes the rather mysterious Ta-Shih, mentioned in Tang dynasty sources as planning to attack the kingdom of Ho-Ling (Java) around about the year 674. Other Chinese sources from the 12th century, and Japanese sources from the 8th century, mention colonies of the Ta-Shih in Southeast Asia. This group might have been Arab Muslims who settled in the region in the 7th century; another group, the Po-sse, may have been local Malay converts. But Tjandrasasmita does not wholeheartedly embrace the theory that Islam arrived in Indonesia soon after the death of the Prophet Mohammad. His description of how Islamic kingdoms emerged on the coasts of Sumatra and Java in many ways aligns with that developed by Western scholars. He notes the late 13th-century gravestone of Sultan Malik al-Shah, found at Samudra, the accounts of Marco Polo, and the importance of economic factors in the spread of the Islamic religion. Although he does acknowledge that evidence for an early arrival for Islam has mostly been ignored, he admits that this evidence is rather sketchy. Instead, he outlines how Islamic polities emerged in north Sumatra. After the 13th century, this process is more visible as a variety of Malay and foreign sources become available. This stage can be distinguished from an earlier period during which Islam may have arrived in the region.[65] The debate over a 7th- or a 13th-century date for the arrival of Islam may simply be a matter of semantics. Arab Muslims may have visited, or even settled in, Southeast Asia at an early date, but the founding of kingdoms or the conversion of the local population may have taken place much later.[66]

In a more general article intended for a non-Indonesian audience, Tjanrasasmita emphasizes a process of development very similar to that of Western scholars. Initial contacts, perhaps as early as the 7th century, occurred around the Strait of Malacca; in the 14th and 15th centuries, Islam emerged on the north coast of Java and from there spread to the rest of the archipelago. This dissemination process was helped by both foreign Muslims and local converts.[67] Conversion was facilitated by trade, marriage, and the activities of the local aristocracy, although Islam was not only an aristocratic religion but also one practiced by the population as a whole. Also of importance were the development of such institutions as the *pesantren* and the work of charismatic figures such as the *wali songo*. The latter drew on the fact that Hindu-Indonesians had "a predilection for mysticism" and "a strong concept of God" and used Sufism as a means to reach potential converts. Hindu art forms such as the *wayang* and Hindu architecture could also be put to use; Tjandrasasmita sees many motifs in Indonesian Islamic structures such as mosques that can be traced back to earlier Hindu-Indonesian norms.

At the center of the Islamization process appears to be the city. New Muslim cities arose under the impetus of foreign contact, and from these sites the religion spread to such distant points as the Moluccas.[68] Tjandrasasmita presents a story of Islam in Indonesia that seems to be above all an Indonesian one. There is little hint of conquest or foreign domination. Instead, Indonesians are exposed to the activities of fellow Indonesians who happen to have converted to Islam. As the new religion spreads, it gains converts and absorbs earlier practices that remain apparent today every time a Javanese goes to mosque. An Islamic history thus complements a nationalist history and in a sense becomes a part of it.

It should not be surprising that Tjandrasasmita was also involved in writing the third volume of the central nationalist history text *Sejarah Nasional Indonesia*, which describes the rise and character of Indonesia's Islamic kingdoms.[69] He entertains the possibility of this process starting at an early date, but in general comes down in favor of it not happening until the 13th century. The spread of Islam is seen as a process in which Indonesians fully participated. He describes it as being a peaceful process encouraged by trade and associated with Islamic mysticism, evident in both cities and the countryside. Muslim kingdoms are shown as the equal of any previous Hindu ones. Although the volume ends rather ominously by noting that Dutch power had increased considerably by the 18th century, the work is clearly "Indo-centric"; foreign colonialists are simply important players in a larger Indonesian game.

In narrating the emergence of Islamic Indonesia, Tjandrasasmita provides a large amount of background information on warfare, the technology of ships and shipbuilding, navigation, trade routes, trade goods, harbors, customs and tolls, and ship ownership during the early modern era. He also discusses urban life and the governance of the various Islamic kingdoms in considerable detail. In general, he offers a strong portrait of an "Age of Commerce" world. For him, there seems to be no contradiction between high-quality academic analysis and a nationalist narrative that celebrates the contributions of Indonesian Muslims to their country's history.

Ambary's *Menemukan Peradaban: Jejak Arkeologis dan Historis Islam Indonesia* (*Discovering Culture: The Archaeological Trail of Islam in Indonesia*), while not discounting the possibility of early Islamic kingdoms, does not emphasize it.[70] Instead, it appears to have the more ambitious motive of using archaeology as a basis for writing a generally more Islamic history of Indonesia. It starts by describing the background to the rise of Islam in Southeast Asia, noting that it was through trade that the region first entered the age of "globalization." Southeast Asia was long open to outside influences: Hindu and Buddhism in the 1st through the 5th centuries, Islam from the 7th through the 13th centuries, and European colonialism from the 17th century. The Hindu-Buddhist tradition had a great impact on local culture, as can be seen in remains of monumental architecture. In a similar manner, the people of Indonesia became familiar with Islam. Muslim traders took up residence in the region, and knowledge of Islam began to intensify within the local population. Religious conversion was associated with political change and the emergence of a common, refined culture. This process can be followed through an examination of archaeological and textual data.[71] It took place in three phases of cultural and social contact between outsiders and the native inhabitants of Southeast Asia. The first stage involved Arab traders and took place within a few centuries of the death of Mohammad. This phase can be documented from gravestones and the writings of Arab geographers. The second stage involved the formation of Islamic kingdoms in the 13th through the 16th centuries. Evidence involves the gravestone of Malik al-Saleh, Malay chronicles, and the writings of Marco Polo. The final stage involved a process of institutionalization, whereby Muslim traders spread out from Aceh, Demak, and Gresik to Borneo, Lombok, and elsewhere. Gravestones are the most important piece of evidence for this latter phase.[72] This reconstruction of the arrival of Islam is not much different from that put forward by Western scholars; Ambary identifies Samudra-Pasai as the first city in Indonesia to accept Islam and places this development in the 13th century.[73]

Ambary pays much more attention to specific manifestations of Islamic culture in Indonesian history, as reflected in material evidence. Beyond a region-by-region description of the archaeology of Islam in

Indonesia, Ambary deals with specific elements of Islamic culture, such as mosque and *kraton* architecture, epigraphy, and gravestones.[74] He sees archaeological research as a vital contribution to understanding Islam's place in the past, present, and future of the country. He describes how the discipline is presently carried out by the Jakarta-based National Archaeological Research Center,[75] which has studied migration patterns and how the local cultures of Indonesia have interacted with "great traditions" such as Hinduism, Islam, and Western civilization to produce a culturally diverse and integrated nation. In presenting a reconstruction of Indonesian history based on archaeological evidence, Ambary points to the overall purpose of his book: to counter a narrative that downplayed Islam's importance in the nation's development. *Menemukan Peradaban* presents a total picture of an Islamic Indonesian culture, a culture whose historical dynamics are as valid and important as one that sees the Republic of Indonesia as but the latest manifestation of Majapahit. The archaeological analysis presented in the book can be interpreted as evidence that an Islamic version of the past is as scientifically rigorous as the earlier histories developed by Western and nationalist-Indonesian scholars and writers. Ambary's work can be placed in a larger context and viewed as an example of "*ummat*-oriented" history, which takes as its starting point the arrival of Islam in Indonesia rather than Gajah Mada. Ambary's work offers a direct challenge to those who would write Islam out of Indonesia's story.

Both Tjandrasasmita and Ambary provide analyses that might present a different view of the Indonesian past than one of a "golden age" of Javanese domination. Tjandrasasmita describes an Indonesia open for trade with the rest of the world and receptive to new ideas, whether in regard to technology or religion. Religious innovations spread through the archipelago mostly through the actions of Indonesians themselves by means of traditional art forms and in harmony with local modes of social organization. Thus, local rulers adopt Islam and found trading centers, the *wayang* is used to explain and propagate Islamic doctrine, and mosques resemble Hindu temples. Ambary attempts a comprehensive history of Islam in Indonesia as reflected in the archaeological record. This is an antidote to the nationalist orthodoxy that tended to downplay Islam's place in the nation's history. He seems to be saying that historical inquiry of the same quality as that carried out in writing the *Sejarah Nasional Indonesia* and of the Dutch in excavating Trowulan,

restoring Borobudur, and interpreting the *Nagarakertagama* will produce a version of Indonesian history that does not marginalize Islam.
In the alternative history, offered by these two archaeologists, Indonesia
was part of a larger Islamic world and was in fact open to many outside influences from India, China, and the West. Local genius adopted
and adapted the best of these influences while retaining a strong local
identity. Islam's arrival in Southeast Asia is seen as a positive event. As
Gajah Mada helped unify the Indonesian Archipelago politically, Islam
helped build a unified Indonesian culture of interest to Muslims and
non-Muslims alike. The modern Republic of Indonesia is the latest
manifestation not necessarily of Majapahit but of a crossroads where
trade and religious currents met and produced a vibrant society. The
notion that an Indonesia seen as historically open to the *ummat* might
also have to be open to other influences is evident in some recent
comments of the Indonesian historian Asvi Warman Adam, who calls
on Indonesians to acknowledge the contributions of Chinese visitors
and residents to the nation's development.[76]

The idea that Indonesia has perhaps been more "Islamic"
than many outside observers have maintained might also lead to a
reassessment of how isolated and unique Indonesia really has been
historically. Indonesia as part of the *ummat* is also part of a wider world;
Islam aids Indonesia in the process of globalization.[77] Majapahit, an
archipelago-wide, Java-centered, hierarchical, Hindu Empire with a
god-king ruling over masses of obedient peasants, might be actually a
bit of an aberration.[78] But this questioning of the standard nationalist
narrative need not lead to increased divisions and conflict among
Indonesians. A new view of the Indonesian past does not imply that
the traditional interpretation is obsolete and that Indonesians can
no longer take pride in the accomplishments of Gajah Mada. There
is no real contradiction between being a Muslim and an Indonesian.
Indonesia can retain a national history, while taking pride of place in
the *ummat*. Stressing Indonesia's Islamic past and Islamic connections
need not separate Indonesian Muslims from their fellow citizens, nor
imply continued hostility to a larger non-Islamic world. In creating
an Indonesian past that pays more attention to Islam, scholars such as
Tjandrasasmita and Ambary might perhaps remove some of the fear
associated with anything that is driven into involuntary exile. Observers both inside and outside of Indonesia might start to understand

that the broad historical forces that brought Islam to Indonesia are the same ones that continue to link this nation with Asia, the Pacific, the West, and, of course, the *ummat*.

Conclusion

Archaeology has been used by independent Southeast Asian nation-states to foster national unity, establish political and cultural boundaries, and legitimize regimes. The problem with using archaeology to make nationalistic claims is not that it is any more scientific or any less biased than historical writings and thus more difficult to manipulate (it is not), but that it tends to show that any modern nation is in fact a recent construct. "Civilizations," as defined by archaeologists, seldom coincide with modern nation-states in regard to borders, religions, languages, supposed ethnicities, material culture, or anything else. Instead, regional and transnational identities seem more apparent. The uniqueness of a regional identity (for example, Balinese over Indonesian) as expressed in particular artifacts (such as dress, architecture, or food) might indeed be corrosive of central power, although this might be less of a danger today than it was at the time of independence, when national languages and identities were in a sense foreign to much of the Southeast Asian population. For example, in his study of life in Modjokuto (Pare), Clifford Geertz describes a town where only a few "intellectuals" spoke the national language and where knowledge of political developments was largely restricted to the visits of outside speakers from the major political parties. Fifty years later, East Java is much less isolated, and the people—whatever their religious or ethnic backgrounds, or first language for that matter—by and large accept, and are indeed proud of, a national identity. In the current context of globalization, the populations of Southeast Asia are exposed to numerous new ideas and styles (the films of Hollywood, Bollywood, and Hong Kong, along with the Internet providing much of this material), while retaining a firm commitment to national cultures they have grown comfortable with, through standardized educational systems, national languages and media, as well as recently shared histories. Similarly, national identities coexist with loyalties to larger worldviews. Howard Federspiel describes the sea routes (which met in Southeast

Asia) as "the linkage between the primary civilizations of Asia—that is, the Islamic world, Brahman India, and Middle-Kingdom China—when all three were at the height of their development and influence between the 7th and 18th centuries."[79] In later years one might add Western civilization to this Southeast Asia blend. None of these civilizations were or are the monopoly of a single country (even "China" consists of two modern polities, Taiwan and the People's Republic; the Indic world consists of the Subcontinent and a much larger cultural zone; and the Islamic world has not been a unified political entity since the 8th century). However, the geographic scope of these civilizations might indicate the existence of substantial tensions between national borders and transnational ideological ties. A modern state might have more difficulty in favoring a national identity over older, larger, and more nebulous ties on the part of its citizens than in suppressing or at least managing loyalties to a village, a city, or a region, especially as the latter might lessen as populations become more urban and mobile. A pertinent question involves the role archaeology might have in favoring broader transnational identities over recently constructed national ones. Can archaeology in fact invalidate national borders by emphasizing transnational linkages?

The answer might indeed be *yes*, if such links are assumed to be more culturally valid than national borders, identities, and histories. Since the fall of Suharto in 1997, there has been some discussion of the desirability of a pan-Southeast Asian, or even worldwide, caliphate, a structure that would logically nullify the concept of an independent Indonesian nation-state, Islamic or secular. Jemaah Islamiyah (JI), a loosely structured organization deemed responsible for the 2002 Bali bombing and several other attacks, supposedly had the construction of a Southeast Asian caliphate as its goal. There may be a large constituency among Indonesian Muslims for a wholesale rejection of the Indonesian national project in favor of a solely Islamic mode of political organization. Instead of trying to bring Islam back into Indonesian history (a goal many Indonesians would feel is overdue), groups like JI might be aiming to take Indonesia out of Islamic history.

First, it might be important to remember that although Indonesia has been an integral part of the Islamic world, it has never been part of any larger Islamic polity. Sultan Agung sent to Mecca for a title, numerous Indonesian pilgrims and scholars visited the Hijaz, and pleas were made at various times for military help from the Ottomans, but Indonesia was never conquered, ruled, or colonized by any outside Muslim power. Nor was there ever any form of trans–Southeast Asian or even Indonesian polity that could be deemed Islamic. Also, though Indonesian Muslims have historically had some interest in the concept of a caliphate, looking with concern on the abolition of the institution by Ataturk in 1924, they have since at least the 1930s been more interested in *Indonesian* independence and unity.

JI members have spoken of a caliphate, but this might simply be the way in which their organization is set up (or even how observers see their group).[80] Talk of caliphates might also be a way in which JI demonstrates its Islamist credentials, a way to distinguish a future Indonesian society from Western forms of knowledge and organization.[81] JI does have, according to some outside reconstructions, connections, especially in terms of personnel, with the Darul Islam (House of Islam) movement, which violently challenged Indonesian national authority, especially in West Java, into the early 1960s.[82] But while the radical Darul Islam rejected nationalist ideology and perhaps the republican form of government, it did not reject Indonesia as a separate entity. In fact, Darul Islam could be seen as simply a more pious version of the "regional rebellions" of the late 1950s. The case of JI is more complicated; it may have indeed started to question the viability of Indonesia as a distinct state; its transnational links—perhaps with al Qaeda, certainly with militants in Malaysia and the Philippines—have been well documented.[83] Of course, these associations may merely be good tactics. On the other hand, there does not appear to be on the part of the group a firm rejection of an Indonesian identity.

Local backing, or at least sympathy, for JI (and by extension any pro-caliphate views the group might harbor) may paradoxically be an issue of Indonesian nationalism. At the time of the Bali bombing in 2002, memories were still fresh in regard to the activities of Laksar Jihad, an armed group with which many Indonesian Muslims, some quite close to the political mainstream, sympathized. The group was perceived as defending Muslims under attack in the Moluccas (accurate or not, many Muslims analyzed the complex local Christian-Muslim conflict in this manner); the sentiment seemed to be that Indonesian Muslims could not be terrorists, only victims, and that foreigners were simply interfering in Indonesia's internal affairs (as they had over East Timor in 1999 and before) in claiming that JI was an armed terrorist organization.

The name itself simply meant "Islamic Organization," and politicians were reluctant to ban or even acknowledge the existence of such an apparently innocuous group. Indonesians denied any domestic terrorist threat up to the 2002 attack, and Vice President Hamzah Haz even met with Abu Bakar Ba'asyir, the group's leader. After the attack, many Indonesians refused to believe that Indonesians were evil or skillful enough to carry out such an attack and instead thought it was some form of foreign conspiracy.[84] While outside observers would be wise to note the strength of ties that seem to cross borders, such as the sympathy exhibited by most Indonesian and Malaysian Muslims toward the plight of their coreligionists in Iraq, Afghanistan, and Palestine, such sympathies should not be exaggerated. JI remains tiny in terms of numbers, and while its attacks can be quite devastating, it has garnered little lasting support from the Indonesian public that might be converted into usable political capital.[85] If it wishes to dissolve the national borders or even radically change national policies, it seems to have little immediate prospect of doing so. That being said, the group has deep roots; many members share close family and educational ties. JI remains committed to a long-term agenda of an Islamic state, and it will continue to take great skill and patience on the part of Indonesian authorities before the group can be neutralized.[86]

Indonesian Muslims do sometimes feel that political and societal arrangements do not always acknowledge the country's Islamic presence. Very occasionally, this feeling is reflected in violent activity, as was the case with JI and, before that, Darul Islam. However, the success of any group or individual in moving Indonesia in a more Islamic direction has more to do with adapting to local conditions and forming useful alliances than to constructing a narrative that does not contain Indonesia.[87] In fact, transnational linkages, as described in the archaeological works of Tjandrasasmita and Ambary, may actually strengthen national identities by showing that historically they have not been incompatible with larger religious ones, nor with particular regional loyalties. There may even be the possibility that focusing on narratives outside of a particular nation-state, in favor of a larger history, might bolster the concept of Southeast Asia as a unified cultural zone. ASEAN is a long way from political integration (or even economic cooperation), but one is reminded of Anwar Ibrahim's comment of feeling closer to a Buddhist Thai than to a Saudi Muslim.

Notes

[1] Dougald J.W. O'Reilly, *Early Civilizations of Southeast Asia* (New York: Altamira Press, 2007), 186–187.

[2] Charles Higham, *The Archaeology of Mainland Southeast Asia: From 10,000 BC to the Fall of Angkor* (Cambridge: Cambridge University Press, 1989), 308.

[3] Ibid., 308–313.

[4] There is a large body of literature on the arrival of Islam in Southeast Asia. Of note are S.Q. Fatimi, *Islam Comes to Malaysia* (Singapore: Malaysia Sociological Institute, 1963); Anthony Reid, "The Islamization of Southeast Asia," in *Charting the Shape of Early Modern Southeast Asia* (Bangkok: Silkworm Books, 1999), 15–34; and M.C. Ricklefs, *Mystic Synthesis in Java: A History of Islamization from the Fourteenth to the Early Nineteenth Centuries* (Norwalk, CT: East Bridge, 2006).

[5] Michael Flecker, "A Ninth Century AD Arab or Indian Shipwreck in Indonesia: First Evidence for Direct Trade with China," *World Archaeology* 32, no. 3 (2001), 335–354.

[6] Anthony Reid, *Southeast Asia in the Age of Commerce 1450–1680, Volume Two: Expansion and Crisis* (New Haven: Yale University Press, 1993), chapter 3.

[7] Clifford Geertz, *The Religion of Java* (Chicago: University of Chicago Press, 1960).

[8] Mark Woodward, "Talking across Paradigms: Indonesia, Islam, and Orientalism," in *Toward a New Paradigm: Recent Developments in Indonesian Islamic Thought*, ed. Mark Woodward (Tempe: Arizona State University, 1996), 25–28.

[9] Ibid., 9.

[10] Mark Woodward, *Islam in Java: Normative Piety and Mysticism in the Sultanate of Yogyakarta* (Tuscon: The University of Arizona Press, 1989), 2, 60.

[11] Ibid., 117, 264. Similarly, Benedict Anderson points out that in the worldview of the traditional *pesantren* (Islamic boarding school), it may be *because* the Koran cannot be understood by its readers that it is all the more powerful as a religious or even a magical text. See "The Languages of Indonesian Politics," in *Language and Power: Exploring Political Cultures in Indonesia* (Ithaca: Cornell University Press, 1990), 127.

[12] Marshall Hodgson, *The Venture of Islam: Conscience and History in World Civilization* (Chicago: University of Chicago Press, 1974), vol. 3, 551.

[13] See A.H. Johns, "Sufism as a Category in Indonesian Literature and History," *Journal of Southeast Asian Studies* 2, no. 2 (1960), 10–23.

[14] See Koentjaraningrat, *Javanese Culture* (Singapore: Oxford University Press, 1985).

[15] Milton Osborne, *Southeast Asia: An Introductory History*, 9th ed. (St. Leonards, NSW: Allen and Unwin, 2003), chapter 1.

[16] See Peter Bellwood, *Prehistory of the Indo-Malaysian Archipelago* (Honolulu: University of Hawaii, 1985), 269–271.

[17] Ian C. Glover, "Some Uses of Archaeology in East and Southeast Asia," in *An Archaeology of Asia*, ed. Mariam T. Stark (Malden, MA: Blackwell, 2006), 25–26. See also "Letting the Past Serve the Present—Some Contemporary Uses of Archaeology in Viet Nam," *Antiquity* 73, no. 291 (1999), 598–599.

[18] David G. Marr, "Sino-Vietnamese Relations," *The Australian Journal of Chinese Affairs* 6 (1981), 46; Peter Bellwood, "Southeast Asia before History," in *The Cambridge History of Southeast Asia, Volume One: From Early Times to c. 1800*, ed. Nicholas Tarling (Cambridge: Cambridge University Press, 1992), 129–132.

[19] Bellwood, *Prehistory*, 275.

[20] For a description of Chinese attitudes and actions toward the region, see Martin Stuart-Fox, *A Short History of China and Southeast Asia: Tribute, Trade and Influence* (Sydney: Allen and Unwin, 2003).

[21] Louise Levathes, *When China Ruled the Seas: The Treasure Fleet of the Dragon Throne, 1405–1433* (New York: Simon and Schuster, 1994).

[22] Ma Huan, *Ying-yai Sheng-lan: "The Overall Survey of the Ocean's Shores" (1433)*, ed. and trans. J.V.G. Mills (Cambridge: Cambridge University Press, 1970).

[23] See *Chinese Muslims in Java in the 15th and 16th Century: The Malay Annals of Semerang and Cerbon*, ed. M.C. Ricklefs, trans. H.J. Graaf and Theodore G. Th. Pigeaud (Melbourne: Monash Papers on Southeast Asia, 1984). The veracity of these documents has been questioned.

[24] Leonard Blussé, *Strange Company: Chinese Settlers, Mestizo Women, and the Dutch in VOC Batavia* (Leiden: KITLV, 1986); Donald Willmott, *The National Status of the Chinese in Indonesia, 1900–1958* (Ithaca: Cornell Modern Indonesia Project, 1961); Leo Suryadinata, *Chinese and Nation-building in Southeast Asia* (Singapore: ISEAS, 1997).

[25] C.R. Boxer, *The Portuguese Seaborne Empire* (Harmondsworth, England: Penguin, 1973).

[26] M.C. Ricklefs, *A History of Modern Indonesia Since c. 1200*, 3d ed. (Stanford: Stanford University Press, 2001).

[27] M.C. Ricklefs, *War, Culture, and Economy in Java, 1677–1726: Asian and European Imperialism in the Early Kartasura Period* (Sydney: Allen and Unwin, 1993).

[28] Reid, *Southeast Asia in the Age of Commerce: Volume Two*, 326–330.

[29] See Harry J. Benda, "Christian Snouck Hurgronje and the Foundations of Dutch Islamic Policy in Indonesia," *Journal of Modern History* 30, no. 4 (1958), 338–347.

[30] Ibid., 339.

[31] See John Smail, "On the Possibility of an Autonomous History of Modern Southeast Asia," *Journal of Southeast Asian History* 2, no. 2 (1961).

[32] For a recent study of the complexity of Southeast Asian responses to colonial rule and borders, see Eric Tagliacozzo, *Secret Trades, Porous Borders: Smuggling and States along a Southeast Asian Frontier, 1865–1915* (New Haven: Yale University Press, 2005).

[33] *Imagined Communities: Reflections on the Origin and Spread of Nationalism*, rev. ed. (London: Verso, 1990), 170–173.

[34] Stuart Robson, *Desawarnana (Nagarakertagama) by Mpu Prapanca* (Leiden: KITLV, 1995) or *Java in the Fourteenth Century: A Study in Cultural History: The Nagara-Kertagama by Rakawi Prapanca of Majapahit*, 5 vols., ed. and trans. Theodore G. Th. Pigeaud (The Hague: Nijhoff, 1960–1962).

[35] "Javanese Historiography: A Synopsis of its Evolution," in *Historians of Southeast Asia*, ed. D.G.E. Hall (London: Oxford University Press, 1961), 87–117.

[36] Delia Noer, "Yamin and Hamka: Two Routes to an Indonesian Identity," in *Perceptions of the Past in Southeast Asia*, ed. Anthony Reid and David Marr (Singapore: Heinemann Educational Books, 1979), 258. There had in fact also been some minor interest in the idea outside of the Dutch East Indies, among Malays worried about any future independent state falling under Chinese domination. See Angus McIntyre, "The Greater Indonesia Idea of Nationalism in Malaya and Indonesia," *Modern Asian Studies* 7, no. 1 (1973), 75–83.

[37] See Daud Tanudirjo, "Theoretical Trends in Indonesian Archaeology," in *Theory in Archaeology: A World Perspective*, ed. Peter Ucko (London: Routledge, 1995), 62–70. See also Jacques Dumarçay, *Borobudur*, ed. and trans. Michael Smithies (Singapore: Oxford University Press, 1978).

[38] Timothy E. Behrend, "Kraton, Taman, Mesjid: A Brief Survey and Bibliographic Review of Islamic Antiquities in Java," *Indonesia Circle* 35 (1984), 29. See also Claire Holt, *Art in Indonesia: Continuities and Change* (Ithaca: Cornell University Press, 1967), and Theodore G. Th. Pigeaud, trans. and ed. F.A. Wagner, *Indonesia: The Art of an Island Group* (London: Methuen, 1962).

[39] *Hasil Pemugaran dan Temuan Benda Cagar Budaya* (Jakarta: Departemen Pendidikan dan Kebudayaan, 1994).

[40] See Anthony Reid, "The Nationalist Quest for an Indonesian Past," in *Perceptions of the Past in Southeast Asia*, ed. Anthony Reid and David Marr (Singapore: Heinemann Educational

Books, 1979), 298. Indonesian scholars such as Sartono Kartodirdjo prefer the term "national history." See *Indonesian Historiography* (Yogyakarta: Kanisius, 2001), 15.

[41] See especially, Sukarno, *Indonesia Accuses! Sukarno's Defence Oration in the Political Trial of 1930*, ed., ann., and trans. Roger K. Paget (Kuala Lumpur: Oxford University Press, 1975), 79, and Muhammad Yamin, *Gadjah Mada: Pahlawan Persatuan Nusantara* (Gajah Mada: A Hero of the Unity of the Archipelago), 6th ed. (Jakarta: Dinas Penerbitan Balai Pustaka, 1960).

[42] S. Supomo, "The Image of Majapahit in Later Javanese and Indonesian Writing," in *Perceptions of the Past in Southeast Asia*, 180–181.

[43] See Michael Wood, *Official History in Modern Indonesia: New Order Perceptions and Counterviews* (Leiden: Brill, 2005).

[44] David Chandler, *The Tragedy of Cambodian History: Politics, War, and Revolution since 1945* (New Haven: Yale University Press, 1991), 6. The use of a term such as "ancient" to describe a civilization contemporary with Baghdad and the Magna Carta might seem odd. Colonial-era European scholars looking at Southeast Asia often sharply distinguished between "ancient" societies such as Angkor, which would not have had any contact with Europeans, and "degenerate" modern societies fit for colonization.

[45] Milton Osborne, *Sihanouk: Prince of Light, Prince of Darkness* (Honolulu: University of Hawaii Press, 1994), 42.

[46] David J. Steinberg, *Cambodia: Its People, Its Society, Its Culture* (New Haven: HRAF Press, 1959), 7.

[47] Ibid., 7.

[48] Chandler, *The Tragedy of Cambodian History*, 6.

[49] Osborne, 42; italics added.

[50] Hong Lysa, "History," in *An Introduction to Southeast Asian Studies*, ed. Mohammed Halib and Tim Huxley (Singapore: Institute of Southeast Asian Studies, 1996), 49–50.

[51] David Chandler, *Brother Number One: A Political Biography of Pol Pot* (Boulder: Westview Press, 1992), 12–13.

[52] Chandler, *The Tragedy*, 6.

[53] Ibid., 284–285.

[54] Ibid., 6.

[55] Anderson, *Imagined Communities*, 183. The original description cited by Anderson appeared in the Cambodian newspaper *Kambuja*, December 15, 1968.

[56] Chandler, *Brother Number One*, 142.

[57] Ben Kiernan, *The Pol Pot Regime: Race, Power and Genocide in Cambodia under the Khmer Rouge, 1975–1979* (New Haven: Yale University Press, 1996), 8.

[58] Elizabeth Becker, *When the War Was Over: Cambodia and the Khmer Rouge Revolution* (New York: PublicAffairs, 1999), 200.

[59] Chandler, *The Tragedy of Cambodian History*, 7. Restoration of the site involved the persistent problem of landmines and continued Khmer Rouge activity; the time and money expended may indicate the importance of Angkor as a symbol. However, the site may simply be seen as a useful source of tourist dollars (echoing Silberman's "touristic archaeology"). See Neil Asher Silberman, "Promised Lands and Chosen Peoples: The Politics and the Poetics of Archaeological Narrative," in *Nationalism, Politics and the Practice of Archaeology*, ed. Philip L. Kohl and Clare Fawcett (Cambridge: Cambridge University Press, 1995), 261.

[60] See John N. Miksic, "Indonesian Publications on Archaeology, 1975–82," *Indonesia Circle* 34 (1984), 45–50.

[61] See, for example, "Recent Archaeological Discoveries at Srivijaya Sites," in *Studies on Srivijaya*, ed. Satyawati Suleiman et al. (Jakarta: Puslit Arkenas, 1980), and *A Preliminary Report of the Excavation of the Urban Sites in Banten (West Java)* (Jakarta: P4N, 1977).

[62] For an analysis of how the tombs of the *wali songo* were treated during the late New Order, when despite regime efforts to reach out to Indonesian Muslim sentiment, the nationalist

orthodoxy could be considered to be in full force, see Michael Wood, "The Historical Past as a Tool for Nation-Building in New Order Indonesia," in *Good Governance: A Workable Solution for Indonesia*, ed. Andi Faisal Bakti (Jakarta: Logos Press, 2000), 81–83.

[63] See A. Hasymy, ed., *Sejarah Masuk dan Berkembangnya Islam di Indonesia* (The History of the Entrance and Growth of Islam in Indonesia) (Jakarta: Almaarif, 1993), and K.H.O. Gadjanata and Sri Swasono, *Masuk dan Berkembangnya Islam di Sumatera Selatan* (Entrance and Growth of Islam in South Sumatra) (Jakarta: University of Indonesia, 1986).

[64] See Ricklefs, *A History of Modern Indonesia*, chapter 1, and Fatimi, *Islam Comes to Malaysia*. See also L.F. Benedetto, *Travels of Marco Polo*, trans. Aldo Ricci, intro. E. Denison Ross (London: George Routledge and Sons, 1931), 281–282; Amando Cortessao, ed., *The Suma Oriental of Tome Pires Book of Francisco Rodriques*, 2 vols. (London: Hakluyt Society, 1944), 137, 143, 182, and *Travels in Asia and Africa 1325–1354*, trans. H.A.R. Gibb (London: George Routledge and Sons, 1929), 272–276.

[65] *Proses Kedatangan Islam and Munculnya Kerajaan-Karajaan Islam di Aceh* (The Process of the Arrival of Islam and the Emergence of Islamic Kingdoms in Aceh), in *Sejarah Masuk*, 360–365.

[66] The reliance on textual evidence in reconstructing early Islam in Southeast Asia is problematic for many reasons. Because of the tropical climate, most manuscripts will not have survived to the present and those that have would present the biased views of a local elite (which might lead scholars to assume that Islamization must have been a top-down process). Foreign sources would have their own sets of assumptions (including simple ignorance of local culture). Archaeology may thus be useful in illuminating the origins of Islam in Southeast Asia. Excavations in Banda give a much earlier date for the arrival of Islam than previously thought (around 1200 as opposed to 1450) based on a paucity of pig bones discovered at various sites. However, such work on sites connected to Islam is not carried out very often. See Peter Lape, "Focus on Islam IV: Archaeological Approaches to the Study of Islam in Island Southeast Asia," *Antiquity* 79, no. 306 (205), 829–836.

[67] "The Introduction of Islam and the Growth of Moslem Coastal Cities in the Archipelago," in *Dynamics of Indonesian History*, ed. Haryati Soebadio and Carine A. du Marchie Sarvas (New York: North-Holland Publishing Company, 1978), 143–145, 148.

[68] Ibid., 149–157.

[69] See Marwati Poesponegoro and Nugroho Notosusanto, eds., *Sejarah Nasional Indonesia* (National History of Indonesia), 6 vols., 4th ed. (Jakarta: Departemen Pendidikan dan Kebudayaan RI, 1990). This set of books functioned as the basis of school textbooks during the New Order period.

[70] Hasan Muarif Ambaray, *Menemukan Peradaban: Jejak Arkeologis dan Historis Islam Indonesia*, ed. Jajat Burhanuddin (Jakarta: Logos, 1998).

[71] Ibid., 53–54.

[72] Ibid., 58–59.

[73] Ibid., 128–129.

[74] Ibid., 163–170, 191–202.

[75] Ibid., 337–339.

[76] Asvi Warman Adam, "The Chinese in the Collective Memory of the Indonesian Nation," *Kyoto Review* 2 (March 2003), 1–12 (online edition).

[77] The writer and politician Roeslan Abdulgani refers to Islam as coming to Indonesia "bearing civilisation [or progress]." Dutch colonialism had, in his opinion, interrupted Indonesia's historic path of development under the guidance of Islam. See *Sejarah Pekembangan Islam di Indonesia* (The History of the Development of Islam in Indonesia) (Jakarta: Pustaka Antara Kota, 1983), 7, 28. Abdulgani, who was close to Sukarno and later worked on developing government ideological training under Suharto, was considered a very secular figure, although he later showed a great deal of sympathy to Islam. As early as the Guided Democracy period, outside observers such as Justus M. Van der Kroef, suspicious of a "nationalist orthodoxy" that emphasized

an inherent Indonesian unity and an Indonesian uniqueness even in the manner of the country's exposure to Islam, called for a history that paid more attention to the importance of outside influences. See "National and International Dimensions of Indonesian History," *Journal of Southeast Asian History* 6, no. 1 (1965), 17.

[78] Anthony Reid points out that historically, centralization was unusual in Southeast Asia; even Majapahit, according to visitors, was quite loosely structured. See "Political 'Tradition' in Indonesia: The One and the Many," *Asian Studies Review* 22, no. 1 (1998), 23–38.

[79] See *Sultans, Shamans and Saints: Islam and Muslims in Southeast Asia* (Honolulu: University of Hawaii Press, 2007), 7.

[80] See Clinton Fernandes and Damien Kingsbury, "Terrorism in Archipelagic Southeast Asia," in *Violence in Between: Conflict and Security in Archipelagic Southeast Asia*, ed. Damien Kingsbury (Singapore: Institute of Southeast Asian Studies, 2005), 21–22. See also International Crisis Group, "Indonesian Backgrounder: How the Jamaah Islamiyah Terrorist Network Operates," Asia Report No. 43, December 11, 2002.

[81] Fernandes and Kingsbury, 20.

[82] International Crisis Group, "Recycling Militants in Indonesia: Darul Islam and the Australian Embassy Bombing," Asia Report No. 92, February 22, 2005. See also Martin van Bruinessen, "Genealogies of Islamic Radicalism in Post-Suharto Indonesia," *Southeast Asia Research* 10, no. 2 (2002), 117–154.

[83] Fernandes and Kingsbury, 22.

[84] Dewi Anggraeni, *Who Did This to Our Bali?* (Victoria, Australia: Indra Publishing, 2003).

[85] International Crisis Group, "Indonesia: Jemaah Islamiyah's Current Status," Asia Briefing No. 63, May 3, 2007.

[86] See International Crisis Group, "Jemaah Isalamiyah in South East Asia Damaged but Still Dangerous," Asia Report No. 63, August 26, 2003, and "Terrorism in Indonesia: Noordin's Networks," Asia Report No. 114, May 5, 2006, for some recent assessments of how successful Southeast Asian governments have been in dismantling JI and what long-term prospects the group might have.

[87] Or in a more leftward direction for that matter; the Indonesian Communist Party owed much of its success to adapting Marxist doctrine to Indonesian norms and through an alliance with Sukarno, who had an uncanny ability to understand and tap into local sensibilities. Similarly, liberal democracy's long-term prospects of flourishing in Indonesia are probably related to how well it can adapt and make itself relevant to local conditions.

Chapter 3

Historical Survey of Borders in Southeast Asia

David Lee

This chapter provides a historical account of the evolution of Southeast Asian borders. The first section shows how the concept of the territorially defined, bordered nation-state evolved gradually in Europe in the 200 years from about 1600 to 1800. From Europe, concepts of borders were exported to Southeast Asia from the 17th to the early 20th century. Precolonial Southeast Asia consisted of nascent states, but the concept of frontiers was thought of more in terms of the allegiance of people than of control over fixed territory.

The chapter next explains how the European powers, principally Britain, France, and the Netherlands, imposed on Southeast Asia the notion of the territorial state. The imperial powers agreed amongst themselves, and with the nominally independent Thailand, on the boundaries for their colonial empires. These boundaries carried over into the post–World War II period and have generally worked to strengthen regional stability. Britain's annexations of Burma reconstituted the precolonial Burman kingdom, France rescued Laos and Cambodia from possible incorporation within other states, and Thailand's borders were effectively determined by Franco-British policy. The Netherlands established the borders of modern-day Indonesia. Malaysia is the legacy of British imperialism and the Philippines of Spanish, and later American, colonialism.

Despite the arbitrariness of Southeast Asian boundaries, they have been generally accepted by the nation-states that emerged in the 20 or so years after World War II and by the larger states that border the region. Nonetheless, in the period from 1945 to the 1960s, Southeast Asian states were relatively weak and struggled with ethnic and other separatist or regionalist forces to maintain control over the territories bestowed on them by international law. The chapter concludes with a section on the effect of globalization and regionalization on Southeast Asian borders. The argument here is that while regionalization and globalization have to some extent made borders more porous, the period from the late 1960s to the present has been one in which Southeast Asian states have generally grown stronger and their borders more important.

European Origins of Southeast Asian Borders

The idea of fixed territoriality, like the state itself, developed in modern Europe and was exported to Southeast Asia. Surveying borders and drawing lines on maps that separate contemporary states are practices that date back only to the 17th century. Before that time, in both Europe and Asia, the frontiers of empires, kingdoms, city-states, and tribal groupings were transient and indeterminate.

However, from the 16th century onward, monarchs in Europe began to centralize authority over their realms, in the process curtailing the strength of rival sources of power such as the landed aristocracy, towns and cities, and the church. In the 200 years from 1600 to 1800, Europe was transformed from a borderless world, with the pope and the Holy Roman Emperor sharing nominal authority over a patchwork of different polities, into a clearly delineated system of highly centralized, territorial polities that are known today as states.[1] Essential attributes that European states possessed were a fixed position in space (territoriality); supreme rule within a bordered realm (sovereignty); and allegiance or loyalty from the permanent inhabitants of the territory that superseded other loyalties.[2]

Distinctions were sometimes made in Europe between the terms *boundary* and *frontier*. A *boundary* can be defined as a "clear divide between sovereignties which can be marked as a line on a map."[3] If states accept a boundary, even if they have not completed the task of laying it down on the ground, then that boundary is said to be *delimited*. If the boundary has also been marked out on the ground, it is viewed as having been *demarcated*. *Frontiers* were sometimes understood as zones rather than lines—as tracts of land separating the centers of two sovereignties.[4]

Precolonial Southeast Asia

Few regions of the world are as clearly demarcated geographically as Southeast Asia. Its southern rim is a volcanic arc consisting of the Sunda Islands of Sumatra, Java, Bali, and Lombok. Its eastern perimeter consists of the Philippines, outside of which lies a deep trench in the Pacific Ocean. To the north, it is bordered by the eastern Himalayas, where the region's greatest rivers begin. The environment of Southeast Asia is characterized by water and forests. Forests were abundant throughout the region because of reliably high rainfalls and temperatures.[5] Today, however, forests in states like Thailand, Burma, Malaysia, and Indonesia are being rapidly depleted largely owing to the huge demand from an industrializing China.[6]

The region is ethnically and linguistically diverse (see map 3–1). This diversity was partly the result of mass migrations into the area from the sea and the land. It was also the result of geographic characteristics of the areas, such as jungles, mountains, and swamps, which have "assisted over time in adding to the diversities among the peoples of Southeast Asia by cutting them off from one another and promoting their distinctiveness in different parts of the region."[7] The process of state-building in Southeast Asia, both before and after European colonization, had an ambivalent effect on this diversity. To some extent, states brought people together, but they also divided the peoples of Southeast Asia from each other.[8]

Most of the people who today inhabit the archipelagic part of Southeast Asia, the region now covered by Malaysia, Indonesia, and the Philippines, are considered to be of the southern Mongoloid type, speaking Austronesian languages.[9] The peoples who inhabit mainland Southeast Asia appear to have originated from the movement of tribal groups southward and westward from southwest China and its frontier region. Tibeto-Burmans seem to have descended the Irrawaddy Valley before the Common Era; and the Shan-Thai-Lao peoples seem to have moved down the Salween and Menam valleys in the early centuries of the Common Era (CE).[10] The Burman peoples restricted the movement of the Shans to plateau country, but the Mon-Khmer peoples of the Menam basin were less effective in resisting the Thais.[11] The Vietnamese were the most Sinicized of the peoples of mainland Southeast Asia. They originated from a kingdom that spanned the contemporary China-Vietnam frontier and later broke away from China and moved southward. In doing so, the Vietnamese fought with and later incorporated the Chams, an Indianized people speaking a Malayo-Polynesian language, and later contended also with the Khmers.[12] Indian civilization had penetrated Southeast Asia by sea from at least the first centuries of the Common Era. It spread gradually over the coastlands of Indonesia and southern Annam (modern Vietnam). The main significance of the

Map 3–1. Ethnic Mosaic of Southeast Asia

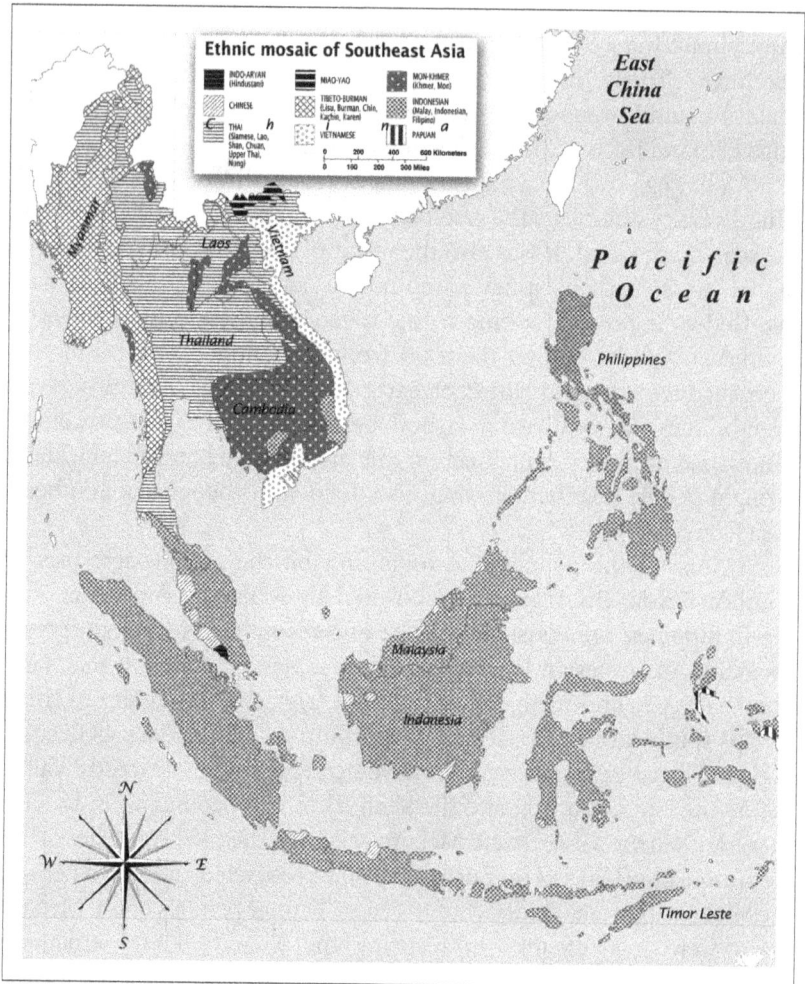

Indianization of Southeast Asia was the importation of the Hindu and Buddhist religions and forms of political organization based on aristocratic concepts of monarchy and the social order.[13]

In the period before the European colonization of the region, kingdoms emerged in Southeast Asia that in some cases formed the nucleus of the bordered nation-states of today. These kingdoms ranged from local chieftaincies to "early kingdoms" that incorporated neighboring areas through tributary patterns rather than through administrative means. From the 9th century CE, some of these kingdoms emerged as imperial kingdoms or super-kingdoms that unified two or more core areas of former kingdoms.[14] Oliver Wolters describes these kingdoms as "mandalas" or "circles of kings" in which larger units formed a tributary relationship with smaller units and expanded and contracted like a concertina.[15]

In mainland Southeast Asia, an Indianized kingdom of Funan, founded in the 1st century CE in present-day Cambodia, gave way to Khmer kingdoms that appeared in the 7th and 8th centuries CE. The greatest of these was the Indianized kingdom based at Angkor. This Khmer Empire expanded westward, contending with the Mons and the Thais of the Menam Valley, and eastward, defeating the Chams in present-day Laos.[16] The Mons were Indianized people closely related to the Khmers who inhabited the lower region of coastal Burma and the Menam Valley. Once a dependency of Funan, Champa had formed a distinct area of Indianized rule from the 2[d] century CE.[17] For one reason or other, the Khmer Empire collapsed in the 14th century.

A fairly stable Vietnamese state emerged in the 1st century CE on the Chinese frontier. The T'ang dynasty set up a protectorate of An-nam (Pacified South) in the 6th century that repelled an invasion from the Chinese kingdom of Nanchao in the 9th century and became increasingly independent thereafter. The Vietnamese subsequently expanded southward, contending with Champa and coming into more intense conflict with the Khmers in the 15th century.[18]

Thai states appeared in the upper Menam Valley in the 13th century, and Shan states emerged in Burma and Assam in the same timeframe.[19] In that century, too, Chiangmai became the seat of the Thai kingdom of Lan Na, to the north of which lay Lao states that merged into the kingdom of Lan Xang in the mid-14th century.[20] Lan Xang, in what is today Laos, was Buddhist and Indian culturally and Thai in its language and leadership.[21] The Thais are an ethnic group, cognate with the Chinese and related to the Shans and Laos, who originated from what are now the Chinese provinces of Kweichow, Kwangsi, and Yunnan.[22] The center of the Thai kingdom later moved to Ayudhya on an island in the Menam where the Thai king was crowned.[23] The Burmans established a kingdom with its capital in Pagan in central Burma in 849 CE and sought in succeeding centuries to exercise hegemony over the Mons, Shans, Chins, and Karens.[24] But their kingdom, later with its seat in Ava, fragmented in the period before British colonization in the 19th century.[25]

Different types of states emerged in precolonial times in archipelagic Southeast Asia. The Indianized kingdom of Sri Vijaya, based in the Strait of Malacca, became from the 8th century the first of a number of states that developed trading empires that held sway in both the archipelago and the peninsula. Sri Vijaya exercised supremacy over Kedah and the isthmus and islands south of the strait and east and north of Sumatra.[26] Another important trading empire was Majapahit, which established itself over a large part of archipelagic Southeast Asia and the Malay Peninsula during the 14th century.[27] These archipelagic trading empires tended to be weaker than mainland super-kingdoms such as those based in Pagan or Angkor since they lacked the resources and populations of the mainland kingdoms and required control of the sea in order to command political supremacy.

The Muslim era in the Middle East dates from 622 CE. However, the new religion did not take root in Southeast Asia for another 700 years. Islam spread throughout Southeast Asia from west to east following trade routes in the period from the 14th century to the early 17th century. In doing so, the new religion established new frontiers between the nascent states of archipelagic Southeast Asia and the Malay Peninsula. After first lodging in Sumatra, Islam spread along the coasts of the islands nominally subject to Majapahit and on the coast of the Malay Peninsula over which Majapahit contended with the kingdom of Siam for suzerainty. When Muslim communities were established, pilgrims followed the trade routes to make the pilgrimage to Mecca, providing contact between Muslims in maritime Southeast Asia and Arabia. Islam gained its most powerful convert in the new state of Malacca on the Malay Peninsula. The Sultan of Malacca carried Islam northward to Pahang and Kedah and southward to the Sumatran river ports. Malacca then cultivated strong trading relationships with such Javanese ports as Demak, Japara, and Tuban. In 1478, the Muslim coastal state of Demak invaded Majapahit, reducing this once-great Hindu-Javanese Empire into an East Javan enclave.[28]

When the era of imperial rule dawned in Southeast Asia, the Vietnamese and Thais were continuing to expand at the expense of the Khmers, and no final solution had been agreed on the limits of the domains of the Burmans, Shans, Thais, and Laos. Alastair Lamb has remarked that "at the moment of colonial impact, it would not have been easy to point to any stable delimited or demarcated boundary in mainland South-east Asia, even though the location of the centres of the power in the region was clear enough."[29] In the sparsely populated world of precolonial Southeast Asia, the allegiance of people and vassal provinces counted for more than the delimitation and control of territory, and the power of Southeast Asian kingdoms was greatest in the capital and weakest at the periphery. Nonetheless, in some ways the territorial and colonial empires that emerged in Southeast Asia in the 19th century resembled the indigenous empires and super-kingdoms that they replaced.[30]

Imperial Frontiers of Southeast Asia

From about the beginning of the 16th century, Europeans began to establish direct contacts with the Southeast Asian region (see map 3–2). The Treaty of Tordesillas, signed on June 7, 1494, divided the world outside Europe into an exclusive duopoly between the Spanish and Portuguese and spurred on these Western European states to extend

Map 3–2. Colonial Boundaries in Southeast Asia

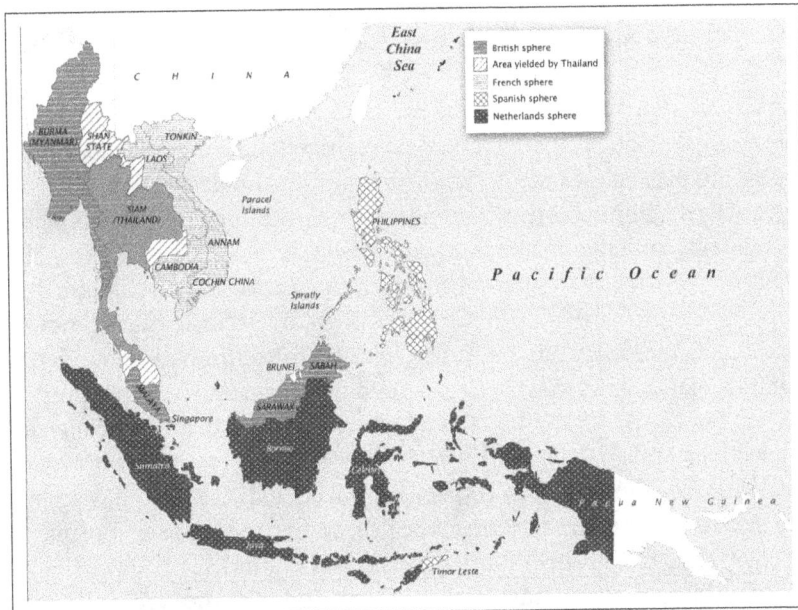

their maritime empires into Southeast Asia. In 1511, the Portuguese captured Malacca, secured a share in the trade of the archipelago, and competed maritime empires into Southeast Asia. In 1511, the Portuguese captured Malacca, secured a share in the trade of the archipelago, and competed with Javanese towns and the Malayo-Muslim state of Aceh in northern Sumatra.[31] This state had extended its control over pepper-producing parts of Menangkabau and parts of Bantam.[32]

In the 16th century, the Dutch East India Company established a presence in the archipelago with a base in Batavia (Jakarta) on the island of Java. The company could neither create a general monopoly nor gain overall political control of the archipelago. But it constrained empire-building in the Indonesian archipelago by other European powers, pursued a monopoly of the trade in fine spices that led to the decay of Aceh, and concentrated increasingly on Java in the 18th century.[33] A Spanish expedition reached what are now the Philippines in the 16th century and established territorial control in Luzon and the Visayas. The Spanish also captured Manila, which had formerly been an outpost of the Sultanate of Brunei.[34] The seizure of the city led to a long conflict between the Spaniards and the Moros, their Muslim opponents in the south. The conflict between Islamic insurgents in the south and the central government based in Manila persists to this day.

On the Southeast Asian mainland, Britain and France were the most important European colonists. From the 18th to the early 20th century, these two powers forced the precolonial kingdoms to "accept a new ordering of political space and a new regime of interstate relations built upon the principle of territorial sovereignty."[35] The British first came to Asia at the beginning of the 17th century as merchants on the subcontinent. While not initially inclined to get involved in Indian politics, the British East India Company became more interventionist in the 18th century, acquiring Bengal in 1757, and then, by degrees, gaining power over the whole subcontinent. It was in order to secure stable boundaries for its Indian Empire that the British became an imperial power in Burma. When the British established their authority in Bengal, the Burmans did likewise in Arakan. It proved difficult for both powers to establish, accept, and enforce a boundary in respect of Arakan and Assam and Manipur on India's northeastern frontier. British efforts to persuade Burma to recognize de facto British supremacy led to a war in 1824.[36]

Although their war aim was not initially the acquisition of Burman territory, the British ended up taking Arakan and Tenasserim.

Because the defeated Burman monarch could not agree to stable relations with his more powerful neighbor, war broke out again in 1852. As
a result of this second war, Burma was forced to surrender Lower Burma
(the Irrawaddy Delta). Then in 1884, when the French approached
the remnant Burman Kingdom to negotiate an agreement, Britain
instigated the third Burma war, which ended in annexation. The frontier
of Burma, Britain insisted, had to be settled between itself and France.
Burma became an administrative subdivision of the British Indian
Empire until 1937, when it became a separate colonial territory, and
then an independent Union of Burma in 1948.[37]

Before British colonization, the Burman state had dissolved into
fragments. The effects of British colonization were not only to put
Burma back together but also to endow it with territory and peoples
over which it previously had only superficial control.[38] There were many
non-Burman tribal groups, such as Shans, Karens, Kachins, and Chins,
that developed firmer and more precise relationships with the British
than they had ever reached with the Burmans.[39] Burma's half-century
as an independent state after the British departure was marked by
recurring conflict between the central government and the non-Burman
hill peoples. Alastair Lamb has speculated on what the consequences
might have been if Britain had restricted itself to its annexations of
1826 and 1852. He contended that, without a British presence in all
of Burma, the Chinese would have penetrated deep into what are
today Burma's Kachin and Karen states. He concluded: "[i]t is hard to
escape the conclusion that the boundaries of modern Burma—and their
associated problems—are very much part of the imperial legacy."[40]

The Thais, like the Burmese and the Vietnamese, had achieved
a form of political unity well before the period of colonial domination
of Southeast Asia. Unlike the Burmese, the Vietnamese, and the
inhabitants of the Malay Archipelago, the Thais were never subjected to
colonial rule. The Thai kingdom, which originated in the 14th century,
was weakened during the early colonial period by the incursions of the
Portuguese and Dutch, but more substantially by war with the Burmans
that ended in the destruction of Ayudhya in 1767. Nevertheless, a
dynasty based in Bangkok revived Thai unity during the time when the
British were expanding their influence in India.[41]

Although the Tenasserim strip remained under Burmese control,
the Thais strengthened their hold of the peninsula, bought the Lao kingdoms of the Mekong under their suzerainty, and penetrated the western

districts of Cambodia. This expanding Thai kingdom was halted by the assertion of British power in Malaya and Burma and of French power in Indochina. The borders of Thailand were determined during the colonial period in Southeast Asian history through negotiations between the imperial powers.[42] British policy in the late 19th century was to minimize the possibility of war with France by maintaining Thailand as a buffer state between the British Indian Empire (incorporating Burma) and the French Indochinese Empire.

The end of the 18th century also saw important changes in the balance of power in archipelagic Southeast Asia and the Malay Peninsula. From about that time, the British East India Company began to ship vast quantities of tea from Canton. Britain thereby acquired a commercial and strategic interest in the Strait of Malacca. After the loss of its American colonies in the 1780s, Britain's overseas interests shifted from North America to Asia. In that decade, a private British trader, Francis Light, persuaded the Sultan of Kedah to cede him the island of Penang in return for British protection against Siam and Burma. During the 1790s, Britain wrested control of Malacca from the Dutch, and in 1811, after France had formerly annexed the Netherlands, Britain invaded Java. Sir Thomas Stamford Raffles was appointed Lieutenant Governor of Java and the dependencies. He subdivided all of the former Dutch dependencies into four administrative units: Malacca, Java, the West Coast of Sumatra, and the Moluccas.

At the end of the Napoleonic wars, the British occupation of Java and Malacca came to an end. Nonetheless, Stamford Raffles sought to counterbalance the reimposition of Dutch control over the Strait of Malacca by establishing a base on the then-unoccupied island of Singapore, an action that increased the tension between the British and Dutch in Southeast Asia. The situation was resolved by the Anglo-Dutch Treaty of 1824 that established a kind of frontier in the Strait of Malacca between the British Empire on the peninsula and Singapore and the Dutch Empire in the archipelago. As Tarling has put it, "Peninsula and archipelago had enjoyed a common past. States—Aceh, Johore, the Portuguese, the Dutch—had previously had a footing on both sides of the straits. Now the straits had become a kind of frontier. In Southeast Asia the sea united; the Europeans used it to divide."[43] By contrast with Burma, where Britain acquired control of a large territory, the "Straits Settlements" of Penang, Malacca, and Singapore were territorially circumscribed and outward looking. They nonetheless restricted Thailand's southward movement over the Malay Peninsula. In 1826, Thailand signed a treaty undertaking to refrain from intervention in the Malay states of Perak and Selangor, and in 1842, Thai troops withdrew from Kedah.

Negotiations among France, Britain, and Thailand resulted in a Thai state less extensive than the Thai kingdom of Ayudhya. In 1828, Ayudhya had claimed authority over the Shan state in Burma, all of the old kingdom of Lan Xang, and most of the kingdom of Cambodia.[44] Thailand's land boundaries consist of a Burma-Thailand section, a Laos-Thailand section in the Mekong valley, a Thailand-Cambodia section stretching from the Mekong to the Gulf of Siam, and a boundary between Thailand and Malaya running from the South China Sea to the Indian Ocean. After the first Burma War, Britain considered placing that territory under a Mons ruler but eventually decided on outright annexation.

The subsequent evolution of Southeast Asia's borders may have worked out quite differently had a separate Mons state been formed in Tenasserim, or had the territory been returned to Thailand (as the British once contemplated), or had British power on the peninsula been centered on Phuket Island rather than on Penang Island much farther to the south. In this last scenario, British Malaya may "have swallowed all southern Thailand."[45] The drawing of the Burma boundary cut off many Shan groups from the Thai city of Chiangmai, with which they had formed close relations. Had the British annexations in Burma not taken the course they did, it is possible that a forward Thai policy may have attempted to incorporate the Shan states.[46]

Just as Thailand's Burma border was established after the British annexations of the 19th century, so was its Laos border determined by French imperial policy. Before the consolidation of French power in Indochina, the Thai kingdom had established political relationships with the Lao peoples to the east of the Mekong River. The intention of the French in the 1880s to expand their influence from Vietnam up the Mekong River threatened to bring about a state of war between France and Thailand. However, partly due to British influence, the Thais agreed with the French in 1893 to terms that ceded the Lao peoples on the east bank of the Mekong to France and that defined the border between Thailand and French Indochina by the course of the Mekong River. The boundary was further redefined to the disadvantage of the Thais in 1904 so as to give France control of the Sayaboury tract to the west of Luang Prabang and part of the old kingdom of Champassak on the west bank of the Mekong.[47] In the 1860s, Cambodia became a protectorate of France. The boundary of Cambodia with Thailand was thereafter defined by a series of Franco-Thai agreements, the first of which in 1867 left Thailand responsible for the western Cambodian province of Siem Reap (the site of Angkor) and Battembang. However, between 1904 and 1907, the French compelled the Thais to surrender the territories to Cambodia by accepting a boundary line on the Dangrek hills that separate the Cambodian plain from the Korat plateau.[48]

The drawing of this boundary was to produce considerable tension after 1953 between Thailand and the independent state of Cambodia. The final part of the Thai border is that with Malaya. The Thai government claimed in the 19th century to control the whole Malay Peninsula, although its authority over the northern part of the peninsula was stronger than in the south. During the course of that century, however, British influence on the peninsula (concentrating on the Straits Settlements, Penang, Malacca, and Singapore) steadily increased, and in 1909, Thailand transferred to British Malaya the states of Kedah, Perlis, Kelantan, and Trengganu. This agreement settled the boundary between Thailand and the British Empire but sowed the seeds of future discord. Several Malay states in the Patani-Singora region, with close ties to Malaya, remained in Thailand.[49]

The boundaries of Vietnam, Laos, and Cambodia were generally established during the period of the French Empire in Indochina from the late 19th century until 1954. The boundary system, established in the late 19th century to demarcate the borders of Vietnam and Laos with China, was carried over into the 20th century and would not be challenged by the People's Republic of China after 1949. In the half-century or so before the French incorporated Vietnam, the country had been briefly administered as a unified state by the Emperor Gia-long based in Hue. However, from the 17th century to the late 18th century, Vietnam had been divided between two dynasties: the Trinh in Tonkin, and the Nguyen in Annam and the south. The French, while treating Vietnam theoretically as a unity, in practice divided the country into the colony of Cochin China and the protectorates of Annam and Tonkin.[50]

What is today the state of Laos owes its existence to French imperialism, and its modern borders are substantially those defined by French officials. Lan Xang, the most powerful Lao kingdom in the precolonial period, had broken up in the 14th century.[51] By the 19th century, there were merely minor principalities such as Luang Prabang, Vientiane, Champas-sak, and Xieng Khouang in the country we now call Laos.[52] Under the mandala system, these Lao principalities offered tribute to both Thailand and the Annamese dynasty at Hue. France exploited these competing relationships and the relative weakness of Thailand. In 1888, it annexed Sipsung Chu Thai, the Thai tribal area that included the city of Dienbienphu, then all the Lao areas on the east bank of the Mekong, and finally, in 1904, the Sayaboury and Champassak tracts. The Sipsung Chu Thai area, an area affiliated with both Laos and Thailand, was incorporated into Tonkin in 1895 and ipso facto into Vietnam.[53] The French did not reconstitute Lan Xang as they would Cambodia. Luang Prabang survived under its own dynasty, but France directly admin-istered the other Lao principalities. But for the accidents of French colonialism, as Peter Lyon has argued, "Laos would now be either part of Thailand (or Vietnam), perhaps rather as the Shan states are tenuously a part of Burma."[54]

By contrast with Laos, the coming of the French Empire in Indochina is what allowed Cambodia to preserve its national identity. Cambodia was the successor of the powerful Khmer Empire, which had been the dominant power on the Southeast Asian mainland until the 13th century. After the collapse of the Khmer Empire, the remnant king-dom that was centered in Phnom Penh fought for several centuries with the Viets and the Thais, who seized the western Cambodian provinces of Siem Reap and Battembang in the 18th century. This process of being squeezed on two sides may well have ended in the extinction of a separate Khmer state if not for the interposition of the French and their establishment of a protectorate there in 1860.[55] Unwilling to fight a war with France, Thailand acknowledged the new protectorate in return for French recognition that Siem Riep and Battembang were part of Thailand. But between 1904 and 1907, the French took from Thailand both Siem Riep and Battembang and the strip leading to the Gulf of Siam from the port of Chantaburi.[56]

Decolonization and the Emergence of Territorially Defined Nation-States

The history of Southeast Asia changed dramatically as result of World War II and the Japanese occupation of the region. The Japanese interlude in Southeast Asia from 1940 to 1945 marked the beginning of the end of European colonialism in the region. Nonetheless, in the period of decolonization that followed the war, the frontiers established in the colonial era would largely remain intact. However, the new nation-states that operated within colonial boundaries were generally politically weak. Their writ did not always run over all of the territorial jurisdictions conferred on them by international law. In many cases, the border areas of the new nation-states served more as buffer zones, contested between weak central governments and ethnic or insurrectionist forces, rather than as delimited boundaries.

At the closing stages of World War II, all the European imperial powers were developing plans to restore their colonial regimes in Southeast Asia. The Dutch government-in-exile viewed the Netherlands East Indies (NEI) as the centerpiece of Dutch overseas interests.[57] It established a provisional government for the NEI in Australia under H.J. van Mook, Minister for Colonies and Lieutenant-Governor. Van Mook expected to return to the NEI in the wings of the allied British-Indian-Australian occupation force. Queen Wilhelmina had announced in 1942 that the Dutch plan for the NEI would be based on "complete partnership" and "self-reliance" (or "internal self-government").[58]

Britain, too, planned to put Burma under the direct rule of officials until 1948 and to allow the Scheduled Areas of ethnic minorities to stay under British rule until they themselves decided to join "Burma proper."[59] It also envisaged a Malayan Union of the peninsular Malay States and the former Straits Settlements of Penang and Melaka and Crown Colony rule for Singapore, Sarawak, and North Borneo.[60] The French were the most conservative of the imperial powers. Their Brazzaville Declaration of 1944 excluded "autonomy and all possibility of development outside the French Empire."[61]

However, the restoration of colonial rule in Southeast Asia was to be short-lived. From 1945 to the mid-1960s, most of the European powers left Southeast Asia and nation-states replaced the European empires, while the boundary system drawn in the colonial period largely remained intact. The first Southeast Asian colony to receive its independence was the Philippines. The United States reoccupied the Philippines at the end of the war, passed the Bell Act ensuring free trade between the Philippines and the United States, and proclaimed the Philippines an independent republic on July 4, 1946. For Burma, the British were envisaging full self-government within the British Commonwealth without spelling out a timetable. However, a police strike in 1946 revealed the colonial authorities to be on the verge of breakdown, and the British thereupon wound up their imperial rule quickly. An important factor in this decision was that the British had always regarded Burma as an appendage to the Indian Raj. With the British having made the decision in 1946–1947 to withdraw from India, Burma had thus "lost its imperial raison d'être."[62]

Partly because of Thailand's alliance with Japan in World War II, the Thai state lost its monopoly over the use of force and only slowly recovered it. The Communist Party of Thailand waged an insurrection between the 1950s and 1980 against an increasingly militarized Thai state in the predominantly Lao northeast.[63] In the 1960s, war in Indochina, the expansion of drug trafficking, and a burgeoning trade in illegal armaments sustained pluralities of armed force in Thailand. Consequently, by the late 1970s, Thailand was divided into two spheres: one controlled by the Thai army in Bangkok, and the "other by Communist revolutionaries in rural strongholds along Thailand's borders with Laos, Cambodia, Burma, and Malaysia."[64] The Malay Muslim part of southern Thailand was the hardest region to integrate. It was the scene of a number of violent secessionist movements from the 1960s to the 1980s.

Burma was another ethnic state that had to struggle to bring about unity from diversity. The first Burmese leader, Aung San, envisaged Burma as a plural nation-state that incorporated diverse political structures. He proposed to confer the status of *Union State, Autonomous State*, or *National Area* on any Burmese territory that possessed such characteristics as a defined geographical area, a unity of language different from Burmese, a fairly large population, and the desire to maintain a distinct unity as a separate entity.[65] Seventy percent of Burma's population consisted of Burmans living in the lowlands. The remaining third consisted of non-Burmese ethnic groups. The larger ones had had their own ethnically based states (as distinguished from nation-states) dating from the non-Burman principalities of the precolonial era. The Kachin state lies in the extreme northwest of the country wedged between China and India. The Shan state (comprising about 3 million of Burma's 24 million in the 1960s and 8 million of 50 million in 2005) is situated in the northeast and has borders with China, Laos, and Thailand. To the south is Kawthule, the territory of the Karens (consisting of about 2 million people in the 1960s and 7 million in 2005). In addition, other minorities reside in Burma such as Indians, Pakistanis, and Chinese. The overwhelming majority of Burma's population are Buddhists of the Theravada variety, but parts of the Karen and Kachen population are Christian, and there are also Muslims in the border region adjacent to what is today Bangladesh.[66]

Aung San and the Shan, Chin, and Kachin leaders agreed to the formation of a Union federal government in 1947. In the Panglong Agreement of the same year, the frontier states and the Shan states pledged their loyalty to the Union. There were four states envisaged in the non-Burmese areas, Shan, Karenni, Kachin, and Karen, and a Chin Special Division. However, Aung San was assassinated and his successor, U Nu, was not as tolerant of ethnic diversity. The first decades of Burmese independence were consequently characterized by various rebellions and ethnic conflicts. In January 1948, Islamic Mujahids started an insurgency, and in 1949, the Karens launched a rebellion, the main cause of which was the refusal of U Nu to create a separate state for the Karens within the Union. According to U Nu, the Karens were scattered over the various parts of Lower Burma rather than being concentrated in a specific area. Two consequences of the 1949 revolt were the purging of Karens from the Burmese national army and the amendment of the Burmese constitution in 1951 to permit the setting up of a Karen state east of Rangoon, later to be known as Kawthule State.[67]

Ne Win, who succeeded U Nu in 1958, induced the hereditary chiefs of the semiautonomous Shan and Kayah states to bring their states into conformity with the rest of the Union by surrendering financial powers to the central government. He also settled the Burmese border with the People's Republic of China, the administration of which had been complicated after 1949 by the retreat of Kuomintang (Chinese nationalist) forces into Burma. This provoked the Chinese Communists to establish defensive posts across the border in Burma in violation of Burmese sovereignty. The withdrawal of most of the Kuomintang forces from Burma in 1954 (some of them moving to Thailand) provided the precondition for the negotiation of the entire Sino-Burmese border between 1956 and 1960. This border essentially followed the colonial border based on the Anglo-Tibetan McMahon line of 1914.[68] Unlike some of the other larger states of Southeast Asia, Burma at no time since independence made any expansionist territorial claims. The boundaries negotiated by the British represented the furthest limits to which any

Burmese government wished to lay claim. The benefit of this policy was stable relations with its larger neighbors, particularly India and China. After the 1960 border demarcation, China abandoned longstanding claims to Burmese territory. The tacit price for this, however, was for Burma to continue a policy of "nonalignment."[69]

Ne Win's policy for Burma was to forge one nation with one kind of citizenship and no special autonomy for the separate states. Indeed, *Burmanization* could be described as the dominant *motif* of actual Burmese policy since independence.[70] By the late 1960s, most minority groups appeared to have accepted this policy. However, some important minorities continued to wage an armed resistance against the central government, including the Shan State Army, the Kachin Independence Army, and the Karen National Union (estimated in 1971 to have 16,000 regular troops). The insurgency of the Karens, Shans, and Karens was intimately connected with the smuggling of opium and heroin, which were exchanged for arms.[71] The threat of secession by some of these states, especially the Shans, at times appeared to be serious. But what secession meant was never entirely clear. The Shan had linguistic relations with the Thai, but Shan ethnic and political identity:

> depended historically on the claim that the Shan system of principalities was connected with the Burman kingdom of Pagan. Shan Therevada Buddhism was more akin to the Burmese style rather than the Thai. Much of the Shan language was influenced by Burmese, which made it less understood in Thailand.[72]

Modern Indonesia, like Burma, became a nation-state after 1949 despite its large population (even in colonial times), fragmentation into over 3,000 islands, religious variegation (Muslims, Buddhists, Catholics, Protestants, Hindu-Balinese, and animists), and ethno-linguistic diversity (over 100 distinct groups). Its predecessor Netherlands East Indies had, moreover, a history of intermittent ethnic strife that needed to be overcome before a cohesive nation-state could be constructed. Examples of such conflict included Sundanese versus Javanese, Javanese versus Ambonese, Batak versus Minangkabau, and Toraja against Bujinese. As Benedict Anderson has argued, Indonesia's "stretch does not remotely correspond to any pre-colonial domain; on the contrary, at least until General Suharto's brutal invasion of ex-Portuguese

East Timor in 1975, its boundaries have been left behind by the last Dutch conquests (c. 1910)."[73]

After twice using force against the Indonesian Republic that had been declared in August 1945, the Dutch were forced by international pressure and military adversity to negotiate with the Indonesian Republic the transfer of sovereignty to a federal United States of Indonesia in 1949. The federal borders of the state were based on administrative divisions established by the Dutch colonial authorities and by the two military actions that had considerably reduced the territory of the Republic in Java and Sumatra. However, Dutch New Guinea was deliberately excluded from the territories transferred from the Netherlands.[74]

Because the federal structure of the new state was tarred with the colonialist brush, it was quickly replaced after 1950 by a unitary structure. In the period from 1950 to the mid-1960s, the new Indonesian Republic established a national unity despite rebellions such as the Darul Islam in West Java, South Sulawesi, and Aceh and the Revolutionary Government of the Republic of Indonesia–Permesta revolt in Sumatra and Sulawesi in 1957–1958.[75] Benedict Anderson has raised the intriguing question of how it is that a nation was created out of such diversity. How, to take one example, did people on the east coast of Sumatra, who are physically, ethnically, and linguistically close to the people on the western littoral of the Malay Peninsula, come to see them as foreigners (Malaysians)? Yet at the same time, how did these same Sumatrans come to see Ambonese, living thousands of miles to the east and sharing no mother tongue, ethnicity, or religion, as fellow Indonesians?

Anderson has argued that the Dutch colonial authorities created a uniform, highly centralized education system in the NEI of which the Dutch-built city of Batavia was the apex. This gave the indigenous elite of the archipelago common experiences, a common language (*Bahasa Indonesia*) based on an ancient interinsular lingua franca, and, through common maps of the colony, "a territorially specific imagined reality which was every day confirmed by the accents and physiognomies of their classmates."[76] By the mid-20th century, he argues, all the major ethnolinguistic groups in Indonesia had become accustomed to the idea that they had a role to play on an archipelagic stage. This partly explains why only one of the rebellions in the 1950s and 1960s, the abortive Republic of the South Moluccas, had separatist ambitions. All the rest were "competitive within a single Indonesian political system."[77]

In the 1950s and early 1960s, Indonesia waged a strong diplomatic and military campaign to incorporate Dutch-administered West New Guinea on the grounds that it was the legitimate successor state to all of the former colonies of the Netherlands in Southeast Asia. The United States decided to support the Indonesian case (which had been strongly opposed by the Netherlands and Australia) in the early 1960s. Consequently, the Netherlands placed West Irian, as it came to be described, under United Nations administration in 1962. In 1963, the Netherlands transferred the territory to Indonesia. The border between West Irian and the Australian-administered external territory, Papua New Guinea, along the 141st meridian and the western bulge of the Fly River was inherited from colonial times.[78] After 1963, it became a relatively stable, delimited boundary between Indonesia and Australia and, from 1975, between Indonesia and Papua New Guinea. The most serious challenge to the administration of the border after 1975 has been posed by the cross-border operations of West Papuan separatists.

The status of the British Borneo territories, which shared a border with Indonesian Kalimantan, proved a thornier problem for the region. From 1946 to 1948, the 11 states in Malaya formed a single Crown Colony known as the Malayan Union. However, due to opposition from Malay nationalists, the union was disbanded and replaced by a Federation of Malaya, which restored the symbolic positions of the rulers of the Malay states. The British accepted the federal solution because it gave them a unified Malaya.[79] This multi-ethnic state, consisting of Malays, Chinese, and Indians, forged a national identity with the help of an intercommunal alliance between the United Malays National Organisation and the Malayan Chinese Association.[80] After achieving its independence in 1957, Malaya cooperated with Britain in the early 1960s to construct a larger federation by uniting Malaya, Singapore, and the British North Borneo states, Sarawak, and Sabah (North Borneo). The plan alienated Indonesia, which feared a British- and Chinese-influenced (through Malaysia's large Chinese minority) state on its border. It also attracted the opposition of the Philippines, which claimed Sabah on the basis of that territory's historic ties with the Sultanate of Sulu.[81]

From 1963 to 1966, Indonesia sponsored an insurgency, described as "confrontation," that involved border crossings from Indonesian Kalimantan into Malaysian Borneo and even military incursions onto the Malay Peninsula. Indonesia's self-proclaimed "right" to a say in the future of its neighbors alienated world and U.S. opinion, and tended to consolidate Malaysia rather than break it up. After the ouster of Indonesia's President Sukarno in 1965 and Singapore's separation from Malaysia in the same year, confrontation was resolved through Malaysian-Indonesian negotiations under Thai auspices. From 1966 onward, the Borneo border between Indonesia and Malaysia, drawn in colonial times, became relatively stable.[82] The mutual agreement between Malaysia and Singapore to allow the latter to separate and form a new state on Malaysia's borders was repeated only once in the postwar history of Southeast Asia. In 1999, international pressure would force Jakarta to allow East Timor to separate from Indonesia.

French Indochina, unlike the Dutch East Indies, was not succeeded by one large Indochinese state but by three separate ones, Vietnam, Laos, and Cambodia. After World War II, Chinese forces took the Japanese-surrendered terrority in Laos and Vietnam down to the 16th parallel, and the British took what was south of it.[83] The latter permitted the restoration of French colonial authority in the south of Vietnam. But in the north the Vietnamese nationalists (Vietminh) consolidated their authority under their Communist leader Ho Chi Minh and laid a wider claim to be the legitimate authority in the whole of Vietnam. Between 1946 and 1954, the Vietminh waged a war of liberation against the French. After defeat at Dienbienphu in 1954, the French were obliged to leave Indochina after having set up a pro-Western state in South Vietnam that claimed authority over the entire nation. An international conference held in Geneva in 1954 divided Vietnam at the 17th parallel leaving two de facto states in Vietnam and two de facto central governments. The Geneva agreements referred to nationwide elections that would unite the country, but they were never held. Between 1956 and 1959, more than 300,000 refugees fled to the south.[84]

From the early 1960s, a National Liberation Front (NLF), otherwise known as Viet Cong, waged an insurgency in South Vietnam against the U.S.-backed government in Saigon with the help of North Vietnam, which infiltrated military and other supplies to South Vietnam via the Ho Chi Minh trail that crossed the Lao and Cambodian borders.[85] The United States contributed military advisors and, after 1965, substantial ground forces to assist the Government of South Vietnam. By the late 1960s, the United States was aware it could not win the war, and in 1973 it signed the Paris Peace Agreements with North Vietnam.

After U.S. withdrawal from Indochina, the forces of Northern Vietnam quickly defeated those of the South and reunited Vietnam on July 12, 1976.

The new state of Laos that emerged after World War II meets Robert Jackson's definition of a quasi-state.[86] The French made it an independent state in the French Union in 1949, and the international community at large accepted it at the Geneva Conference of 1954.[87] However, in its history up to the 1970s, Laos could only be considered a state by cartographic and diplomatic convention. For one thing, the state of Laos contained only a small minority of ethnic Lao. The prime minister of Laos, Souvannaphouma, estimated in 1967 that there were about 3 million Lao in Laos but more than 16 million in northeast Thailand.[88]

After the Geneva Conference of 1954, Laos was subject to a de facto division in which the Royal Lao Government, with Thai and American support, managed to control the rice-growing area on the east bank of the Mekong, while the Communist Pathet Lao controlled the highlands and the two northern provinces, Phong Saly and Sam Neua.[89] An international agreement in Geneva in 1962 arranged for the unification and neutralization of Laos. However, the arrangement quickly unraveled, North Vietnamese troops gave strong support to the Pathet Lao and infiltrated supplies to South Vietnam through Laos, and the United States bombed North Vietnamese–held territory inside the Lao border. In 1975, after the fall of Saigon, the Pathet Lao proclaimed a Lao Democratic Republic in all of Laos.[90]

Cambodia, a small territorial remnant of the Khmer Empire, was granted independence by the French in 1953. One of the most pressing tasks for the new state was to persuade its neighbors to accept the borders that had been drawn for the protectorate in colonial times. Cambodia's leader, Prince Sihanouk, saw Vietnam and Thailand as the biggest threats to the new state's territorial integrity. In an effort to persuade China to restrain the Vietnamese and the Thai from acting to Cambodia's detriment, Sihanouk adopted a strictly nonaligned policy in the Cold War. He did, however, negotiate for the United States to supply military assistance to the Royal Khmer Armed Forces. However, border incursions by South Vietnamese troops in pursuit of Viet Cong and U.S. overflights within Cambodian airspace precipitated a breach in Sihanouk's relations with the United States and South Vietnam in 1963. Soon thereafter, Sihanouk tried to reach a border settlement directly with North Vietnam. The North Vietnamese in turn declared that the borders would have to be negotiated with South Vietnam's NLF, which recognized the inviolability of Cambodia's borders in 1967.[91] In 1968, Sihanouk repaired his relationship with the United States, which in 1969 recognized the sovereignty, neutrality, and territorial integrity of the Kingdom of Cambodia with its existing frontiers. The agreement was not respected. In the same year, U.S. President Richard Nixon authorized the secret bombing of border sanctuaries in Cambodia used by the North Vietnamese and the Viet Cong. Cambodia was consequently engulfed in the Indochina war; Sihanouk was replaced by right-wing General Lon Nol, who was himself deposed. After the fall of Saigon, the indigenous Cambodian Communists, the Khmer Rouge, came to power under their leader Pol Pot.[92]

Regionalism, Globalization, and the Consolidation of Southeast Asian Borders

The period from the late 1960s to the present has been characterized by increasing regionalism within Southeast Asia and by globalization. Regionalism involves states in a particular area associating for the purposes of security and economic liberalization. In 1967, Brunei, Indonesia, Malaysia, Singapore, Thailand, and the Philippines formed the Association of Southeast Asian Nations (ASEAN) as a gesture of reconciliation between previously antagonistic neighbors.[93] They believed that working toward mutual economic development would be conducive to regional stability. ASEAN agreed to create a Zone of Peace, Freedom, and Neutrality in 1971 and concluded a Treaty of Amity in 1971. The ASEAN states vociferously opposed Vietnam's invasion of Cambodia in 1978 and its establishment there of a pro-Vietnamese regime. However, after ASEAN helped to broker a solution in Cambodia between the pro-Vietnamese regime and its opponents in the early 1990s, Vietnam was permitted to join the organization in 1995, followed by Laos and Burma in 1997 and Cambodia in 1999.

Globalization entails the reduction of geographical and legal barriers to the movement of goods and services, capital, technology, ideas, and culture. According to some theorists, the interaction of globalization and regionalization, particularly from the 1980s, has meant that states are becoming weaker and borders less important.[94] In some respects, the integrating effect of regionalization and globalization has made Southeast Asian borders more porous. For example, the ease with which capital crossed borders in the 1980s and 1990s had as one consequence the crippling currency devaluations in Indonesia, Malaysia, and Thailand during the Asian financial crisis of 1997–1998. However, globalization and regionalization have also had the contrary effect that states have become stronger and borders more salient. Southeast Asian states that had been relatively weak from the 1940s to the 1960s consolidated their territoriality from the 1970s to the present.

Thailand, for example, obtained a monopoly of force in the 1980s after the insurgent communist force dissolved. This allowed the Thai government to wind up groups that it had previously permitted to act as countervailing forces to the communists in its borderlands: the Shan army and remnants of the Kuomintang. In the 1980s and 1990s, the Thais saw their future economic prosperity as dependent on opening their borders to trade and investment flows and developing secure trade routes with the other major trading centres in the Mekong Basin. To achieve their objectives, they therefore commenced several infrastructure projects that extended Bangkok's control over peripheral areas. These included highways from the eastern seaboard to centers in Laos, Vietnam, and China; a highway from the west coast across the Kra Isthmus, and a Thai-Burma development zone to capture a portion of the freight trade from Singapore and Penang. Insofar as Thailand became increasingly subject to international pressures in such areas as control of drug trafficking and prevention of the proliferation of HIV–AIDS, border control became more important.

In response to international pressure, the Thais began to enforce their antidrug policies more strictly and consequently to regulate cross-border movements of people and goods more rigorously. The Lao state, too, has extended authority in the last quarter of a century in its borderlands over areas such as smuggling, illegal logging, and protecting its environment and wildlife.[95] Laos even fought a small-scale war with Thailand in the late 1980s, provoked by the illegal teak logging activities of Thai generals inside Laos.[96]

Burma provides a similar example of a state that became stronger in the 1980s and 1990s. Before that time, both China and Thailand had derived a strategic advantage from the ethnic secessionist movements operating in Burma's borderlands. However, this changed after the 1980s when China sought to persuade Burma's State Law and Order Council

(SLORC) to open a trading route through Burma from Yunnan to the Indian Ocean. China consequently withdrew military aid from the ethnic secessionists and encouraged the SLORC to negotiate ceasefires with secessionists operating on its border. Similar developments occurred on Burma's Thai border when Thai opinion began to turn against the ethnic separatists. Fighting within Burma has led to hundreds of thousands of people fleeing across the border into Thailand. The Thais have classified some groups, such as the Karenni and Karen, as refugees. However, despite being regarding as the Thais' ethnic cousins, the fleeing Shan are classified as illegal Burmese workers.

Border tensions between Cambodia under the Khmer Rouge and Vietnam reached their height in 1978 with the massacre of ethnic Vietnamese and their sympathizers in eastern Cambodia. In December of that year, Vietnam launched an invasion of Cambodia, toppled Pol Pot, and installed a pro-Vietnamese government.[97] Cambodia's Chinese allies immediately retaliated by invading Vietnam on February 11, 1979, partly because of the fear that Hanoi's close relations with Moscow would lead to the militarization of the Sino-Soviet border. After 3 weeks of fighting, China withdrew, leaving the border issues unresolved.

In the quarter-century after the war with China, Vietnam realized that unsettled border issues not only posed a security threat to Vietnam but also negatively affected "Vietnam's sovereignty in terms of both protecting its national territory and its people."[98] Accordingly, Vietnam reached border agreements with neighboring states through a process of consensual dialogue. In joining ASEAN in 1995, Vietnam accepted a regional framework for conflict management and a code governing interstate conduct. From 1992 to 2004, Vietnam completed talks on five land and maritime disputes with Malaysia, Thailand, China, and Indonesia. The final demarcation of Vietnam's border with Laos was concluded in 1990. Despite its dependence on Vietnam, Laos did not give up substantial areas of territory to Vietnam, and the borderline was very close to the 1945 border between Tonkin and Annam.[99] On December 30, 1999, Vietnam signed a treaty with China that settled the border dispute between the two countries. Within its borders, Vietnam maintains the largest army in Southeast Asia (over 400,000), which is deeply embedded in the economy and actively involved in construction projects on Vietnam's borders and in mountainous areas where security is problematic.[100] Since the 1990s, the central government also became more active in strengthening border controls to counter smuggling and the spread of avian influenza.

The United Nations helped to broker an end to the civil war in Cambodia between the pro-Vietnamese government and a coalition of Sihanoukists and Khmer Rouge in the early 1990s. After national elections produced a coalition government in 1992, Phnom Penh steadily consolidated its authority, including over western Cambodia where the Khmer Rouge had conducted an illicit and highly lucrative trade in timber, gems, and drugs. By the end of the 20th century, it was possible to describe Cambodia tentatively as a "territorially integrated state."[101]

In the 1990s, Indonesia's political stability and sense of national identity was gravely affected by the upheaval caused by the East Asian financial crisis of 1997–1998 and the successful effort by the peoples of the former Portuguese colony East Timor to wrest independence from Indonesia in 1999. The financial crisis ended more than 30 years of President Suharto's New Order. The East Timor crisis inflicted grave damage on the authority of the Indonesian army. From 1949 to the late 1990s, Indonesia's territorial integrity had been achieved through a combination of military force, political and administrative control from the center (inherited from colonial times), and the application of policies aimed at mitigating cultural and political differences. For example, throughout most of Indonesia's history as a nation-state, political parties were not permitted to form on a sectional or geographic basis. Post-Suharto Indonesia now has to cope with the challenges of other genuinely separatist movements: the Free Aceh Movement and the West Papuan independence movement.

Moreover, in addition to these separatist movements, there are other regionalist causes, whether conceived religiously, ethnically, or on a nationalist basis. Such movements tend to argue that politicians based in Java are not sharing power or resources fairly with peripheral areas. Examples of such regional movements include oil-rich Kalimantan, Riau, Maluku, and West Kalimantan, where there is significant communal disorder. However, the tendencies toward fragmentation of the Indonesian state are producing new kinds of state policy aimed at encouraging national unity in Indonesia's diverse provincial borderlands. Such policies include President Habibie's proposal to extend regional autonomy within Indonesia's unitary constitution and the multifaceted efforts designed to conciliate the peoples of West Papua and Aceh.[102]

Conclusion

The region of Southeast Asia is clearly demarcated geographically. But natural barriers within this region, such as rivers, mountains, and swamps, encouraged the ethnically and linguistically diverse peoples of the region to set up political communities separated by notional or natural frontiers. These polities and their frontiers waxed and waned according to military and economic fortune. They were also reshaped by the world religion of Islam, which swept over the Malay Peninsula and insular Southeast Asia from the 14th to the 17th century. Before European colonization of Southeast Asia, regional political communities thought more in terms of the allegiance of people rather than control over fixed territory.

But from 1600 to 1800, Europe was transformed from a borderless continent into one of bordered nation-states, each of which claimed sovereignty over its territorial jurisdiction. European colonizers, particularly Britain, France, and the Netherlands, imported the notion of the territorial state and delimited borders to Southeast Asia. From the late 18th century to the early 20th century, European imperial powers interacted with indigenous polities to draw boundaries in Southeast Asia that were largely inherited by the nation-states that succeeded the European empires after World War II. For three decades after World War II, these states or quasi-states were nonetheless relatively weak and struggled to maintain control over the territories conferred on them by international law.

Regionalization and globalization since the late 1960s have worked in some ways to fade the clarity of the state frontier in Southeast Asia by making the exercise of sovereign authority in certain domains difficult (for example, state control over local currencies). However, in other respects Southeast Asian states have strengthened their hold over their territorial domains in the era of globalization and regionalization. In general, the state boundaries drawn up by the colonial powers had no necessary coincidence with the divisions created by "language, community, religion, or 'ethnicity.'"[103] But it is not clear that an effort to redraw boundaries in a way that did coincide with language, community, religion, or ethnicity would be more conducive to regional stability than the existing boundaries.

Notes

[1] Charles Tilly, *Coercion, Capital and European States AD 990–1990* (Oxford: Basil Blackwell, 1990).

[2] Christopher W. Morris, *An Essay on the Modern State* (Cambridge: Cambridge University Press, 1998).

[3] Alastair Lamb, *Asian Frontiers: Studies in a Continuing Problem* (Melbourne: F.W. Cheshire, 1968), 4–5.

[4] Ibid., 6–7.

[5] Anthony Reid, *Southeast Asia in the Age of Commerce 1450–1680, Volume One: The Land Below the Winds* (New Haven: Yale University Press, 1988), 1.

[6] Jane Perlez, "Forests in Southeast Asia Fall to Prosperity's Ax," *The New York Times*, April 29, 2006.

[7] Nicholas Tarling, *Southeast Asia: A Modern History* (Melbourne: Oxford University Press, 2001), 3.

[8] Nicholas Tarling, *Nations and States in Southeast Asia* (Cambridge: Cambridge University Press, 1998), vii–ix.

[9] Reid, *Land Below the Winds*, 3.

[10] Anthony Reid, *Southeast Asia in the Age of Commerce 1450–1680, Volume Two: Expansion and Crisis* (New Haven: Yale University Press, 1993), 203–204.

[11] Tarling, *Southeast Asia: A Modern History*, 6.

[12] Damien Kingsbury, *South-East Asia: A Political Profile* (Oxford: Oxford University Press, 2001), 232–234.

[13] Charles A. Fisher, *South-east Asia: A Social, Economic and Political Geography* (London: Methuen, 1967), 83–88.

[14] Anthony Reid and Lance Castles, eds., *Pre-Colonial State Systems in Southeast Asia* (Kuala Lumpur: Council of the Malaysian Branch of the Royal Asiatic Society, 1975).

[15] Oliver W. Wolters, *History, Culture, and Region in Southeast Asian Perspectives* (Singapore: Institute of South East Asian Studies, 1982), 6–8.

[16] Ian Mabbett and David Chandler, *The Khmers* (Oxford: Basil Blackwell, 1996).

[17] Brian Harrison, *South-East Asia: A Short History* (London: Macmillan & Co., 1954), 35.

[18] Keith W. Taylor, *The Birth of Vietnam* (Stanford: University of California Press, 1983).

[19] *Shan* is a Burmese term and *Thai* is the indigenous name.

[20] David K. Wyatt, *Thailand: A Short History* (New Haven: Yale University Press, 1984), 67.

[21] Martin Stuart-Fox, *The Lao Kingdom of Lān Xāng: Rise and Decline* (Bangkok: White Lotus, 1998).

[22] Mayoury and Pheuiphanh Ngaosyvathn, *Kith and Kin Politics: The Relationship between Laos and Thailand* (Manila: Journal of Contemporary Asia Publishers, 1994).

[23] Reid, *Expansion and Crisis*, 69–73.

[24] Michael Aung-Thwin, *Pagan: The Origins of Modern Burma* (Honolulu: University of Hawaii Press, 1985).

[25] William J. Koening, *The Burmese Policy, 1752–1819* (Ann Arbor: University of Michigan Press, 1990).

[26] Oliver W. Wolters, *The Fall of Srivijaya in Malay History* (Ithaca: Cornell University Press, 1970).

[27] Reid, *Expansion and Crisis*, 173–176.

[28] Harrison, 50–60.

[29] Lamb, 42.

[30] Tarling, *Southeast Asia: A Modern History*, 20.

[31] Sanjay Subrahmanyam, *The Portuguese Empire in Asia, 1500-1700* (London and New York: Longman, 1993).

[32] Reid, *Expansion and Crisis*, 256–259.

[33] C.R. Boxer, *The Dutch Seaborne Empire, 1600-1800* (London: Hutchinson, 1965).

[34] Reid, *Expansion and Crisis*, 272.

[35] Paul Battersby, "Border Politics and the Broader Politics of Thailand's International Relations in the 1990s," *Pacific Affairs* 71, no. 4 (Winter 1998/1999), 474.

[36] Oliver B. Pollak, *Empires in Collision: Anglo-Burmese Relations in the Mid-Nineteenth Century* (Westport: Greenwood, 1979).

[37] Tarling, *Southeast Asia: A Modern History*, 80–86; Lamb, 146–156.

[38] Lamb, 146–147.

[39] John F. Cady, *A History of Modern Burma* (Ithaca: Cornell University Press, 1958).

[40] Lamb, 149.

[41] Wyatt, 158–160.

[42] Thongchai Wininchakul, *Siam Mapped: A History of the Geo-Body of a Nation* (Honolulu: University of Hawaii Press, 1994), 62–80.

[43] Tarling, *Nations and States*, 54.

[44] Kingsbury, 145.

[45] Lamb, 163.

[46] In 1943, Thailand actually invaded the Shan regions of Burma and incorporated them, although these territories were subsequently retroceded; Kingsbury, 153.

[47] Martin Stuart-Fox, *A History of Laos* (Cambridge: Cambridge University Press, 1997), 21–29.

[48] Lamb, 168–169.

[49] J.R.V. Prescott, *Map of Mainland Asia by Treaty* (Melbourne: Melbourne University Press, 1975), 418–423.

[50] Alexander B. Woodside, *Vietnam and the Chinese Model: A Comparative Study of Nguyen and Ch'ing Civil Government in the First Half of the Nineteenth Century* (Harvard: Harvard University Press, 1971).

[51] Lamb, 175–176.

[52] Stuart-Fox, *History of Laos*, 13–19.

[53] Lamb, 177–178.

[54] Peter Lyon, *War and Peace in South-East Asia* (Oxford: Oxford University Press, 1969), 86.

[55] Ibid., 78–80.

[56] Lamb, 168–169.

[57] Nicholas Tarling, ed., *The Cambridge History of Southeast Asia. Volume Two, Part Two, From World War II to the Present* (Cambridge: Cambridge University Press, 1999), 13–18.

[58] Ibid., 17.

[59] Hugh Tinker, ed., *Burma: The Struggle for Independence, 1944-1948* (London: HMSO, 1983–1984).

[60] A.J. Stockwell, *British Policy and Malay Politics during the Malayan Union Experiment, 1942-1948* (Kuala Lumpur: Malaysian Branch of the Royal Asiatic Society, 1978).

[61] Anthony Short, *The Origins of the Vietnam War* (London: Longman, 1989), 40.

[62] Tarling, *Cambridge History of Southeast Asia*, 25.

[63] Wyatt, 287–290.

[64] Battersby, 475.

[65] Tarling, *Cambridge History of Southeast Asia*, 80–81.

[66] Josef Silverstein, *Burmese Politics: the Dilemma of National Unity* (New Brunswick: Rutgers University Press, 1980).

[67] Kingsbury, 110–112.

[68] Lamb, 155–158; Prescott, 352–356.

[69] Robert H. Taylor, *The State in Burma* (London: C. Hurst & Co., 1987).

[70] Maung Maung, *Burma and General Ne Win* (London: Asia Publishing House, 1969).

[71] Alfred McCoy, *The Politics of Heroin in Southeast Asia* (New York: Harper & Row, 1972).

[72] Tarling, *Cambridge History of Southeast Asia*, 120.

[73] Benedict Anderson, *Imagined Communities: Reflections on the Origin and Spread of Nationalism* (London: Verso, 1991), 120.

[74] George McT. Kahin, *Nationalism and Revolution in Indonesia* (Ithaca: Cornell University Press, 1952).

[75] Audrey R. Kahin and George McT. Kahin, *Subversion as Foreign Policy: The Secret Eisenhower and Dulles Debacle in Indonesia* (Seattle: Washington University Press, 1997); Clive J. Christie, "Nationalism and the 'House of Islam': The Acehnese Revolt and the Republic of Indonesia," in *A Modern History of Southeast Asia: Decolonization, Nationalism, and Separatism* (Singapore: Institute of Southeast Asian Studies, 1996).

[76] Anderson, 122.

[77] Ibid., 132.

[78] Paul W. van der Veur, *Search for New Guinea's Boundaries: From Torres Strait to the Pacific* (Canberra: Australian National University Press, 1966).

[79] Tarling, *Nations and States*, 18.

[80] Tarling, *Cambridge History of Southeast Asia*, 82.

[81] Michael Leifer, *The Philippine Claim to Sabah* (Switzerland: Inter-Documentation, 1968); Lela Garner Noble, *Philippine Policy towards Sabah: A Claim for Independence* (Tucson: Association for Asian Studies, 1977).

[82] J.A.C. Mackie, *Konfrontasi: The Indonesian–Malaysia Dispute, 1963–1966* (Kuala Lumpur: Oxford University Press, 1974).

[83] David Marr, *Vietnam 1945: The Quest for Power* (Stanford: University of California Press, 1995).

[84] Stanley Karnow, *Vietnam: A History* (London: Penguin, 1991), 203–239.

[85] Tarling, *Cambridge History of Southeast Asia*, 280.

[86] Robert H. Jackson, *Quasi-states: Sovereignty, International Relations, and the Third World* (Cambridge: Cambridge University Press, 1990), 21. Quasi-states "are often deficient in the political will, institutional authority, and organised power to protect human rights or provide socio-economic welfare. The concrete benefits which have historically justified the undeniable burdens of sovereign statehood are often limited to fairly narrow elites and not yet extended to the citizenry at large whose lives may be scarcely improved by independence or even adversely affected by it. These states are primarily juridical."

[87] Lyon, 86.

[88] Ibid., 85.

[89] Stuart-Fox, *History of Laos*, 78–98.

[90] Ibid., 99–135.

[91] David Chandler, *A History of Cambodia*, 2d ed. (Boulder: Westview Press, 1983); Milton Osborne, *Politics and Power in Cambodia* (Melbourne: Longman, 1973).

[92] David Chandler, *Brother Number One: A Political Biography of Pol Pot* (Bangkok: Silkworm

Books, 1992).

[93] Michael Leifer, *ASEAN and the Security of South-East Asia* (London: Routledge, 1989).

[94] For example, Martin van Creveld, *The Rise and Decline of the State* (Cambridge: Cambridge University Press, 1999).

[95] Stuart-Fox, *History of Laos*, 204–205.

[96] Ibid., 198.

[97] Stephen P. Herder, "The Kampuchean-Vietnamese Conflict," in *The Third Indochina Conflict*, ed. David W.P. Elliott (Boulder: Westview Press, 1981), 21–67.

[98] Ramses Amer and Nguyen Hong Thao, "The Management of Vietnam's Border Disputes: What Impact on its Sovereignty and Regional Integration?" *Contemporary Southeast Asia* 27, no. 3 (December 2005), 439.

[99] Ibid., 432.

[100] Lawrence E. Grinter, "Vietnam Pushes on 30 Years after War," *Asia Times*, April 28, 2005.

[101] Battersby, 479.

[102] Grayson Lloyd, *Indonesia's Future Prospects: Separatism, Decentralisation and the Survival of the Unitary State*, Current Issues Brief 17, Department of the Parliamentary Library, 1999–2000.

[103] Tarling, *Nations and States*, 55.

Chapter 4

Borderlands, Terrorism, and Insurgency in Southeast Asia

Zachary Abuza

Borderlands and Militancy

At the end of the Cold War, the greatest security threat to Southeast Asia appeared to be coming from China, a rising superpower whose insatiable thirst for oil, gas, and other natural resources led it to grab territory in the South China Sea in the 1990s. Yet after 9/11, an unexpected threat to the region emerged: Islamist terrorism and insurgency. Today, Southeast Asian states are confronted by both inter- and intrastate violence, the latter complicated by the fact that substate actors work across national boundaries. There are myriad militant organizations in Southeast Asia of varying sizes and degrees of overtness and radicalism. Some have purely parochial agendas and focus on the "near enemy," such as Darul Islam, Gerakan Aceh Meredeka (GAM), the Pattani United Liberation Organization (PULO), and the Laskar Jihad, while others, such as Jemaah Islamiyah (JI) and Rabitatul Mujiheddin, have a pan-regional agenda and focus on the "far enemy." Many organizations, such as the Moro Islamic Liberation Front (MILF), Kampulan Mujiheddin Malaysia (KMM), Laskar Mujahideen, Laskar Jundullah, Rohinga Solidarity Organization, Gerakan Mujiheddin Islami Pattani (GMIP), Barisan Revolusi Nasional–Koordinasi (BRN–C), and Abu Sayyaf Group (ASG), straddle that divide; while they may have a domestic agenda, such as a desire for a homeland, they have forged tactical alliances and operate transnationally to achieve their goals. These organizations are linked with varying degrees of cooperation that change over time.

Traditionally, terrorism has been confined within national borders, usually on the periphery of Southeast Asian countries in areas such as southern Thailand or the Philippine island of Mindanao. In these regions, dominated by an ethnic minority, state institutions have been weakest, and the people have lagged behind in most measures of socioeconomic development. As such, low-level insurgencies erupted, but the demands were clearly parochial. If there was an "international" component to them, it was that they operated transnationally: that is, sanctuary or their key logistical operations were based in neighboring countries. The Association of Southeast Asian Nations (ASEAN) was founded in 1967 as a very loose organization based on the shared threat of communism. But the five founding members—Indonesia, Singapore, Malaysia, the Philippines, and Thailand—continued to have disputed borders and mutual suspicion over their neighbors' intentions. The fact that governments often did not crack down on the operations of their neighbors' insurgent groups only heightened the fear. For example, GAM used to engage in significant fundraising in Malaysia, where there was a large exile community; indeed, the head of one state government was a descendent of the Acehnese royal family. Rebels in southern Thailand were key arms smugglers for GAM as well as some of the Filipino groups. The Moro National Liberation Front (MNLF) and MILF both used Sabah for fundraising and as a secure rear area. Likewise, the Malayan Communist Party (MCP) was based in southern Thailand. As long as these groups were not actively plotting against the "host" state, the government tended to look the other way, despite political pressure from its neighbors. In some cases, the state actively supported the militants. Nowhere is this more evident than with Thailand, which not only gave sanctuary to the Khmer Rouge from 1979 to 1991, but also allowed the Chinese to arm them.

The ASEAN states became more willing to cooperate in the 1980s and 1990s, and they accorded the militants a less permissive operating environment. For the most part, security cooperation was the result of the region's rapid economic growth. States saw little benefit to ongoing turmoil in neighboring countries, which hurt burgeoning intraregional trade and the development of "growth triangles" and other economic zones. State-state cooperation reaped more rewards. Even the Thai government in the 1980s saw little to be gained from the continued insurgency in Cambodia and declared its intention to "turn battlefields into marketplaces."

Perhaps because neighboring states became less hospitable operating environments, insurgent groups began to act more transnationally. Beginning in the 1990s, terrorism started taking on a more international form. With the return of fighters from Afghanistan and greater transnational links among Islamists vested in the creation of Islamic states, tied loosely to financing in the Middle East and to al Qaeda, the region became an incubator for a sophisticated, highly motivated terrorist organization known as Jemaah Islamiyah.

While this chapter cannot delve into the histories of each of these insurgent groups and movements, they share a number of important characteristics. First, they operate where weak states are at their weakest—where the authority of the state has collapsed or was always marginal and the provision of social services is often negligible. These organizations try to supplant or usurp the authority of the state. While most are unable to provide social services, they work assiduously to impose their laws and social mores on the society.

Second, many of the Islamic movements in Southeast Asia have legitimate grievances. Economically speaking, in all Southeast Asian countries, the Muslim *pribumi* or *bumiputera* communities are less well off. The growth of Islamic extremism around the world since the Iranian revolution of 1979 has had less to do with theology than with the failure of the domestic political economies of the groups' countries.

Third, they operate in border regions, where by definition cultures overlap and minorities face some degree of persecution and have legitimate socioeconomic grievances. Often the ethnic balance has been in flux because of official policies of migration and resettlement of the ethnic majority in an attempt to pacify the region. The ethnic minorities believe that their culture is under assault and chafe at national assimilation policies that discourage the use of local languages and undermine cultural mores.

Fourth, as these groups exist in border regions, many of their members are dual citizens, or the movements can rely on a large base of supporters, diaspora communities, or coreligionists across the border. These conflict areas are often the legacy of colonial empires and arbitrary mapmaking. The current Thai insurgency, for example, is being contested by Malay Muslims who had been incorporated into the kingdom of Siam in a 1902 border treaty with Great Britain.

Fifth, in all of these countries, the inability of weak states to control all of their territories has allowed insurgents to establish sanctuaries to train and regroup. For example, there were seven jihadi training camps that the Indonesian government was unable to shut down until 2002–2003. In 2010, Indonesian authorities discovered a

JI camp in Aceh. Such camps are small and easily hidden. And despite U.S. military exercises in Mindanao and the provision of more than $500 million in military aid since fiscal year 2002, JI members captured in Malaysia, Indonesia, and the Philippines have all confirmed that JI training, now occurring in conjunction with ASG, continues in MILF-controlled territories, albeit on a smaller scale than in the 1990s. Central to the U.S. policy is the tenet that al Qaeda and its affiliates will never again be allowed to take over a country as they did in Afghanistan. The reality, however, is that groups like JI are able to take over portions of ungoverned territory in regions that are on the fringes of the state and often prone to sectarian and lateral conflicts. The silver lining of the Iraq conflict is that it seemed to have absorbed the attention of international jihadists. But will a region like Southeast Asia, several of whose states have been directly identified in al Qaeda statements, remain off their radar screen as Iraq winds down?

Sixth, these organizations emerge because governments are usually unwilling and unable to cooperate with their counterparts. This mistrust and animosity are the legacy of history as most ASEAN states either have territorial disputes with their neighbors, or have at times supported substate actors challenging their neighbors. The lack of transnational cooperation in policing, military operations, and intelligence-sharing is an incentive for organizations to operate transnationally, conducting portions of their operations across multiple jurisdictions, so that no security service has a clear idea of what they are doing. They rely on cross-border trade and smuggling to fund their activities and arm their movements.

This chapter looks at several different case studies, including JI, MILF, ASG, and several Thai insurgent groups. The MILF, ASG, and the Thai insurgents all represent the interests of disaffected ethnic and sectarian minorities and are fighting for an independent homeland. Their constituents lag behind the ethnic majorities in almost every measure of socioeconomic development. All of these groups are strongest on the fringes of the state, along the border, where they rely on diaspora communities and their coreligionists, and where government authority is weak, corrupt, and abusive. Even JI, which has a transnational agenda, established two different paramilitary arms in 1998–1999 that were engaged in sectarian bloodletting in the outer islands of Indonesia's sprawling archipelago.

The Regional Caliphate: Jemaah Islamiyah

Jemaah Islamiyah was an al Qaeda–affiliated terrorist group in Southeast Asia committed to establishing a pan-Islamic caliphate that would include Indonesia, Malaysia, southern Thailand, and Mindanao. The degree of its affiliation to al Qaeda is now uncertain. JI was founded in 1992–1993 by Abdullah Sungkar and Abu Bakar Ba'asyir, disaffected members of Darul Islam who had become frustrated with the organization's *dawa*, or "quietest approach," to implementing an Islamic state, and the gradual political emasculation of Islamists following the 1965 coup by Suharto.[1] JI was established with the explicit intent of being a covert organization that would bring down the secular state through force and some political struggle.[2] Sungkar and Ba'asyir founded the group while living in exile in Malaysia, and it really developed among the large community of exiled Indonesians. JI's leaders sought the approval of the al Qaeda leadership in the group's founding and received financial and materiel support from al Qaeda; several top JI leaders were concurrently members of al Qaeda, and its chief operatives were trained in al Qaeda's Afghan camps beginning in the late 1990s. JI established two paramilitaries, the Laskar Mujahideen (in the Moluccas) and the Laskar Jundullah (in Central Sulawesi), that engaged in sectarian bloodshed immediately after Indonesia's strongman Suharto fell in May 1998 and the subsequent abolishment of *dwi fungsi*, which gave the Indonesian armed forces a civil-administrative function in the provinces. JI was quick to take advantage of the collapse of the authoritarian and overly centralized secular state. JI began its bombing campaign in 2000 and, since the Bali attacks of October 2002, has perpetrated roughly one major attack a year and has employed seven suicide bombers, making it the most consistently lethal al Qaeda–affiliated group in the world.

While JI was an Indonesian-centric organization, it always operated transnationally and, according to its founding documents, it established regional command structures called *mantiqi*s to take advantage of different legal jurisdictions: *Mantiqi* 1 covered peninsular Malaysia, Singapore, and southern Thailand; *Mantiqi* 2 covered Java and Sumatra Indonesia; *Mantiqi* 3 comprised the Philippines, Brunei, eastern Malaysia, Kalimantan, and Sulawesi Indonesia; and *Mantiqi* 4 was being developed to establish cells in Australia and Papua (formerly Irian Jaya). Each *mantiqi*, in turn, had subregional commands (*wakalah*) and, beneath those, cells (*fiah*). To a degree, there was a functional division of labor among the *mantiqi*s to take advantage of the different circumstances and capabilities of each state. For example, *Mantiqi* 1 was the logistical hub for up to 100 JI operatives who were sent to Afghanistan for training in al Qaeda camps, in addition to running its own camp in southern Malaysia.[3] It was responsible for establishing dozens of front companies that could be used to channel al Qaeda funds and procure weapons and bomb-making materiel. In many cases, JI members established businesses, received contracts and business from JI supporters, and then plowed the proceeds back into the organization. According to the Singapore government's White Paper, "All JI-run businesses had to contribute 10% of their total earnings to the group. This money was to be channeled into the JI's special fund called *Infaq Fisbilillah* (contributions for the Islamic cause or jihad fund)."[4] Because the socioeconomic conditions were better in Malaysia and Singapore, the *mantiqi* was a key fundraising arm for JI.

Mantiqi 2 provided the bulk of the membership—nearly 2,000 members. Following the fall of Suharto in May 1998, JI developed its two paramilitary arms. It ran a network of training camps, including seven in Sulawesi and one in Kalimantan. The Indonesian cell was also very important in liaising with al Qaeda–linked Islamic charities, especially al Haramain and the International Islamic Relief Organization, and became a very important conduit for foreign funding.

Mantiqi 3 was important in terms of being a major logistics cell for the network responsible for acquiring explosives, guns, and other equipment, as well as for liaising with the MILF, which began running training facilities for JI members in 1996. Camp Hudaibiyah was established by Nasir bin Abbas as a sub-camp of the MILF's headquarters, Camp Abu Bakar. These camps included not only top JI trainers but also senior al Qaeda trainers, such as Omar al-Faruq, al-Mughira al-Gaza'iri, and Omar al-Hadrani.[5] Cell members procured explosives and small arms used by the JI's two paramilitary arms that were engaged in sectarian conflict in Indonesia starting in 1999. Several hundred JI members went through these camps.

The sectarian conflict really is the key to understanding JI. The group did not start the sectarian conflicts, though it was quick to take advantage of them. The conflicts erupted with the collapse of the New Order regime whose policies of forced transmigration fundamentally altered the ethnic, religious, economic, and political balances in the outer islands—regions where state power was always weaker and that were quicker to collapse following the end of the New Order regime. JI fomented sectarian conflict by sending seasoned operatives to lead the jihad, establishing its own paramilitaries, and creating a network of charities (often Saudi-funded) to support the conflicts. The sectarian fighting, which gave young men a sense of defending their religion and reinforcing their Manichean world view, became JI's primary recruitment and indoctrination tool.

Although the government brokered the fragile Malino Accords in the Moluccas and Sulawesi in 2002, there was an alarming uptick in attacks, including bombings, targeted assassinations, and raids on military/police facilities, between 2004 and 2007. State authority was tenuous and unable to control outbursts of violence. Attacks, including the beheadings of three schoolgirls in October 2005, were meant to undermine confidence in the state. In 2007, Indonesian police recovered JI documents from a central Javanese safe house that outlined JI's new structure and agenda: conflict zones, particularly Poso, were front and center of the organization's attempt to regroup and indoctrinate a new generation of militants. As such, the Indonesian security forces increased their capacity in these zones.

In 1999–2000, JI held three meetings in Malaysia to establish linkages to broaden JI's network and forge alliances with other Islamist organizations in the region. Counterterrorist operations following 9/11 prevented the Rabitatul Mujiheddin, which included Bangladeshi, Thai, and Indonesian organizations, from developing deeper operational ties.

While transnational operations have always been essential for JI, they are also one of its greatest vulnerabilities. Since 9/11, there has been a dramatic improvement in interstate security cooperation, though it still needs to be strengthened and institutionalized. Where such cooperation has taken place, there have been some significant breakthroughs. In particular, the maritime triborder region of Malaysia's Sabah State, Indonesia's Kalimantan (especially around the border town of Nunukan), and the Sulu Archipelago—the jumping-off point for Mindanao—has been JI's Achilles' heel. Top JI operatives Zulkifli bin Hir and Mustaqim were arrested coming into Malaysia and Indonesia, respectively, from MILF camps in Mindanao.

A handful of JI leaders still at large, including Umar Patek and Zulkifli, are believed to be confined in Mindanao or the Sulu Archipelago, unable or unwilling to risk being exfiltrated back into Indonesia and Malaysia. The MILF uncharacteristically violated the ceasefire with government forces in August 2006 when two police were killed while moving to arrest Zulkifli, who was in a MILF-controlled region. After more than 500 arrests across the region, JI is organizationally much weaker than it was in 2001–2002. While it is still able to perpetrate attacks in Indonesia, it is clearly in a regrouping mode. To that end, its ability to lie low and train in MILF camps is essential for its survival.

An important 17-man JI cell in central Java was broken up in June 2005 as part of the investigations into the 2003 Marriott hotel and 2004 Australian embassy bombings. Among other things, the cell leaders, Abdullah Sunata and Encen Kurnia, had an important role in sending members to the Philippines for training. Between December 2004 and mid-2005, they dispatched four separate teams to Mindanao. Senior JI leaders Dulmatin and Umar Patek had also called on the central Java cell to send operatives to Mindanao for suicide attacks.[6] Likewise, the Malaysian government announced that they arrested 12 individuals between March 16 and April 3, 2006, who were part of the Darul Islam organization who were planning a string of bombings.[7] The Malaysian authorities went to great lengths to insist that the 12 individuals—including 3 or 4 Indonesians, 2 Filipinos, and 6 Malaysians—were members of neither JI nor the KMM.[8] The group arrested in Malaysia appears to have been playing a logistical support role for JI. They were arrested off the coasts of Sandakan and Tawau, on the eastern coast of Sabah, on the island of Borneo.[9] Tawau is near the Indonesian port city of Nunukan, which has always been a center of smuggling and illegal immigration. Tawau and Nunukan are both departure points for trips across the Sulu Archipelago into Mindanao, where JI has had sanctuary in territory controlled by the MILF. "The role of Darul Islam Sabah was to help Indonesian militants transit to the southern Philippines, smuggle weapons from the southern Philippines to Indonesia, and obtain military training in the southern Philippines," the Malaysian police chief explained.[10]

The maritime border has also been vulnerable to seizures of weapons and explosives. On October 13, 2005, Indonesian authorities arrested three Malaysians and an Indonesian who were caught smuggling 175 kilograms of ammonium nitrate and 900 detonators and fuses into Nunukan from Sabah. It is believed that these materials came from the southern Philippines.

Malaysia established a successful maritime police interdiction force in Sabah in 2003. The United States has a small military presence in the Sulu Archipelago and has shared intelligence with its Philippine counterparts. Roughly 500 U.S. Special Forces troops are deployed in Mindanao and Sulu, where several hundred Abu Sayyaf militants are protecting a small number of JI members. In 2006, there were reports that elite Australian Special Air Service units had conducted maritime interdiction training and operations with Philippine forces. The Australian government recently gave the Philippine armed forces some 10 riverine small craft to use to patrol the maritime border near Malaysia and Indonesia.

Insurgency and Terrorism in the Philippines: The Moro Islamic Liberation Front and Abu Sayyaf Group

Armed secession, led by the MNLF, began in the southern Philippines in 1972. Attempts to broker a peace in 1976 failed and war resumed, though the MNLF entered into a peace agreement with the government in 1996. In 1978, the MILF broke away from the MNLF and continues its struggle for an independent Islamic state for the Bangsamoro people. The MILF fields roughly 9,000 men and controls significant territory in central Mindanao and Basilan. It has been involved in a peace process with the government since 1997 that has been interrupted by major government offensives in 2000 and 2004. A ceasefire signed in mid-2004 was monitored by a 60-man Malaysian-led contingent, but by 2006, the armistice had frayed, both due to local Muslim politics and frustration over the stalled peace process. Although an apparent breakthrough was reached in November 2007, the Philippine cabinet and supreme court rejected the draft autonomy agreement, prompting the MILF to return to war. Talks have resumed, but the MILF is awaiting the resumption of talks under the administration of President Benigno Aquino, who was elected in mid-2010.

The MILF has legitimate grievances. Waves of government-sponsored Christian migration have greatly reduced the amount of territory with a Muslim majority. In 1900, 76 percent of people in Mindanao were Moro; in 2000, only 18 percent were. In 1976, 13 provinces had a Muslim majority and were eligible for a plebiscite, yet by 2006, it was only 6 provinces, but Muslims were still a minority within many cities in those provinces. Moreover, the Muslim regions of Mindanao tend to have the lowest levels of human development.[11] The United Nations Development Programme's Philippine Development Report notes that 7 of the 10 provinces with the lowest human development index are in Muslim regions of Mindanao.[12] The people in the five provinces of the Autonomous Region of Muslim Mindanao—Basilan, Lanao del Sur, Sulu, Maguindanao, and Tawi-Tawi—have the lowest life expectancy, some of the lowest education rates, highest instances of child mortality, and lowest levels of per capita income.

In addition to the MILF threat, the armed forces of the Philippines are confronted with operations against the Abu Sayyaf Group in the Sulu Archipelago and against a resurgent Communist Party of the Philippines–New People's Army that has never been stronger in eastern and northwestern Mindanao. In June 2006, then-Philippine President Gloria Macapagal Arroyo ordered an offensive against the New People's Army in an attempt to destroy the movement within 2 years.

The MILF control significant territory in central Mindanao, where they have established rudimentary government structures, including a three-tiered sharia court system and a limited shadow government in regions under central government control. While the MILF criticizes "Imperial Manila" for its lack of concern for development in Mindanao, the group has done very little to offer anything beyond the most basic educational and social services to the population in the vast zones under its control.

Though the MILF has an ethno-nationalist agenda and has been more focused on the "near enemy," it has forged tactical alliances with al Qaeda and Jemaah Islamiyah in return for funding and training, all at a time when state sponsorship from Libya was waning.[13] Beginning in 1996, members of the al Qaeda–linked Jemaah Islamiyah established training camps in MILF territories. One such facility, Camp Hudaibiyah, was established by Nasir bin Abbas, who would go on to head JI's *Mantiqi* 3. Several hundred JI operatives received training from the MILF and from a succession of al Qaeda trainers, including Omar al-Faruq, who, at the time of his arrest in 2003, was the top al Qaeda operative in the region.

The MILF relationship with JI and al Qaeda is changing, as many of its first-generation leaders and field commanders who fought in Afghanistan have died. The MILF is led by a less ideological generation of leaders—in particular, its chairman Ebrahim el haj Murad, who has sought a negotiated settlement.

Nonetheless, JI continues to receive sanctuary from the MILF in Mindanao. While the training of JI members is down from the rate of the 1990s, it is still going on. The arrests of Zulkifli (in Malaysia), Mustaqim (in Indonesia), and Taufiq Riefqi and Rohmat (Zaki) (in the Philippines) shed further light on the continuance of JI training in Mindanao. What is most interesting about these arrests is that they contradict the MILF's assertions that they have "no formal ties" with JI and attribute any such relations to those of "lost commands" and "rogue commanders." Yet all have confirmed that training took place in Butig, Lanao del Sur, the MILF's largest base camp at present, and the seat of its vice chairman, Aleem Abdul Aziz Mimbintas. Other evidence of the ongoing relationship surfaced after the arrest of Dulmatin's wife, Istiada Oemar Sovie, and two children on October 3, 2006, in Jolo. Sovie not only shed important light on how JI militants traveled from Java to Kelimantan, to Sabah, to Tawi-Tawi in the Philippines, but also confirmed that her husband had lived in MILF camps and trained their fighters from 2002 to late 2005.[14] Like Nasir bin Abbas, she debunked the MILF's claims that any ties between the MILF and JI are through "lost commands." She made clear that the JI men always received sanctuary in MILF territory and that MILF operatives had received training from her husband.

Continuing this relationship makes perfect sense for the MILF. For one thing, they have not been punished for it; the government of the Philippines has pleaded with the U.S. Government not to put the MILF on the Foreign Terrorist Organization list for fear of undermining the peace process. Second, most in the MILF see the JI members as fellow mujahideen whom they have known since Afghanistan. Third, there is a commitment to a global agenda, a religious obligation to help other jihads. Fourth, ties with the ASG, which is comprised mainly of ethnic Tausigs, is important for the MILF vis-à-vis its competition with the MNLF, which too is dominated by Tausigs. Fifth, the MILF has low expectations for the outcome of the peace process and the government's seriousness and intentions to actually implement it. The group cannot afford to cut ties to JI and al Qaeda. The MILF does not like to employ terrorism but will use it when it suffers battlefield losses—usually to good effect in that it ends the offensives.

Although the MILF and the government established the Ad Hoc Joint Action Group (AHJAG) in 2004 to go after JI and Abu Sayyaf terrorists and other lawless elements, they have not arrested or turned over a single individual. They did force ASG chieftain Khadaffy Janjalani as well as JI leaders Dulmatin and Umar Patek out of their territory in late 2004 or early 2005. The AHJAG was disbanded when the peace process stalled in 2006.

The Abu Sayyaf Group was founded in 1991 by Afghan war veteran Abdurrajak Janjalani, who received seed money from Osama bin Laden. The group for the most part is an ethnic Tausig organization that extends throughout the Sulu Archipelago, from Zamboanga, Basilan, Jolo, and Tawi-Tawi, near Malaysia's Sabah State. ASG was involved in a number of cross-border raids including the notorious kidnapping of 20 foreigners and a Filipino from a dive resort on the Malaysian island of Sipidan in April 2000. It is a small (roughly 400 members organized in very loose autonomous cells) but exceptionally violent organization.

In 2002–2003, JI forged an alliance with ASG and brought it into MILF camps for training. The MILF provided sanctuary for ASG members on Basilan and Jolo during Philippine-American operations in 2002 and 2004–2006. MILF and JI operatives were blamed jointly for the Davao airport and Sasa Wharf bombing in Davao in 2003, which left 38 people dead. The 2004 bombing of a Superferry killed 116. Since 2004, terrorist operations in the Philippines have often included members from all three organizations, and it has become all but impossible to disaggregate them. The ASG has provided very important logistical services to JI—in particular, escorting JI operatives from Sabah and Nunukan into MILF camps. For example, one ASG operative, Muhair dela Merced, was arrested in December 2004 while escorting three JI members into the country. JI operatives have also trained in ASG facilities in Tawi-Tawi.

The Insurgency in Southern Thailand: GMIP, BRN–C, and PULO

Thailand has faced an Islamist secessionist movement since January 2004, which has led to the deaths of more than 4,200 people. There have been thousands of bombings and over 800 arson attacks. Militants have assassinated more than 2,000 people and beheaded over 40. Ten of the 33 districts in the deep south are "plagued by violence," according to the ministry of the interior, and the number is increasing. Yet little is actually known about the insurgents' structure and capacity. To date, there has not been a single credible claim of responsibility, nor have the insurgents publicly stated their goals or political platform other than in printed pamphlets. Their unwillingness to disclose any details has worked to their advantage and left Thai intelligence in a quandary. Unlike the insurgency from the 1960s to the 1990s, when groups were sharply divided over their goals and ideology and proved absolutely incapable of working together, today's organizations share a common Islamist agenda and are demonstrating unprecedented coordination and cooperation. Organizations are not trying to discredit each other to build up their power base at others' expense. The groups most responsible to date are the BRN–C, GMIP, and to a much lesser extent, the PULO and its splinter, New PULO.

Like the Philippines, Thailand has a Muslim minority population comprised of ethnic Malays in its southern regions. The Muslim population is roughly 5 million and constitutes about 7 percent of the overall population concentrated in the three provinces of Narathiwat, Yala, and Pattani, historically known as Pattani Raya (Greater Pattani), as well as three districts in the provinces of Songkhla and Satun. Ninety-nine percent are Sunni and most speak Bahasa Malayu, which is written in Yawi, an Arabic script. Approximately 360,000 Buddhists live in the three provinces (28 percent of the total population), primarily in urban areas.

Insurgency is not new to southern Thailand, the borders of which were fixed by the 1902 Anglo-Thai agreements and Britain's colonization of Malaysia. For most of the post–World War II era, the region has been plagued by insurgency, but it had died out by the mid-1990s for several reasons. The first was that the Thai groups were notoriously fractious and divided along ideological lines. Some groups supported autonomy, some independence, some an independent Islamic state, and some union with Malaysia. The MCP was at odds with the agenda of the Muslim and ethno-nationalist movements. In short, the groups could never come together and coordinate their operations, despite a few attempts to reconcile. Second, there was considerable cross-border cooperation between Malaysia and Thailand. The Thais provided the Malaysians with assistance in combating the MCP and even gave Malaysian forces the right of hot pursuit into Thai territory. In return, Malaysia restricted Malay separatist activities in the country. Third, the Thai government addressed many of the underlying grievances and effectively employed amnesties.

By early 2001, a new generation of insurgents emerged who had rejected both the peace process and amnesty in the 1990s and incubated in the region's increasingly radical mosques and *pondok*s or *madrassas*.

The insurgency has taken on decidedly sectarian and religious tones. More than 15 percent of the Buddhist community has fled. While some contend that the violence is simply about narcotics and cross-border smuggling routes, which is not untrue, the sheer amount of violence, the brutality of some acts, and the victim types suggest political and religious agendas, not mere criminality. To date the insurgents have not clearly outlined a platform, goals, or agenda. By analyzing the patterns of violence and victims, the insurgents appear to have a fourfold short-term agenda: they are making the region ungovernable, trying to force heavy-handed government responses, imposing their Islamist values and political controls over the population, and destroying secular institutions. To date, over half of their victims have been fellow Muslims. Insurgents have increasingly and systematically targeted the pillars of the economy. The mid-term goal is to create *hijrah*, a secure base of operations governed by sharia law.

The transnational aspects of the conflict are essential to any resolution, and to date, they have served as a hindrance. An interesting question is why there has not yet been any violence in the Muslim majority province of Satun. While some observers have pointed to the greater prevalence of Thai language and integration into Thai society, others have pointed to the province's key strategic location. The ports along Satun's western coast are too important for the infiltration and exfiltration of militants—any attacks would bring the region under greater scrutiny. But there is also another aspect: the two bordering Malaysian states, Perlis and Kedah, are under firm United Malay National Organization/Barisan Nasional[15] control and, thus, policing efforts along the border have been more effective. The most violence-prone province during the Thai insurgency, accounting for 42 percent of all violent incidents, was Kelantan, the only state currently controlled by the Islamist opposition party PAS. Political leaders and local policemen in Kelantan have been far more sympathetic to the plight of the Pattani.

Thai officials have long asserted (with scant evidence) that insurgents train and enjoy sanctuary in Malaysia, assertions that have infuriated Malaysian leaders. In the mid-1990s, the Malaysians arrested a key suspect and turned him over to the Thai police who, after interrogating him, summarily executed him. This provoked widespread condemnation from the Malaysian authorities, who expressed an unwillingness to provide greater cooperation. The most important insurgent captured to date, Jaekumae Kuteh, was arrested in Malaysia, not because of what he was orchestrating in Thailand, but because he was planning an attack in Kuala Lumpur to punish the Malaysian government for cooperating with the Thais.

In short, there is a reason that so few insurgent leaders have been arrested: there is so little cooperation between the two sides. Though the respective militaries have increased the number of joint patrols along the border, the reality is that it is a long, mountainous border covered in places in a thick jungle canopy. The border remains highly porous and accommodating to the insurgents. Police cooperation and intelligence sharing are nascent.

Although the Thai government claims to have made more than 2,200 arrests of insurgents, nearly all of them were low-level members or youths who were merely suspected of belonging to the insurgency. Moreover, more than 90 percent have been freed as the government has been unable to garner enough evidence to convict them. To date, the most important arrests have been on Malaysian, not Thai, soil. And yet there is still little cooperation between the two states. From 2004 to 2006, the Thaksin administration repeatedly blamed Malaysia in the media for coddling terrorists. This "bullhorn" diplomacy was disastrous and made it much more difficult for Malaysian Prime Minister Badawi to cooperate, as anger toward Bangkok's handling of the insurgency provoked anger across the political spectrum in Malaysia. The Islamist opposition party PAS resolutions were quickly endorsed by the ruling United Malay National Organization, making it hard for Badawi to ensure cooperation from his ministries. In 2005, for example, 131 individuals from a village where two marines were gruesomely murdered crossed over into Malaysia asking for asylum. This brought intense media scrutiny and put unwanted international attention on Thai policies. Although Malaysian authorities returned 1 individual of the 131, as he had a longstanding warrant for his arrest, they would not repatriate the rest; they refuse to extradite dual citizens.

Resolution of the insurgency was all but impossible with Thaksin's botched policies and subsequent bilateral relations with Malaysia. Following the September 19, 2006, coup, in which Thaksin was ousted from power, relations with Malaysia improved markedly. The government of caretaker Prime Minister Surayud Chulanont made many important overtures to the Muslim community and reforms in the counterinsurgency policies including: publicly apologizing to the Muslim community for the previous government's policies; reinstating key institutions for local governance and dispute resolution that Thaksin had scrapped in 2002; dropping charges against some 58 protestors; abolishing blacklists and death squads; and being willing to implement sharia law. The junta tried to put in place clear lines of command and control, which had been appallingly absent. Surayud made two fence-mending trips to Kuala Lumpur and announced that the military had entered into secret talks with the insurgents in late 2005.

In short, resolving the southern crisis was the one thing that Prime Minister Surayud felt very comfortable doing, and he threw himself into it. Nonetheless, violence spiked after the coup. The rate of attacks and killings in the following 6 months soared; May and June 2007 were the most violent months in the insurgency. Moreover, parallel secret talks in both Malaysia and Europe failed completely as they did not include representatives of the two leading insurgent groups, the GMIP and the BRN–C.[16]

Sadly, little came of any of Surayud's other policy announcements. In mid-2007, the new Thai army commander, General Anupong, launched his own "surge" of forces in southern Thailand and ordered a more visible presence of security forces. When democracy was restored in early 2008, Thaksin's allies were able to establish the government, to the military's chagrin. Prime Minister Samak Sondaravej and his successor were so fearful of another military coup that they gave the military free rein in the south. It was simply not a priority for the government. As such, most of Surayud's promises and policy proposals were not implemented.

When the Democrat Party came to power in December 2008, there was once again hope that the south would be a priority, as the region is the Democrats' traditional heartland. Nonetheless, violence escalated in 2009 to mid-2010. Between the Democrats' assumption of power and September 2010, over 700 people were killed and 1,300 wounded. Though most victims have been gunned down, there have been over 250 bombings. The insurgency shows no signs of abating.

Conclusion

While a number of insurgencies have been resolved, including the MNLF's agreement with the Philippines in 1996, and the 2005 agreement between the GAM and Indonesia, some continue to this day. The MILF is moving closer toward a peace agreement with the Philippines, though the devil will be in the details of implementation. Power sharing with the MNLF will further complicate any peace accord. Until that agreement is signed, the MILF have no incentive to cut its ties to groups such as JI. Despite its focus on Indonesia, JI remains a transnational entity, with training camps in the Philippines and operatives based in Southeast Asia and parts of South Asia. Sporadic sectarian conflict in the Indonesian provinces of the Moluccas and Central Sulawesi are part of JI's attempts to rebuild its depleted ranks. The insurgency in southern Thailand shows little sign of abating, despite the government's profound interest in reaching a durable settlement. In all of these cases, insurgency remains based both in the nation's periphery, where state power is at its weakest, and in places such as neighboring states where the insurgents are capable of basing some of their operations. The threat of transnational terrorism in the region after the 2002 Bali attacks did lead to an increase in interstate cooperation, but much more needs to be done.

Notes

[1] Darul Islam (DI) was founded in 1947 by Sekarmadji Maridjan Kartosuwiryo with the espoused goal of establishing an Islamic state in Indonesia (Negara Islam Indonesia). To that end, Indonesia's anticolonial war against the Dutch was in reality a triangular war, with Kartosuwiryo's forces battling Sukarno's nationalists as well as the Dutch. Kartosuwiryo was captured and executed in 1962, and the group fell into disarray and factionalized. Under Suharto's New Order (1965–1998), DI in some ways paralleled the Egyptian Muslim Brotherhood under Anwar Sadat. Though the organization was illegal, it had become nonviolent, and individual membership was quietly tolerated by the regime. Jemaah Islamiyah (JI) is a direct offshoot of Darul Islam, and many JI members are the children of DI members. JI has also been able to tap effectively into DI networks for operations, which has extended the group's reach. In many ways, DI is the foundation upon which JI has been built, though it is clear that many (but not all) in DI reject the al Qaeda strategy of targeting the far enemy.

[2] JI's primary organizational and philosophical document, the "General Guidebook for the Struggle of Jemaah Islamiyah," outlines the role of clandestine cells and describes the struggle using the language of guerrilla warfare.

[3] Ministry of Home Affairs, *White Paper: The Jemaah Islamiyah Arrests and the Threat of Terrorism* (Singapore: Ministry of Home Affairs, 2003), 6.

[4] Ibid.

[5] Romesh Ratnesar, "Confessions of an al Qaeda Terrorist," *Time*, September 16, 2002; BIN Interrogation Report of Omar al-Faruq, June 2002.

[6] Eva C. Komandjaja, "Police Search for Two JI Members in Philippines," *The Jakarta Post*, August 16, 2005; Jim Gomez, "Terror Suspect Details Training, Plots," Associated Press, March 23, 2005; INP, "Interrogation of Suyatno," Semerang, July 16, 2003; INP, "Interrogation of Machmudi Hariono," Semerang, July 18, 2003; INP, "Interrogation of Joko Ardiyanto," Semerang, July 19, 2003.

[7] Wong Chun Wai and Lourdes Charles, "Terror Group Busted," *The Star*, May 31, 2006.

[8] "Track Down Remnants of Darul Islam Group–PM," Bernama, June 1, 2006, available at <www.bernama.com.my/bernama/state_news/news.php?id=201272&cat=nt>.

[9] Wong and Charles.

[10] "Malaysian Group Helped Top Indon Terror Suspects Flee to Philippines, Police Say," *Sun-Star*, June 1, 2006, available at <www.sunstar.com.ph/static/net/2006/06/01/malaysian.group.helped.top.indon.terror.suspects.flee.to.philippines.police.say.html>.

[11] United Nations Development Programme.

[12] Ibid.

[13] When Salamat Hashim broke away from the secular Moro National Liberation Front in 1978, he moved his headquarters to the Jamaat Islamiya compound in Lahore, Pakistan. From there he oversaw the Moro and Southeast Asian participation in the jihad in Afghanistan in the 1980s. He did not return to Mindanao until 1988. His writings clearly depicted the Moro struggle as part of a global struggle. Moreover, they envisaged a pan–Southeast Asian Islamic state, of which Mindanao would be the nucleus. Links to transnational movements grew in 1991 when Osama bin Laden's brother-in-law, Mohammed Jamal Khalifah, moved to the Philippines and established branches of the Muslim World League, its sister organization, the International Islamic Relief Organization (IIRO), and the al Qaeda–linked Muwafaq. Through these charities and a host of smaller local charities, Khalifah was able to fund Ramzi Yousef and Khalid Sheikh Mohammad's Bojinka Plot in 1994–1995, the Moro Islamic Liberation Front (MILF), and the Abu Sayyaf. Many MILF officials held key positions within the IIRO.

[14] Johna Villaviray-Giolagon, "Dulmatin, His Wife, and Her Stories," *The Manila Times*, October 12, 2006.

[15] The United Malay National Organization (UMNO) is the dominant political party in Malaysia, having ruled since the country's founding in 1957. The Barisan Nasional, the ruling political party coalition of which UMNO is the primary member and controlling force, also includes the Malaysian Chinese Association and the Malaysian Indian Congress.

[16] One channel was through former Malaysian Prime Minister Mahathir Mohammed, who flew to Bangkok in November 2005, where he had an audience with the king and received his blessing to facilitate the talks. This process represented an end-run around the Thaksin government. In fact, the crown authorized the military to hold the talks secretly and independently of the National Security Council's sporadic talks in Europe. The government announced, "Core leaders of both the Pattani United Liberation Organisation (PULO) and Bersatu have contacted us through senior figures in Malaysia to propose peace talks." Other groups represented were the Barisan Revolusi Nasional Kongres, the Pattani Islamic Liberation Front, and the Muslim Mujahideen Movement of Pattani. A number of domestic and foreign press reports added that these insurgent groups had not only signed on to the talks in principle but had also signed a draft plan titled "Joint Peace and Development Plan for South Thailand." A military team was sent to Saudi Arabia to meet Tuanku Bilor Kortor Nilor, the former secretary-general of the PULO, whom the team hoped to enlist in contacting the separatist leaders. Yet the talks did not include representatives from the two groups most responsible for the violence: the Gerakan Mujiheddin Islami Pattani and the Barisan Revolusi Nasional Coordinasi, which have little incentive to negotiate. The government held talks primarily with the leaders of Bersatu and PULO, who have no effective control over the insurgency. As one official conceded, "They [separatist leaders at the negotiation] have told us that they have no influence over this generation of insurgents. . . . These village-based militants are an entirely new generation with no interest in negotiation. They are behind most of the violence in the region." See "Mahathir Arranged Meetings Between Thai Officials, Separatist Leaders," *The Nation*, October 6, 2006; "Gen Sonthi: Leaders Made Contact with the Authorities," *Bangkok Post*, October 5, 2006; "Authorities Seek Two Key Rebel Leaders," *Bangkok Post*, October 12, 2006; Connie Levett, "Thai Rebels Ready to Strike a Deal," *The Age*, October 7, 2006; "Separatists 'End Call for Independence,'" *The Nation*, October 12, 2006.

Chapter 5

The Maritime Borderlands: Terrorism, Piracy, Pollution, and Poaching in the South China Sea

David Rosenberg

The South China Sea is both a borderland for the nation-states of Southeast Asia and China as well as a maritime superhighway in the world economy. The South China Sea can also be seen as an open-access, common-pool resource that connects states and markets with substantial fisheries, hydrocarbons, and biodiversity resources. Bordered by some of the world's most rapidly urbanizing and industrializing countries, the South China Sea is also the hub of the industrial revolution of Asia. All of these factors combine to make it an area of growing concern over conflicting territorial claims, piracy, poaching, pollution, drug trafficking, illegal migration, and terrorism threats.

The South China Sea has been seen as a borderland at least since 1608, when Hugo Grotius formulated *Mare Liberum, The Freedom of the Seas, or the Right Which Belongs to the Dutch to Take Part in the East Indian Trade.*[1] It remains a contested borderland with territorial disputes over the Spratly Islands, among others. This chapter examines how the nation-states around the South China Sea are attempting to create regional regimes to deal with common transboundary problems in their maritime borderlands. From the wide range of possible issues, four examples will be considered: terrorism, piracy, pollution, and poaching.

Over 500 million people live within 100 miles of the South China Sea coastline. Many of them depend on it for their sustenance and livelihood. The South China Sea provides the habitat and spawning grounds for the world's most productive source of shrimp and tuna. It also has a remarkable amount of biological diversity and immense genetic resources, including over 30 percent of the world's coral reefs.

The South China Sea is also one of the world's busiest international sea lanes. More than half of the world's oil tanker traffic passes through the region's waters. Over half of the world's merchant fleet (by tonnage) sails through the South China Sea every year. The port cities of Hong Kong and Singapore are the two busiest container shipping ports in the world. For the many export-oriented, energy-importing countries of East Asia and Southeast Asia, the South China Sea is the main artery of transportation for vital energy imports and commodity exports.

Economic growth, however, has had several unintended negative consequences. The waters of the South China Sea have become a pool of pollution and an area of conflicting territorial and resource claims. Fish catch rates have been declining despite, or perhaps because of, intensified efforts by more numerous fishing vessels. Countries around the South China Sea have been more concerned about maximizing their national economic growth and ensuring adequate energy supplies than about preserving their common natural resources.

Maritime security concerns in the South China Sea are also increasing. Foremost among these are the conflicting territorial claims to many of the islands and reefs in the sea. The Spratly Islands are claimed by six countries and occupied by three of them. These territorial claims are especially important as an anchor for asserting an exclusive economic zone (EEZ) around the disputed islands and the oil and natural gas resources they are thought to contain. Freedom of navigation through the strategic chokepoints of the Straits of Malacca, Lombok, and Sunda is another major security concern. Perhaps the most frequent source of low-level conflict involves fishing vessels competing for dwindling fish stocks. The porous borders of countries around the South China Sea have exacerbated other security problems of trafficking in drugs, refugees, and forced labor.

The large volume of shipping in the region has created opportunities for attacks on merchant shipping. Over the past 2 decades, more than half of the world's reports of piracy took place in or around the South China Sea. As a result of piracy and the post-9/11 terrorist threat, there has been heightened international scrutiny of ports and shipping containers. Coastal states are modernizing their naval and coast guard forces and patrols to secure their sea lanes as well as their maritime resources.

The South China Sea is also the strategic maritime link between the Pacific Ocean and the Indian Ocean. For major naval powers, freedom of navigation through its sea lanes is of paramount importance for their naval fleets. The declaration of EEZs by coastal states has led to numerous overlapping and multiplying jurisdictional claims and legal confusion over the right to exercise innocent passage through territorial seas by warships, and the right to conduct military surveillance activities in the EEZ of a coastal state. One tragic result of this confusion was the collision between a U.S. EP–3 surveillance aircraft and a Chinese fighter jet in Chinese EEZ waters near Hainan Island on April 1, 2001, and the ensuing political crisis. Another example, also near Hainan Island, occurred in March 2009, when five Chinese ships confronted an unarmed U.S. ocean surveillance ship, the USNS *Impeccable*, and engaged in "reckless and dangerous maneuvers," according to Pentagon reports.

Governing the South China Sea borderlands is becoming more important due to the increase in shipping of energy imports and container exports. The volume of oil tanker traffic—already high—will increase substantially with the projected increase in Chinese oil imports. Almost all of this additional Asian oil demand, as well as Japan's oil needs, will be imported from the Middle East and Africa. Most tankers pass through the strategic Strait of Malacca into the South China Sea. The largest supertankers going to Japan use the wider Lombok Strait east of Bali. Clearly, there is a growing concern among coastal states and user states to ensure safety and security for the vessels passing through these contested and congested borderland waters.

The Stakeholders

There are two sets of stakeholders with interests in governing activities in the South China Sea borderlands. Countries with extensive coastlines bordering the sea, such as Indonesia, Malaysia, Vietnam, and China, mainly want to protect their recently declared sovereign rights and resource control in their EEZs that extend up to 200 nautical miles beyond their coastlines, as authorized by the 1994 United Nations Convention on the Law of the Sea (UNCLOS).[2] They want to safeguard their tourism, fisheries, and other environmental resources from the proliferating transit shipping traffic. About 80 percent of all shipping through Southeast Asian waters is international transit traffic. Coastal countries want international shippers to share the burden of providing safety of navigation.

Nonregional countries with major shipping and naval interests, such as the United States and Japan, want to maintain freedom of navigation through the straits and sea lanes of the South China Sea for their oil tankers, container ships, and naval vessels. The United States sends its warships, including aircraft carriers from the Pacific Fleet, through the South China Sea in support of its military missions in the Arabian Sea and Persian Gulf. The sea is the vital artery that connects Japan with its Middle East energy suppliers.

Some countries do not neatly fit into this dichotomy. For example, Singapore, a coastal state with very little coastline, is a major hub in the world economy with a vital interest in maintaining safe and secure shipping, and therefore it shares many concerns with the United States and Japan. China, a coastal state with an extensive coastline and EEZ resource claims, is also a major trading and ship-owning country with a growing dependence on vital energy imports.

All these regional and international stakeholders have many overlapping interests—for example, promoting safe navigation through the sea. On other issues, such as antipiracy or antiterrorist enforcement measures, however, they have had conflicting views.

From this brief overview, we can see three distinct emphases emerging to attempt to control the borderlands of the South China Sea. First, international stakeholders want to preserve freedom of the seas and the straits of the South China Sea and its archipelagic waterways for their commercial and naval vessels. Second, sovereign nations along the coastline want to extend and assert their EEZ claims as population growth, consumer demand, and technology have increased their economic and political interests in exploiting those zones. Third, there has been a countervailing movement, especially evident in the UNCLOS, to ensure environmentally sustainable resource use and to preserve the natural biodiversity of the sea as a public trust rather than for private exploitation. The following four brief case studies will show how these emphases emerge and how coastal and international stakeholders with varying capabilities are pursuing different interests and organizational forms of governance for the South China Sea.

Maritime Terrorism

Maritime terrorist attacks or threats—politically or ideologically motivated attacks against ships—have been scarce around the South China Sea. Those few that have occurred were within the territorial waters of coastal states. For example, Singapore foiled a terrorist plot in

2002 to hit visiting U.S. naval vessels using a smaller boat rigged with explosives. The most notable maritime attack to date was carried out by the Abu Sayyaf Group on Superferry 14 in Manila Bay in February 2004, with 116 people killed or missing and presumed dead. Sam Bateman contends that terrorists appreciate the consequences of a ferry disaster: "They know that cruise vessels and ferries might have iconic value, and that an attack on one of them could cause many casualties with maximum public impact."[3]

Some notable factors militate against a successful terrorist attack in the South China Sea. Targets are less accessible at sea. A maritime terrorist attack would require a very complex and expensive coordination of efforts. An attack, even if successful, could be much less visible than a terrorist attack on land. So far, there have been no terrorist attacks or hijacking attempts in the maritime borderlands of the South China Sea, compared with dozens of terrorist attacks against churches, hotels, and other land-based targets. Overall, the probability of a maritime terrorist attack appears low.

The greatest concern about the threat of maritime terrorism in Southeast Asia was shown by the George W. Bush administration after the September 11, 2001, attacks on the United States. Admiral Thomas Fargo, then-commander of U.S. forces in the Pacific, while on a visit to Singapore and Malaysia warned that the threat of seaborne terrorism needed to be taken as seriously as attacks from the air. He was accompanied by Defense Secretary Donald Rumsfeld, who anticipated U.S. forces would be hunting terrorists in the Strait of Malacca "pretty soon."[4]

Three major international maritime security initiatives were launched by the Bush administration, all with implications for governing the territorial seas as well as the high seas of the South China Sea: the Container Security Initiative (CSI), the Proliferation Security Initiative (PSI), and the Regional Maritime Security Initiative (RMSI). While the first two are global in scope, the third was directed specifically at the Strait of Malacca. The CSI, first proposed by the U.S. Customs Service in January 2002, aims to identify high-risk containers and to use technology to screen them in the originating ports rather than in the destination ports in the United States. In order to be approved as a CSI port, a government must agree to allow U.S. Customs personnel to supervise the screening of U.S.-bound containers; purchase screening equipment to detect illicit narcotics and radiological, chemical, biological, or conventional weapons; submit to U.S. Customs an electronic manifest of the containers' contents at least 24 hours before arrival; and install new container screening and security technologies.

The initiative constitutes a major change in global shipping practices by shifting inspection from the arrival port to the loading port. There was no significant opposition to the measure; to the contrary, it was implemented widely and relatively quickly and smoothly. By the end of 2002, 18 of the world's top 20 container ports were in compliance. By 2006, nearly 50 ports had been certified as CSI-compliant. Many ports and states have complied with CSI requirements because the economic incentives—getting one's goods to market as soon as possible—are high. The CSI Web site warns noncompliant ports that their U.S.-bound containers may be suspended or banned in the event of a terrorist strike or catastrophe.

The PSI aims to seize shipments of weapons of mass destruction (WMD) and missile-related equipment and technologies by sea, land, or air before they can fall into the hands of terrorist organizations or their state sponsors. Participating states agree to a statement of interdiction principles that includes a commitment to board suspicious vessels sailing within their national waters and suspicious vessels flying their own flag in international waters, and to "seriously consider providing consent" to boardings of their own flagged vessels by other PSI states.

Washington has negotiated bilateral ship boarding agreements with several major flag states, including Panama, Liberia, Cyprus, and Belize. Under the PSI, if a vessel registered in the United States or any partner country is suspected of carrying proliferation-related cargo, either one of the parties to the agreement can request authorization for boarding, search, and possible detention of the vessel and its cargo.

While many countries support the PSI, Singapore and Thailand are the only ones from Southeast Asia that have done so publicly. Despite considerable pressure from Washington to fully and publicly participate in PSI, key maritime nations such as China, India, Indonesia, and Malaysia have so far not joined. A major obstacle for the PSI is that most of the parts for WMD are dual-use, having both civilian and WMD applications. The potential interdiction of dual-use materials may thus threaten legitimate commerce. It is also very difficult to provide assurances that decisions about interdiction will not be politically influenced or based on who is sending or receiving the shipment. China has reservations about the efficiency and legality of the

PSI because it could be detrimental to its legitimate commercial shipping and trade interests. Indonesia and Malaysia are more concerned about arms smuggling, illegal migration, poaching, pollution, and piracy than WMDs. As Mark Valencia succinctly puts it, "WMD are simply not Malaysia's or Indonesia's chief concern."[5]

The RMSI focused specifically on counterterrorism measures in the Strait of Malacca. Admiral Fargo introduced the initiative in a speech to Congress on March 31, 2004, saying that "we're looking at things like . . . putting Special Operations Forces on high-speed vessels so that we can use boats that might be incorporated with these vessels to conduct effective interdiction in, once again, these sea lines of communications where terrorists are known to move about and transit throughout the region."[6]

Malaysia and Indonesia immediately and vehemently rejected the idea of U.S. troops in the area, emphasizing their own capabilities in tackling any terrorist threat. Malaysian Deputy Prime Minister Najib, who concurrently served as defense minister, emphasized that the presence of foreign forces in the region or any interdiction operations in the strait would not be tolerated.[7]

Washington began to backpedal on the idea. Secretary Rumsfeld and Pacific Fleet Commander Admiral Walter Doran stated that Admiral Fargo's earlier comments on the RMSI had been misreported. They said the plan was still very much in its early stages, and it would focus primarily on intelligence sharing, not a U.S. troop presence. The U.S. Navy has since pursued bilateral security agreements in the region. In June 2005, for example, it began a series of bilateral naval antiterrorism exercises in Southeast Asia as part of the annual Cobra Gold exercise regime. In the joint U.S.-Singapore training drill in the South China Sea, more than 15,000 troops took part along with naval aircraft, a submarine, and 12 ships. A major emphasis of the exercise was preventing a maritime terrorist strike on the high seas. From Singapore the U.S. Navy traveled to Malaysia, Thailand, Brunei, Indonesia, and the Philippines to continue separate bilateral exercises.

The three U.S. counterterrorism initiatives have encountered mixed results: CSI has been widely accepted, RMSI was initially rejected, and PSI gets mixed reviews. Most Southeast Asian nations, with the exception of Singapore, have resisted the strong U.S. pressure. However, they have been more willing to accept technical and capital assistance that would help them to respond to not only a terrorist threat, but also their own pressing maritime borderland concerns such as piracy, pollution, and poaching.

The results of these bilateral and multilateral efforts can be seen in the improved counterterrorist response capabilities in the region. For example, in March 2010, Singapore, Malaysia, and Indonesia stepped up security in the Strait of Malacca following warning of possible attacks on oil tankers. A Thai naval attache in Singapore said the original warning came from Japan, which informed the International Maritime Bureau (IMB) that ships in the strait could be hijacked. Sea patrols and air surveillance were increased, and ships were advised to take precautions and stay in patrolled waters. An Indonesian official said that 13 suspects had been detained from a militant training camp in the province of Aceh, at the northern end of the strait. The swift coordinated response proved effective. The threat did not materialize, shipping routes did not change, and insurance costs were not raised. "Trade continues as normal," reported the Joint War Committee at Lloyd's Market Association.[8]

Piracy: Scope and Trends

Piracy is an ancient, persistent, and elusive problem in Southeast Asian waterways. Since the 1990s, about half of the reported events of piracy in the world have taken place in and around the South China Sea. Following the usage of the IMB, this includes the international legal definition of piracy as both theft on the high seas as well as armed robbery or theft in the territorial waters or ports of coastal states.

Piracy appears to be largely related to the economic conditions of seafarers and fishermen. For example, the big increase in piracy in Indonesian waters and ports around the turn of the 21st century may be attributed to the country's sharp economic downturn and domestic instability in the wake of the 1997 currency crisis. Some piracy trends suggest criminal syndicate involvement: more attackers are armed, more vessels are being hijacked, and more crew members are injured or held for ransom.[9]

Coastal states have been under considerable pressure from international user states to curb piracy. Indonesia, in particular, has been portrayed in the media as not doing enough to suppress it. Several factors impede antipiracy efforts: uncertainties over legal jurisdiction, disputed sovereignty, and uncoordinated efforts at recovery of crew, cargo, or ships. Even when pirates were detected, "hot pursuit" across national boundaries was seldom attempted.

A closer examination of the data on piracy shows that the problem might not be as alarming as sometimes portrayed by the media, at least not in economic terms. For example, in 2005 over 63,000 ships sailed through the Straits of Malacca and Singapore. In the same year, the IMB reported 12 cases of actual and attempted attacks on ships in the straits. Hence, the probability of attack is a relatively low rate of 0.019 percent, or 19 out of 100,000. Moreover, many of these reported piracy attacks were little more than cases of petty theft against ships at anchor in port. The IMB estimates that the average haul of an attack is under $10,000.[10]

Many ship owners are reluctant to report pirate attacks to the authorities or to otherwise assist in their investigation. In fact, many shipping companies explicitly prohibit ship masters from reporting pirate attacks. Apart from reflecting badly on the company's image, reporting an attack may mean that the victim vessel will be detained in harbor for investigation, and the cost of such delays may easily exceed the losses incurred by a pirate attack. If suspected pirates are arrested, crew members of the victim ship may be unable or unwilling to bear the expense or risk of testifying at the trial.

Many low-cost antipiracy measures are available, such as equipping the superstructure with proper locks and providing antipiracy training. However, ship owners and insurance companies have little economic incentive to implement such measures. That reluctance, rather than the neglect or incompetence of coastal states, may be the main reason why piracy persists in the South China Sea.

Representatives of the governments of Indonesia and Malaysia have frequently asked shipping companies and the international community to share the costs of policing the Strait of Malacca against pirates. Their requests, however, are met with little enthusiasm from most international actors involved—with the notable exception of Japan, which has funded a number of initiatives to provide training and resources to the law enforcement authorities in the region. Contrary to the popular impression from news media reports, most ship owners have not seen piracy as a menace to international shipping.

For some coastal states, any proposed international coordination to combat terrorism or piracy is a lesser priority than other issues such as maintaining control over newly acquired EEZ resources. With a coastline twice as long as the circumference of the Earth, and with no more than a few dozen operating vessels to patrol its territorial waters, the

Indonesian navy and marine police face a range of problems, including illegal fishing, illegal migration, human trafficking, drug smuggling, and marine pollution. The Indonesian government has estimated that the country loses $4 billion each year due to illegal fishing alone—several times more than the estimated cost of all pirate attacks worldwide.

Regional concerns about terrorism and piracy changed substantially after June 2005, when the Joint War Committee of the London marine insurance market listed the Malacca Strait and certain areas in the southern Philippines as "prone to hull war, strikes, terrorism and related perils" (together with areas such as Iraq, Lebanon, and Somalia). As a result, marine insurance premiums were increased for vessels transiting these areas despite very strong protests by regional governments and ship owners. The Joint War Committee removed the listing in August 2006 after regional governments—with the assistance of international organizations and user states—instituted several security measures. The International Piracy Control Center in Kuala Lumpur and the International Maritime Organization's Piracy Reporting Centre in London stepped up monitoring efforts. The Association of Southeast Asian Nations (ASEAN) Regional Forum convened a meeting of maritime specialists to coordinate coast guard action, information exchange, and investigation of piracy reports. Japan's Antipiracy Coast Guard Program provided additional antipiracy technologies and training.

Singapore has taken the most forceful measures to address maritime security threats. It was the first Asian port to join the U.S.-sponsored CSI and has provided sea security teams to escort selected vessels transiting the Strait of Singapore. It has restricted circulation of small craft and ferries within the port area and increased surveillance efforts by installing tracking devices on all Singapore-registered small boats to identify their location, course, and speed. Together with Indonesia, it operates a radar tracking system on Batam Island to identify, track, and exchange intelligence on shipping in the Singapore Strait.

In 2003, Malaysia and Thailand started coordinated naval patrols along their maritime frontier. Following this, in 2004, Singapore, Malaysia, and Indonesia began coordinated naval patrols in the Strait of Malacca. In September 2005, the "eyes in the sky" initiative began with air patrols over the strait by the three coastal states. The Philippines, meanwhile, has proposed building on its maritime border patrol exercises with Malaysia and Indonesia by formalizing a tripartite agreement to exchange information and intelligence.

Piracy has historically been a pretext for foreign intervention, but coastal states are now insistent that antipiracy measures should be locally initiated and led. They are willing to accept external assistance—especially to modernize their naval and coast guard capabilities—but they contend that ultimately they must have the capability for implementation. Slowly and erratically, they are acquiring that capability. As a result of these monitoring efforts and antipiracy patrols, piracy substantially declined in the key shipping lanes from 2004 to 2008.

However, since then, pirate attacks have been increasing worldwide, with 406 incidents recorded in 2009, the most since 2003. This has occurred despite high-profile patrols mounted by multinational navies in hotspots like the Gulf of Aden and Malacca Strait. The most dramatic of these were the ship hijackings by Somali pirates, including the seizures of the Ukrainian MV *Faina*, with its cargo of heavy tanks and weapons, in September 2008 and the fully laden Saudi-owned tanker *Sirius Star* 2 months later.

The international community responded quickly. The United Nations (UN) passed four resolutions on piracy, the European Union and North Atlantic Treaty Organization authorized the deployment of multilateral counterpiracy forces, and several countries contributed naval resources to antipiracy efforts off the coast of Somalia, including China, Denmark, France, India, Iran, the Netherlands, Pakistan, Russia, the United Kingdom, and the United States.

This quick antipiracy response for the Horn of Africa had little effect on piracy around the South China Sea. The IMB reported 13 attacks in the South China Sea in 2009, the highest in 5 years. There were nine attacks in the Singapore Straits, up from six in 2008. Thirty-two Singapore-flagged vessels were set upon by pirates in 2009—a 5-year high. Maritime piracy remains a global criminal activity.[11]

Many shippers have improved their onboard deterrents. Many states have collaborated to dispatch naval warships to those regions most affected by piracy. The UN has applied pressure through the Convention for the Suppression of Unlawful Acts against the Safety of Maritime Navigation (SUA Convention). In addition, UN Security Council resolutions reaffirmed the power of navies to pursue pirates. In the case of Somalia, they expanded these powers by authorizing pursuit on land.

Through these efforts, hundreds of pirates have been captured over the last 2 years. However, few of the captured pirates have been brought to trial, and many have been released without prosecution. The dilemma led participants in one workshop to conclude that despite more than 400 years of experience with pirates, nation-states have not found a viable and sustainable solution to this crime. Ultimately, what is needed is the integration of three vital components: better operational definitions of piracy in international law, criminalization of piracy and enforcement in national jurisdictions, and coordinated naval operations.[12]

Transboundary Pollution: Lessons of the 1997 Smoke Haze Crisis

Transboundary air pollution over the South China Sea takes many forms, including carbon and sulfur emissions from the smoke-stacks of coal-fired power stations, aluminum smelters, and cement and steel factories, along with motor vehicle emissions of additional particulate and aerosol pollution. However, the relatively sudden and costly smoke pollution from Indonesian forest fires in 1997 precipitated a highly publicized transboundary air pollution crisis. The 1998 State of the World Report noted that:

> [a] plume of smoke larger than the continental United States has spread across Southeast Asia, turning the skies dark and leaving at least 20 million people choking on air that has become a toxic soup, killing hundreds outright. The areas affected include Brunei, Indonesia, Malaysia, Papua New Guinea, the Philippines, Singapore, Thailand, and Vietnam. The massive forest and peat fires swept Borneo and Sumatra in the fall of 1997 and sent life-threatening pollution to cities more than 1,000 kilometers away.[13]

Forest fires are not normal in tropical rainforests, but the immediate cause was clear: the fires were started by pulp, palm oil, and rubber plantation owners to clear natural forest in Indonesia. Then they spread to at least 2 million hectares of forest and underground peat deposits. Tens of millions of people were sickened, hundreds died, and schools, transportation, and businesses were shut down. Enormous amounts of carbon dioxide were added to the atmosphere.

ASEAN has discussed and passed resolutions on regional environment issues for several years. In 1995, ASEAN ministers agreed on a landmark plan specifically related to the South China Sea to combat air and marine pollution and control hazardous wastes. The accord outlined measures for preventing and controlling forest fires, including an early warning system; however, there were few concrete changes in the underlying cause: the practices of domestic and multinational commercial loggers, corporate traders, and state forest management agencies in Indonesia.

There was broad agreement that the smoke haze problem originated in Indonesia and therefore was Indonesia's responsibility to resolve, not ASEAN's. However, not until the 1997 forest fires did ASEAN overcome its longstanding custom of noninterference and begin movement toward a framework convention on regional air pollution. ASEAN environment ministers met in December 1997 to devise a Regional Haze Action Plan (RHAP). They met again in early 1998 to coordinate firefighting efforts. Malaysia would concentrate on fire prevention, Singapore on satellite monitoring, and Indonesia on fire-fighting. Detailed satellite data on smoke haze is now accessible to all ASEAN countries. The Asian Development Bank supported the plan with a $1 million grant to Indonesia for an advisory technical assistance program and another $1 million grant to ASEAN for a regional technical assistance program for strengthening ASEAN's capacity in preventing and mitigating transboundary atmospheric pollution resulting from the forest fires.

A genuine regional effort has emerged to deal with a problem that transcends national boundaries. As a result of the RHAP, the tackling and controlling of forest fires and the resulting smoke haze are no longer an individual undertaking of the affected countries, but rather a coordinated response by the ASEAN member countries. If this initiative continues to enjoy strong leadership, it could become an important precedent in formulating a collective response to other regional environmental problems. Unfortunately, there has not been continuous strong leadership for the RHAP. The 1997–1998 currency crises and subsequent political instabilities disrupted the full institutionalization of the RHAP. Pervasive smoke haze reoccurred in 2006 despite widespread satellite monitoring efforts and warnings about rising economic and health costs. So far, the RHAP has not been able to compel compliance and enforcement; it has limited effectiveness.

Poaching

For centuries, the South China Sea has been an abundant source of fish for food security and employment opportunities for coastal countries. However, as coastal urban populations have grown and as fishing technology has improved, competition for the shared fish stocks of the China seas has intensified considerably. Poaching, or illegal, unreported, or unregulated fishing, has become widespread. Fish catch rates began to decline in the 1970s, with sharper declines registered in the mid-1980s. As a result of bottom trawlers coming into widespread use in the 1990s, many species are now on the brink of extinction. Clearly, the coastal countries have good reason to cooperate to avoid a tragedy of the commons.

Given the migratory pattern of many species and the common pool nature of the South China Sea, no single country would be able to manage or conserve the common migratory fish stocks. Where EEZ claims overlap, UNCLOS calls for establishing joint resource management areas and provides guidelines for doing so, even where conflicting territorial claims are unresolved.

Several joint resource management areas have been established that straddle the borderlands of maritime Southeast Asia, such as the 1979 Malaysia-Thailand Joint Authority for the Gulf of Thailand (see map 5–1). One recent area merits examination as it incorporates the key components of successful regional resource management, the joint resource management agreements between China and Vietnam in the Beibu or Tonkin Gulf. The agreements took effect in 2004, have a term of 15 years, and address three key issues. First, they reaffirm each country's exclusive rights over fishery resources and fishing activities in its own EEZ. Second, they establish general principles for reciprocal fishing access in each other's EEZ. Third, the agreements create a cooperative management regime for their shared fishery resources.[14]

The agreements established a Joint Fishery Committee (JFC) with representatives from each country to conduct research on the status of fisheries, consult with fishing industry interests, and make recommendations on access to fishing zones, fishing quotas, types of species to be caught, and other conditions for fishing.

The JFC establishes areas for joint fisheries management in the common sea between the coastal countries. In addition, the agreement also includes a buffer zone for fishing boats. This attempts to regulate the many small-sized fishing boats with limited communications and navigation equipment near the China-Vietnam shoreline. Some are not even motorized. Illegal entry by mistake is inevitable and understandable. Hence, Chinese and Vietnamese negotiators established this buffer zone to avoid unnecessary disputes by unintentional illegal entry.

The JFC has the power to decide on conservation and management measures, including the allocation of fishing quotas and the

Map 5–1. South China Sea Maritime Claims

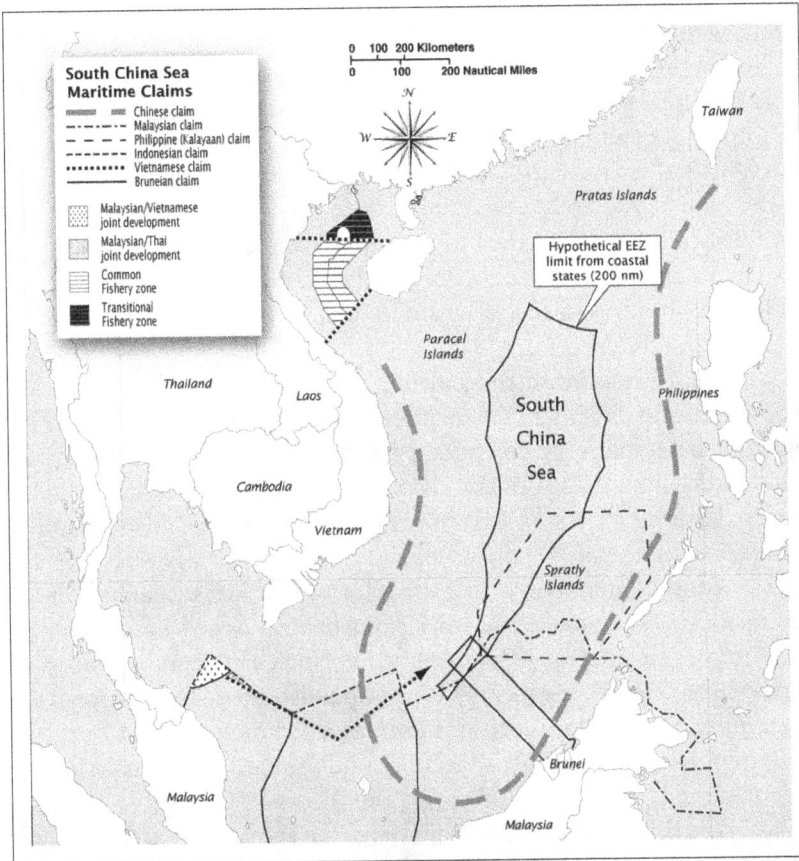

maintenance of fishing order. Its major responsibility is to determine each year how many fishing vessels of each country to permit in the joint resource management areas. Fishing vessels of one country need to apply for a license to fish in the other country's EEZ. They have to comply with the terms of the joint fisheries agreement as well as the domestic laws and regulations of that country. Any violation is subject to legal procedures of the country controlling the EEZ where the fishing takes place. In the case of seizure or detention, the fishing vessels and crew must be promptly released upon posting a bond or other form of security.

The Sino-Vietnamese agreement for the Beibu/Tonkin Gulf is distinctive in that it establishes a cooperative fisheries management program within demarcated maritime zones. It is a permanent body with full operational authority, including a dispute settlement mechanism.[15] The contracting parties have made an effort to carry out periodic joint patrols to prevent illegal fishing. They have also conducted monitoring, surveillance, and control of fishing vessels, including boarding and inspection. However, few workable enforcement mechanisms have been established. Many fishermen find it difficult to accept that they cannot fish in waters where they have done so for years. Hence, monitoring and enforcement efforts need to be strengthened to improve the effectiveness of the agreements.

From a resource management perspective, the main limitation of these agreements is that they focus on managing fishing activity in designated areas that only comprise part of the fishery ecosystem. Many fish stocks migrate seasonally from the management zones to unrestricted fishing waters, which remain open for unrestricted exploitation of fish stocks.

Another limitation is that the JFCs have little transparency or accountability. They make their decisions behind closed doors with no public participation or dispute settlement mechanisms for redress of grievances. The JFCs generally do not publish their deliberations, the data upon which their decisions are based, or the results of scientific findings. Hence, it is difficult to fully understand the rationale for the regulations.

Notwithstanding these limitations, the agreements are important pioneering efforts. The key ingredients to the success of these agreements are a clear maritime boundary delimitation agreement, specific rights and responsibilities for the contracting parties, and compelling reasons for cooperative fisheries management. As long as ecosystems do not match political jurisdictions, cooperation is imperative for sustainable fisheries.

Conclusion

The number and intensity of regional maritime problems in the South China Sea are increasing. However, there are few effective multilateral regimes there. With the notable exception of managing shipping traffic, there have only been a few ad hoc, issue-specific agreements with varying degrees of effectiveness. What explains this limited progress?

One reason is that the international user states themselves have divergent priorities. For example, U.S. policy in the region has often been driven primarily by its global war on terrorism. Japan is primarily interested in antipiracy measures, reflecting its acute vulnerability to any disruption to its trade and raw materials flows.

A second reason for limited progress is that many coastal states give top priority to protecting national sovereignty and controlling their recently acquired ocean resources. In cases where EEZ claims overlap, joint resource development agreements have been negotiated, as in the Tonkin Gulf. Other conflicting territorial claims, as in the Spratly Islands, remain unresolved but have been deferred for future consideration.

A third reason for limited cooperation is that military and intelligence-gathering activities are becoming more intensive, intrusive, controversial, and dangerous. There is general agreement that the exercise of freedom of navigation and overflight in and above EEZs should not interfere with the rights of the coastal state. However, there is still disagreement about when overflights become intrusive eavesdropping missions to scout the defenses of potential rivals.

A fourth reason is that many governments in the region have limited enthusiasm about America's antiterrorism efforts. They remain sensitive to any infringement of sovereignty, especially by the naval forces of user states. This was clearly evident in the initial rejection by Indonesia and Malaysia of the U.S. proposal for RMSI and in the wider regional opposition to Japan's early and ambitious proposal for a regional Ocean Peace Keeping arrangement.

A fifth reason is the divergence between unilateral and multilateral methods of regime building. CSI and PSI "not only change the rules by which the high seas are governed, but they change the way in which those rules are determined."[16] The Bush administration introduced CSI and PSI unilaterally and then negotiated a network of formal bilateral agreements to include other countries. They represent a sea change, a substantial departure from the multilateral, negotiated consensus process that characterized development of UNCLOS. Kerry Lynn Nankivell asserts that CSI and PSI indicate a new form of regime formation—"cooperative unilateralism"—that represents "the gradual movement away from the Westphalian to a hegemonic system of states." Some were concerned about "American praetorian unilateralism."[17] Valencia finds that:

> most of the PSI's shortcomings stem from its ad-hoc, extra-UN, U.S. driven nature. Bringing it into the UN system would rectify many of these shortcomings by loosening U.S. control, enhancing its legitimacy, and engendering near universal support. Whether or not the PSI is formally brought into the UN system, its reach and effectiveness could be improved by eliminating double-standards . . . and increasing transparency.[18]

Despite the many factors inhibiting regional cooperation, coastal state governments and user states recognize they have shared interests in ensuring that the resources and sea lanes of the South China Sea are used effectively and sustainably. But they differ markedly on the means for achieving them.

The most promising recent areas for regional cooperation concern safety, security, and environmental protection in the Straits of Malacca and Singapore. In September 2006, Malaysia and the International Maritime Organization (IMO) organized a meeting in Kuala Lumpur of coastal states, major shipping nations, and shipping companies. Working groups on safety of navigation and maritime security were established to undertake projects on issues such as the removal of shipwrecks, the establishment of a hazardous and noxious substance response center, the installation of automatic identification system transponders for small ships, and the placement of tide, current, and wind measurement systems.

Substantial voluntary contributions have been made by China and Japan for these projects. Some have advocated a toll-road or user-pays system to help fund pollution cleanup and navigational aids. The United States and many shippers, however, strongly oppose the introduction of any fees. They prefer to see greater transparency and accountability in any use of funds for maritime safety and security. They would also like to see Malaysia and Indonesia ratify the 1979 Convention on Maritime Search and Rescue, the SUA Convention, and the Regional Cooperation Agreement on Combating Piracy and Armed Robbery against Ships in Asia. Given the limited funding and compliance with international conventions, there is still no effective governance of the sea lanes of the South China Sea. The current situation is far from the most ambitious proposal by the World Bank, UN Development Programme, and IMO to construct a Marine Electronic Highway, a shipping traffic control system similar to the global air traffic control arrangement, with comprehensive, integrated electronic information, navigation, and control systems.

Whatever their conflicting claims and mutual suspicions may be, political leaders in the coastal states are beginning to understand that they must cooperate in order to manage the increase in shipping traffic, to address maritime security threats, and to use the resources of the South China Sea sustainably. While some progress has been made, there is as yet no durable agreement on how to share the burden for providing safety and security in the region.

Regional problems require regional solutions, but they are taking many different forms, including cooperative unilateralism as in the case of the U.S.-initiated Container Security Initiative, multilateral institutionalization as in the case of the UNCLOS, or through a network of similar bilateral and regional agreements on specific issues such as joint fisheries committees and coordinated naval patrols. Clearly, there are many ways for coastal and international stakeholders with varying capabilities and diverse interests to manage the common transboundary issues in their maritime borderlands. The nation-states of Southeast Asia that have only recently extended their sovereignty and resource claims to EEZs in the South China Sea are in no rush to negotiate them away.

Notes

[1] Hugo Grotius, *Mare Liberum, The Freedom of the Seas, or the Right Which Belongs to the Dutch to Take Part in the East Indian Trade* (1608), trans. Ralph Van Deman Magoffin (New York: Oxford University Press, 1916).

[2] United Nations Convention on the Law of the Sea, 2006. Full text, related agreements, and ratifications are available from the United Nations Web site at <www.un.org/Depts/los/index.htm>.

[3] Sam Bateman, "Ferry Safety: A Neglected Aspect of Maritime Security?" Institute of Defence and Strategic Studies *Commentaries* 31 (2006).

[4] "U.S. to Hunt Malacca Terrorists," *Channel News Asia*, June 23, 2004.

[5] Mark J. Valencia, "The Proliferation Security Initiative: Making Waves in Asia," *Adelphi Paper* 376 (Abingdon and New York: Routledge, 2005), 59.

[6] "Crack U.S. Troops May be Used to Flush Out Terrorists in Key Southeast Asian Waterway," *Channel News Asia*, April 5, 2004.

[7] John Burton, "Countries Oppose U.S. Offer to Patrol Malacca," *Financial Times*, April 5, 2004.

[8] Neil Chatterjee, "Security Raised in Malacca Strait after Terror Warning," Reuters, March 4, 2010, available at <www.reuters.com/article/idUSTRE62335120100304>.

[9] Catherine Zara Raymond, "Piracy in Southeast Asia: New Trends, Issues, and Responses," *Harvard Asia Quarterly*, May 24, 2006.

[10] International Maritime Bureau, Piracy Reporting Centre, 2005, 5.

[11] "World Pirate Attacks Soar," *Straits Times*, January 14, 2010, available at <www.straitstimes.com/BreakingNews/SEAsia/Story/STIStory_477258.html>.

[12] Elizabeth Andersen, Benjamin Brockman-Hawe, and Patricia Goff, "Suppressing Maritime Piracy: Exploring the Options in International Law," workshop report, *One Earth Future*, 2009, available at <www.oneearthfuture.org>.

[13] Lester Brown, *State of the World 1998*, WorldWatch Institute (New York: Norton, 1998), xvii.

[14] Zou Keyuan, "The Sino-Vietnamese Agreement on Maritime Boundary Delimitation in the Gulf of Tonkin," *Ocean Development and International Law* 36 (2005), 13–24.

[15] Nguyen Hong Thao, "Maritime Delimitation and Fishery Cooperation in the Tonkin Gulf," *Ocean Development and International Law* 36 (2005), 25–44.

[16] Kerry Lynn Nankivell, "The Container and Security Initiatives: A First Look," *CANCAPS Bulletin* 41 (May 2004).

[17] R. Ramakrishna, "9/11, American Praetorian Unilateralism and the Impact on State-Society Relations in Southeast Asia," *IDSS Working Paper* 26 (Singapore: Institute of Defence and Strategic Studies, June 2002).

[18] Mark J. Valencia, "The Proliferation Security Initiative in Perspective," *Policy Forum Online 06-41A*, Nautilus Institute (May 25, 2006), accessed at <www.nautilus.org/fora/security/0641Valencia.html>.

Chapter 6

Bilateral and Multilateral Trade Arrangements in Southeast Asia: Forces for Integration?

Dick K. Nanto

A tangled web of regional and bilateral trade agreements within Southeast Asia and between the Association of Southeast Asian Nations (ASEAN) and countries outside the region is causing national borders to ripple as their restraining effects on trade flows are pushed from inside to outside the ASEAN states (see map 6–1). While intra-ASEAN boundaries are fading, those that separate ASEAN from non-ASEAN states are both becoming more distinct and stretching to include several other trading partners. The driving force behind these trends is globalization and the free trade agreements that follow. This is causing a fundamental shift in economic relationships among countries in this part of Asia and how they view the cartographic delineations that surround them.

As bureaucratic resistance to the international spread of manufacturing and consumption dissipates, the economic constraints of country borders also are becoming less binding. Supply chains now resemble botanical diagrams of trees. Their roots cross national boundaries as they seek to pull in components for assembly from multiple sources. Their branches reach toward the sunshine of demand and carry the finished products to be sold into any country with marketing space. Markets once local have become national, markets once national have become regional, and markets once regional have become global.

Nearly absent from this push for globalization has been ideology. For much of the post–World War II period, ideological battles pushed some nations apart and pulled others together. East Asia was divided into blocs with communist countries on one side confronting the United States and its allies on the other. The ideological clash often manifested itself in struggles for political ascendency, and, in the cases of Vietnam

Map 6–1. Trade Arrangements in Southeast Asia

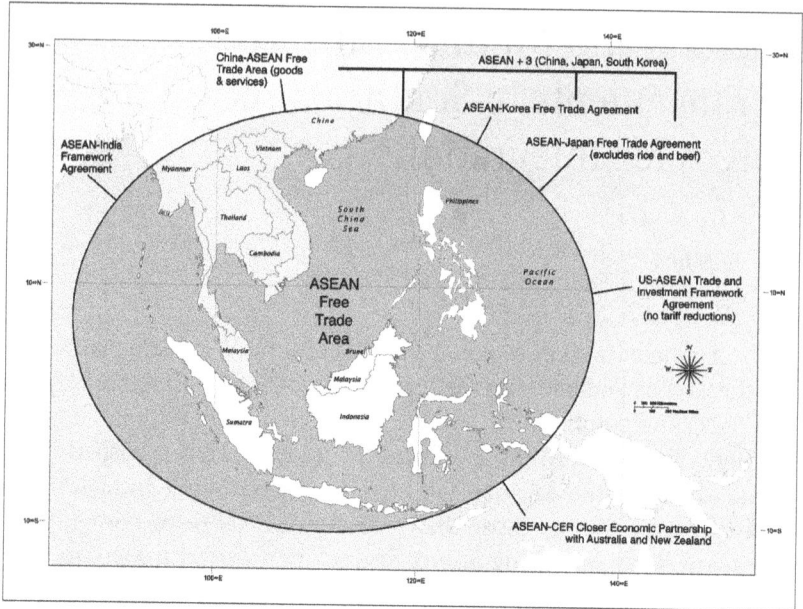

and Korea, the great power rivalry led to open warfare. During this time, international trade flows tended to be channeled by political alliances. The American market served both as the anchor of the Asia Pacific economy and the preferred export destination for many of the noncommunist countries. China and the Soviet Union also maintained trading blocs. Some businesses danced around the limits set by the ideological propensities of their respective governments, but by and large, trade flows settled into channels of least political, as well as economic, resistance.

Governments also used trade policy, particularly the protection of certain industries, as a tool of development. The export-led industrialization practiced by Japan, South Korea, and Taiwan called for protection of infant industries while promoting industrial competitiveness by inducing them to venture into international export markets. For Southeast Asian nations, this often meant that selling certain manufactures in relatively open though distant markets, such as those in the United States, became easier than exporting them to a neighboring country. The revolutions in communications and shipping exacerbated this trend.

Currently, Southeast Asia is riding the crest of a third wave of industrialization. The first was more of a wake than a wave as Japan quadrupled its national income over the 1960s. Then came the Asian tigers of South Korea, Taiwan, Hong Kong, and Singapore as they emulated the Japanese model and crashed through markets around the world. Now, Thailand, Malaysia, and Indonesia are joining with China in a new wave of industrialization that is establishing Asia as a preferred manufacturing platform for industries across the globe. These waves of industrialization, combined with a revolution in information technology and communications, have created ideal conditions for the countries of Southeast Asia to rethink their economic relationships with each other, to reduce border barriers, and to join together in regional trade arrangements.

U.S. Trade Policy and Challenges

As U.S. policy toward economic arrangements in East Asia evolves, it is turning on matters of intensity, inclusiveness, and final structure. Should the United States intensify its efforts to either hinder or support the architecture? Who should be included in the arrangements? Should the groupings be exclusively Asian? The current U.S. policy appears to be to hedge by not trying to block attempts to create exclusive Asian free trade agreements (FTAs) but doing deals to keep from being cut out from their benefits. On the security side, U.S. interest in stability, counterterrorism, and nonproliferation in East Asia is so great that the United States has sought a seat at the table when Asians meet to address security issues. An American presence is not as crucial in trade because most transactions are done by private entities on a win-win basis. FTAs can lower barriers for participants but not raise them to outsiders.

At the core of U.S. concern over the developing regional architecture in East Asia is the growing influence of China. A danger exists that if China comes to dominate regional institutions in East Asia, it could steer them down a path inimical to U.S. interests. Some Asian nations, however, are wary of excessive Chinese influence and are hedging and maneuvering against possible Chinese dominance.

The Obama administration was late in addressing issues of international trade because of the urgency of dealing with the global financial crisis and the push for health care legislation. In 2009, most U.S. trade policy relied on existing mechanisms to protect American industries from unfair trade and from surges in imports (such as increased tariffs on imports of tires from China) and on taking no action on pending free trade agreements with Colombia, Panama, and South Korea. During the debate on health care, the Obama administration could scarcely afford to offend constituencies, such as the labor unions, by pursuing measures to liberalize trade. In March 2010, following the passage of the health care legislation, the administration was able to turn its attention to other pressing issues, including international trade policy.

In Congress, the Democratic majority still was wary of additional free trade agreements. This generally reflected public opinion. In November 2009, the Pew Research Center found that 85 percent of survey respondents said that protecting jobs should be a top foreign policy priority and that economic issues were the greatest international problem confronting the United States, followed closely by the wars in Afghanistan and Iraq. As for FTAs, 43 percent said that they were good for the country, while 32 percent said that they were bad. According to the Pew survey, 53 percent thought FTAs lead to job losses, 49 percent to lower wages, and 42 percent to slower economic growth.[1]

Members of Congress have cited specific arguments against approving the three pending free trade agreements (anti-labor activities in Colombia, potential tax havens in Panama, and the protected automobile market in South Korea), but the inaction seems to reflect a general reluctance to approve any FTAs at all unless they are likely to create, rather than destroy, U.S. jobs. Other trade policy issues in Congress have been China's undervalued currency, trade enforcement, consumer safety for imported goods, and environmental protection as it relates to trade.

A majority of Representatives had signed on to the proposed Trade Act of 2009 (H.R. 3012). This bill would require biennial reviews of certain free trade agreements and would provide that implementing bills of new agreements not be subject to expedited consideration unless such agreements included certain standards with respect to aspects such as labor, human rights, the environment and public safety, and food and product safety. The bill also would require the President to submit a plan to Congress for the renegotiation of existing trade agreements to bring them into compliance with such standards.

The Obama administration's 2010 Trade Policy Agenda has included the following: doubling U.S. exports over the next 5 years (National Export Initiative); maintaining a commitment to a rules-based global trading system (including a balanced Doha Round agreement); enforcing trade rights (including intellectual property rights and trade rules); opening markets abroad to enhance U.S. job growth and innovation; working to resolve outstanding issues in pending FTAs and build on existing trade and investment arrangements; facilitating progress on national energy and environmental goals; and fostering stronger partnerships with developing and poor nations. The administration also is exploring the possibility of negotiating a multilateral agreement providing for free trade in environmental goods and for removing nontariff barriers to environmentally friendly services.

With respect to the Asia Pacific region, the 2010 Obama Trade Agenda states:

> The Asia-Pacific region, encompassing Asia and the Americas, already constitutes the largest share of the world economy, and that share will continue to grow in the coming decade. If the United States is to benefit from more exports, job expansion, and accelerated innovation through trade, the Asia-Pacific must take a central place in our trade agenda. And countries in that region must see the United States as a committed and engaged trading partner if we are to remain similarly at the center of its network of intensifying trade relationships.[2]

With respect to regional trade arrangements, the Obama administration is pursuing two initiatives. On March 15, 2010, the United States entered negotiations to join a regional Asia Pacific trade agreement known as the Trans-Pacific Partnership (TPP) agreement. The United States, Australia, Peru, and Vietnam are seeking to join the four existing members of the pact: Singapore, Chile, Brunei, and New Zealand. The administration believes that the TPP is the strongest vehicle for achieving economic integration across the Asia Pacific region and advancing U.S. economic interests there. It intends to build on the most forward-looking aspects of existing FTAs to shape a broad, deep, and high-quality 21st-century regional trade agreement. A new focus is on the efficiency of regional business supply chains and the concerns of small- and medium-sized businesses. The supply chain focus initially will attempt to harmonize regulations dealing with product safety and other such aspects of transnational manufacturing.

The administration also holds out the prospect that other countries (such as South Korea) will join the TPP negotiations and that, over the long term, the TPP will become the basis for a Free Trade Area of the Asia Pacific (FTAAP), which is the second regional trade initiative of the Obama administration. This would span the 21 economies of the Asia Pacific Economic Cooperation (APEC) forum and is the only regional trade proposal that includes Taiwan. The administration said that it intends to work with trading partners in the region to build consensus and advance work on critical trade and investment issues leading up to 2011 when the United States will host the APEC Leaders' Meeting in Honolulu.

In addition, the Obama administration supports ASEAN integration and intends to continue working with ASEAN to build economic relationships in the region.[3] U.S. policy has been to conclude bilateral FTAs with individual Asian countries and work toward a U.S.-ASEAN FTA that would serve as a counterweight to the China-ASEAN FTA. In August 2006, ASEAN and the United States signed a Trade and Investment Framework Agreement that may serve as a precursor to an FTA.

A question for the United States is whether the development of regional free trade arrangements in Asia represents a shift in power, a shift in problems, or a shift in paradigm.[4] The rise of China along with Japan and South Korea's economic power already has caused a shift in the manufacturing activity toward Asia. While the United States still is the largest economy in the world, the combination of ASEAN plus China, Japan, South Korea, Australia, and India would form a trading bloc that would be roughly equal in size to North America or the European Union. It is not clear, however, if China's participation in regional trading arrangements would increase or blunt its ability to exercise power.

Does the rise of an Asian trading bloc based on ASEAN or one spanning the Pacific Ocean provide an opportunity to shift problems from ad hoc or single-nation solutions toward multilateral resolution? In the 21st century, more and more problems are international in nature and can be resolved only through international cooperation and coordination. Financial crises, climate change, nonstate terrorism, contagious diseases, and product safety are as much global as national problems. Regional groupings of countries, whether as formal economic communities or merely publicity and social venues, may provide impetus for greater cooperation on and awareness of such issues. Even though the ultimate resolution of such problems depends on national responses, international coordination helps to ensure that each country adopts the best practices and that burdens are borne equally among countries.

Even though pre–World War II empires often had free trade and easy movement of labor, the nation-state remained the focus of most economic policy. International trade was conceptualized as country A exchanging goods with country B according to each country's comparative advantage. The paradigm began to shift in the postwar period with the formation of the European Community, the North American Free Trade Agreement, the Eurozone, and other economic groupings of countries. This coincided with the development of global supply chains by businesses, cheap telecommunications, reliable and low-cost shipping, and the fracturing of the manufacturing processes into segments that could be located almost anywhere in the world. The shift in paradigm is that while sovereign governments may view trade as between nations, companies view much of it as within their supply chain. They seek regulatory structures that are harmonized from country to country and that allow them to focus on the development, production, and sales of products rather than on border barriers, certificates of origin, and differing regulatory regimes. Businesses seek trading arrangements that are inclusive (more members) and extensive (cover more aspects of the economy).

Why Join Together?

The role of nations in legitimate economic activity is to provide the conduit for it to occur, to facilitate it, to regulate it, and in some cases to own it. In the case of international trade, however, the problem for nations is that the space above national borders tends to be anarchic and without order or standards of behavior. In facilitating trade in this anarchic space, governments establish trading rules, cede preferential benefits to other nations through formal mechanisms, and establish neutral institutions as umbrellas for supranational rulemaking and dispute settlement, or they may intervene to impair the trade of certain countries for political purposes (such as by imposing economic sanctions).

After the retreat from trade during the Great Depression and World War II, nations sought to fill the anarchic void by first establishing the General Agreement on Tariffs and Trade and then, in 1995, the 153-member World Trade Organization (WTO).

Unlike international political interaction, international economic transactions tend to be self-generating and positive-sum because they provide benefits to both buyers and sellers (each side gains from the exchanges). Otherwise, the transactions would not occur. In cases, however, private parties may gain from trades but impose losses on nations (such as in illicit weapons or drug trade). In this sense, economic transactions differ from zero-sum security exchanges, such as war, in which one side's gain is the other side's loss.

Countries join in free trade and other economic agreements to gain certain advantages. The benefits of FTAs for exports, imports, or investments usually go beyond those available through global concessions agreed to multilaterally under the WTO. The organization's rules allow for FTAs, but they can only lower barriers between signatory countries. They cannot raise them for other nations.

As with the European Union or the North American Free Trade Agreement, preferential trade arrangements usually follow existing trade patterns. FTAs do not spring into existence *ex nihilo*, although in some cases, they are pursued for strategic rather than purely economic reasons.

Trading arrangements and economic institutions also provide a platform for countries to take leadership roles and to spread their influence. The end of the Cold War brought unipolarity, with the United States as the sole remaining superpower. Asian nations recognize that the United States will continue to exercise major influence in the region, but ASEAN and China both are using their leadership in trade negotiations to climb the international diplomatic ladder. Beijing, in particular, sees regional trade and other economic arrangements as a vehicle to promote economic interaction with countries that may be wary of its growing strategic and political reach. For China, leadership of exclusive Asian organizations, including regional trading blocs, may help it reclaim what it considers to be its historical position as the "center kingdom of the world" and leader of Asia.

The economic effects of trade agreements are manifested in both trade diversion and trade creation. FTAs divert existing trade toward the signatory countries but may also create more trade overall. In addition, free trade and other trade agreements may lock in market access or other benefits provided by one government that are under risk of being withdrawn by successive governments. They also may induce governments to take politically difficult actions, such as opening agricultural markets or providing labor rights or protection for the environment, that may be too risky for politicians to undertake without external pressure and a scapegoat to blame.

Any change in the rules of trade creates winners and losers—those who can take advantage of the new trading regime and those who will be harmed by it. Those hurt tend to be in industries previously protected by tariffs, regulations, or other government action. Under a theoretical cost-benefit calculus, a government should pursue an FTA if the gains exceed the losses by a sufficiently large margin that even if the gainers compensate the losers, society still emerges with a net gain. In real life, however, governments that enter into FTAs rarely compensate losers sufficiently. The problem is that gains under a liberalized trading regime tend to be incremental and diffuse and usually are manifest in the form of lower prices for imports that also force down prices of competing products made domestically. Those benefitting tend to be consumers, retailers, and buyers of foreign-made equipment and supplies. Those losing tend to be in import-competing industries or those traditionally protected from imports. These typically include textiles, unionized industrial sectors (such as steel and automobiles), and agriculture. Transferring some of the benefits of liberalized trade from the gainers to the losers is difficult indeed.

FTAs typically proceed through evolutionary stages with respect to intensity (greater liberalization) and expansiveness (more members). International trading relationships begin with unorganized trade and investment flows based on comparative economic advantage. As shown in figure 6–1, trade then can be brought under broad international trading rules such as those stemming from normal trade relations (most favored nation status) or from the WTO. Trade furthermore can be placed under a preferential arrangement with special access privileges or reduced barriers but not necessarily free trade. As a precursor to a preferential trading arrangement, the United States uses Trade and Investment Framework Agreements to strengthen bilateral trade and support economic reform in partner countries through regular senior-level discussions on commercial and economic issues. Other countries use Framework Agreements that may provide for an "early harvest" of trade concessions and launch discussions on a future FTA.

Japan and several ASEAN countries have negotiated partial FTAs called Economic Partnership Agreements, which have established free trade in most manufactured goods but have usually excluded sensitive sectors, such as agriculture. In some cases, these agreements are long on promise but short on actual trade concessions. They also may map a path toward a full FTA. An FTA usually provides for elimination of tariffs on goods, liberalized access to services and investment flows, as well as other provisions. The FTA member nations, however, usually do not have common external barriers (a customs union). The most extensive trading arrangement is a common market, which goes beyond an FTA. Its members have free trade among themselves plus common external barriers, and the arrangement allows for the free movement of labor and capital among member states. As trade arrangements become more intensive, they also can become more expansive by including other countries.

In Southeast Asia, most trade agreements have been driven by the market. They also have been competitive. The benefits available under a preferential trade agreement usually induce competing demands as other countries seek the same trade advantages or risk losing business for their exporters or investors. In some cases, countries have negotiated bilateral FTAs for political and security as well as economic purposes. The United States, for example, has sought FTAs with countries with large Muslim populations (Malaysia, Jordan, Morocco, Oman), with strategic locations (Singapore, Thailand, Mexico, Canada, and Central American countries), or with sensitive military considerations (South Korea, Israel).

Trade specialists debate whether FTAs complement or compete with multilateral trade negotiations under the WTO. While some see FTAs as centrifugal forces working against global trade liberalization, others see them as centripetal forces that will lead eventually to global free trade. One argument is that WTO agreements tend to result in "lowest common denominator" outcomes, whereas FTAs can go beyond multilateral agreements by providing deeper concessions between like-minded nations. Rather than lowering barriers somewhat for many countries under a WTO agreement, through FTAs, nations can slash

Figure 6–1. Types of Trading Arrangements by Intensity of Economic Integration

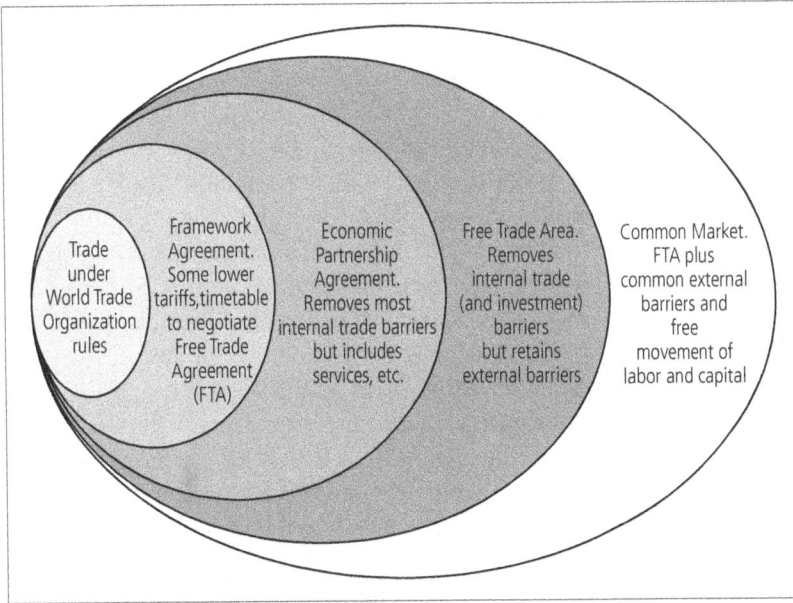

| Trade under World Trade Organization rules | Framework Agreement. Some lower tariffs, timetable to negotiate Free Trade Agreement (FTA) | Economic Partnership Agreement. Removes most internal trade barriers but includes services, etc. | Free Trade Area. Removes internal trade (and investment) barriers but retains external barriers | Common Market. FTA plus common external barriers and free movement of labor and capital |

barriers or eliminate them for a select number of their major trading partners. In 2010, as WTO multilateral negotiations under the Doha Development Agenda stalled, many view the proliferation of FTAs as providing a fallback position for countries should the negotiations fail completely. The FTAs have provided a secondary strategy that leads to trade liberalization even without the multilateral negotiations. In that sense, FTAs have detracted from the WTO negotiations.

The complex web of free trade agreements in the world is becoming denser each year. In February 2010, the WTO reported that it had been notified of more than 465 regional trade agreements and that 267 were in force. Many others were being negotiated. The complexity of rules for overlapping FTAs may increase transaction costs for businesses as they, for example, have to cope with increasing paperwork to meet the rules-of-origin requirements to qualify for free trade status. In some cases, businesses are opting out of taking advantage of lower FTA tariffs because the documentation required to show country of origin is too onerous.

ASEAN and Bilateral FTAs in East Asia[5]

The Southeast Asian economies are dwarfed by those of Japan and China to the north and North America and the European Union across the oceans. ASEAN's combined gross domestic product of $1.45 trillion in 2009 was less than 10 percent that of the European Union ($16.42 trillion) or North America ($16.47 trillion for NAFTA). Still, the region is growing quickly. To put the region into perspective, the ASEAN combined gross domestic product in 2009 was only about half again as large as that of South Korea. This is a major reason for forming a free trade area. ASEAN manufacturers need markets of a size sufficient to generate economies of large-scale production. Taking into account ASEAN's FTAs (although they have only partial coverage) with China, Japan, South Korea, Australia, New Zealand, and India, however, the ASEAN-centric, hub-and-spoke FTA configuration of an ASEAN + 6 is nearly the same size ($14.58 trillion) as the other two economic centers of the world.

In 1992, ASEAN created an ASEAN FTA (AFTA) among its member nations. Under this arrangement, tariffs on the products covered by the FTA for the ASEAN 6 (Brunei Darussalam, Indonesia, Malaysia, the Philippines, Singapore, and Thailand) dropped below 5 percent or were eliminated in 2010, while the newer members (Burma, Cambodia, Laos, and Vietnam) have until 2020 to do the same. In 2005, this deadline was moved up 5 years to 2015. The AFTA covers all manufactured and agricultural products traded within ASEAN and includes services. However, 734 tariff lines in the General Exception List, representing about 1.09 percent of all tariff lines in ASEAN, are permanently excluded from the free trade area for reasons of national security, protection of health and human, animal, or plant life, or for artistic, historic, or archaeological reasons.[6]

The ASEAN FTA has made significant progress in lowering barriers to trade within the region. ASEAN implemented the FTA through a series of agreements. The most significant was a Common Effective Preferential Tariff (CEPT) Scheme for AFTA, an agreement that defines the trade categories to be included and sets deadlines for member countries to reduce tariffs to below 5 percent. As of January 1, 2010, 99.5 percent of the tariff lines in the ASEAN inclusion lists under the CEPT for ASEAN Free Trade Area (CEPT–AFTA) stood at 0 to 5 percent. Intra-ASEAN trade almost tripled to $458.1 billion in 2008 as compared to 2000, when all 10 member states joined the CEPT–AFTA.

AFTA is a work in progress. The member nations are expanding the coverage of the FTA to include more services, such as mutual recognition of nursing qualifications. They also have established 11 priority sectors to be liberalized. These include automobiles, electronics, information technology, health care, wood-based products, rubber-based products, textiles and apparel, agriculture-based products, fisheries, air travel, and tourism. In December 2006, the ASEAN leaders signed an agreement that crafted a road map for action on liberalizing these prioritized sectors.

While ASEAN has been fostering closer economic, political, and cultural relations among its member states, the organization also has concluded various agreements with other nations that provide some immediate trade liberalization and contain provisions for negotiations that are to lead to formal FTAs. Since ASEAN is not a common market, it may negotiate an FTA agreement with a non-ASEAN country, but each individual member must sign it and implement it as if it were a bilateral agreement. ASEAN does not have common external tariff rates. Individual ASEAN countries also may pursue bilateral FTAs on their own. ASEAN views itself as the core of a regional FTA in East Asia. Currently, there are various proposals for membership, such as ASEAN + 3 (the addition of Japan, China, and South Korea) and ASEAN + 6 (ASEAN + 3 and Australia, New Zealand, and India).

In November 2002, ASEAN and China signed a Framework Agreement on Comprehensive Economic Co-operation. This provided for an ASEAN–China Free Trade Area (ACFTA) that took effect on January 1, 2010, between China and the more industrialized ASEAN 6. By 2015, Burma, Cambodia, Laos, and Vietnam are to follow. ASEAN also has concluded an FTA with Australia and New Zealand that is in force (but has not yet been ratified by Cambodia, Indonesia, and Laos).

In November 2007, Japan and ASEAN endorsed a free trade agreement under which tariffs would be eliminated on 90 percent of imports by both sides, but key items such as rice and beef would remain protected. ASEAN has a similar agreement with India that currently covers goods but may be widened to include services and investment.[7] With South Korea, ASEAN has signed an FTA pact that covers goods trade only. In December 2005, Thailand refused to sign the agreement because South Korea excluded rice from the 4,000 items that are to have import tariffs cut to below 20 percent and then to 0 by 2009 (with an additional 5 years for the newer ASEAN member nations).[8] In 2008, Thailand and South Korea concluded negotiations that brought Thailand into the ASEAN–Korea FTA and gave Thailand more flexibility than other ASEAN nations in cutting or waiving its tariffs or both.[9] Services and investment have also been added to the original agreement. In 2010, the India-ASEAN FTA came into force.

Table 6–1 shows the extent to which the ASEAN and other Asian nations have been linking their economies through free trade and other economic agreements. Almost all of the countries in the region have either concluded FTAs or are negotiating or discussing the possibility of negotiating them with each other. The glaring exception is Taiwan, which because of pressure from Beijing has been unable to conclude FTAs with countries of the region. Taiwan, however, is a member of the WTO and has FTAs with some Central American nations.

The two-tiered nature of ASEAN membership manifests itself in the various FTAs. The more developed ASEAN 6 countries generally have more FTAs and quicker timetables for liberalization than the new ASEAN members (Burma, Cambodia, Laos, and Vietnam).

Among individual ASEAN countries, Singapore has been most aggressive in seeking FTA deals. As a city-state, it has long served as an *entrepot* for the region with virtually free trade and a hospitable environment for foreign businesses. In addition to being a part of the ASEAN Economic Community, it has concluded free trade agreements with the United States, China, Japan, South Korea, Australia, New Zealand, India, Jordan, Panama, and the European Free Trade Association. Singapore also is a member of the Trans-Pacific Strategic Economic Partnership Organization (an FTA among Singapore, New Zealand, Chile, and Brunei) that is seeking to expand membership to include the United States, Australia, Peru, and Vietnam. It has ongoing negotiations with Mexico, Canada, Pakistan, Costa Rica, Ukraine, and the European Union.

Likewise, Thailand, the Philippines, Indonesia, and Malaysia have been initiating talks and signing various types of trade agreements. Negotiations for FTAs between the United States and Malaysia and Thailand have hit snags and currently are on hold. Cambodia and Laos are far behind in the FTA process. They barely have been able to sign trade agreements, let alone free trade or other types of preferential trade arrangements. Laos is not a member of the WTO, but Cambodia joined in 2004.

Table 6–1. Free Trade Agreements, Negotiations, and Discussions by ASEAN Members and Selected Other Nations, 2010

	China	Japan	South Korea	Taiwan	ASEAN	Singapore	Indonesia	Thailand	Malaysia	United States	Australia	New Zealand
China[a]		D	D	D	FTA	FTA	PF	FTA	FTA		N	FTA
Japan[b]	D		N		FTA	FTA	FTA	FTA	FTA		D	
South Korea[c]	D	N			FTA	FTA	FTA	FTA	FTA	FTA–U	N	
Taiwan[d]	D											
ASEAN[e]	FTA	FTA	FTA								FTA	FTA
Singapore[f]	FTA	FTA	FTA				FTA	FTA	FTA	FTA	FTA	FTA
Indonesia[g]	PF	FTA	FTA		FTA			FTA	FTA	D	FTA	FTA
Thailand[h]	FTA	FTA	FTA		FTA	FTA			FTA	N	FTA	FTA
Malaysia[i]	FTA	FTA	FTA		FTA	FTA	FTA			D	FTA	FTA
Philippines[j]	FTA	FTA	FTA		FTA	FTA	FTA	FTA		D	FTA	FTA
Vietnam[k]	FTA	FTA	FTA		FTA	FTA	FTA	FTA		N	FTA	FTA
Australia[l]	N	N	D		FTA	FTA	FTA	FTA	FTA	FTA		FTA
New Zealand[m]	FTA				FTA	FTA	FTA	FTA	FTA	N	FTA	

Source: Country trade ministries, news articles, and bilaterals.org.

Notes: FTA = existing Free Trade Agreement (may not be fully implemented); FTA–U = unratified FTA; PF = partial FTA (many sectors not included or plan for future FTA implementation); N = FTA negotiations; D = FTA discussions.

[a] China also has FTAs with Hong Kong, Macao, and New Zealand; partial FTA with Chile; negotiations with Pakistan, the Southern Africa Customs Union, the Gulf Cooperation Council, Iceland, Norway, and Costa Rica; discussions with India.

[b] Japan also has FTAs with Mexico, Chile, Switzerland, and Brunei; negotiations with India and Peru; discussions with Canada and Mongolia.

[c] South Korea also has FTAs with Chile, European Free Trade Association (EFTA), India, and European Union (EU) (unratified); negotiations with Canada, Japan, Mexico, Peru, Australia, and New Zealand.

[d] Taiwan or Chinese Taipei also has FTAs with Panama, Guatemala, Nicaragua, El Salvador, and Honduras; negotiations with Dominican Republic.

[e] ASEAN also has an FTA with India; negotiations with EU.

[f] Singapore also has FTAs with India, EFTA, Jordan, Panama, Peru, Gulf Cooperation Council, Brunei, Chile, and New Zealand; negotiations with Mexico, Canada, Pakistan, Costa Rica, Ukraine, and EU.

[g] Indonesia also has an FTA with India waiting approval; discussions with Egypt.

[h] Thailand also has an FTA with Bahrain, a partial FTA with India, is a member of The Bay of Bengal Initiative for Multi-Sectoral Technical and Economic Cooperation with Bangladesh, Bhutan, Burma, India, Nepal, Sri Lanka, and Thailand that aims for an FTA by 2017; negotiations with Peru, Chile, EFTA, and Papua New Guinea; discussions with EU.

[i] Malaysia also has an FTA with Chile and Brunei, negotiations with New Zealand; discussions with India.

[j] Philippines also has an FTA with EFTA; discussions with Chile and Israel.

[k] Vietnam has an FTA with the Andean Community; negotiations with New Zealand, EFTA, and the UAE. It also is joining the negotiations on a Trans-Pacific Partnership (TPP).

[l] Australia also has an FTA with the United States, with the Pacific Island Countries Trade Agreement (14 members), and Chile; negotiations with China, the Gulf Cooperation Council, Japan, South Korea, and the TPP.

[m] New Zealand also is a member of the TPP; negotiations with the Gulf Cooperation Council, Hong Kong, South Korea, and India.

Among the less industrialized members of ASEAN, Vietnam has been the most active in pursuing FTAs. It has been trying to catch up with its more market-oriented neighbors in Southeast Asia. In 2009, it approved and began implementing the Vietnam-Japan Economic Partnership Agreement. Also, along with the United States, Australia, and Peru, Vietnam has entered into negotiations to join the Trans-Pacific Partnership (TPP). For Vietnam, however, joining the TPP would be a huge policy leap that would require a large number of concessions and new laws. The negotiation, moreover, is likely to take a considerable period of time, and Vietnam could drop out once it sees what actually will be required. Congressional consideration of any such agreement would be still further into the future, and how Congress would view an FTA with Vietnam is a large question. Just the possibility of such a trans-Pacific FTA, however, may induce other countries, such as South Korea, to join the negotiations. If so, the TPP could become the foundation for a free trade area of the Asia Pacific as envisaged by APEC and its 21 member economies.

"ASEAN Plus" and Other Regional FTA Proposals

ASEAN has played a major role in the effort to form regional organizations in Asia. It has an advantage in exercising leadership in this respect because, compared with China or Japan, it carries less political and historical baggage. ASEAN tends to be a more neutral party in both the big power rivalry and in the wrangling over history often indulged in by China and South Korea against Japan. ASEAN initiatives engender less suspicion even though some ASEAN countries also have territorial disputes with China and bitter memories of Japanese military actions during World War II. Several of the proposals for free trade areas in the region, including ASEAN + 3 (APT) and ASEAN + 6, have ASEAN at the center. The association also views itself as a fulcrum in relations between Australia/New Zealand and Northeast Asian countries, and it houses the headquarters for the APEC forum and Asian Development Bank.

Regional FTAs can address what is called the "spaghetti (or noodle) bowl problem" resulting from the proliferation of FTAs and similar preferential trade agreements in Asia. Businesses face a plethora of trade rules under the various agreements that may or may not coincide with each other. A regional FTA that harmonizes the rules and tariff rates contained in the various bilateral FTAs of the countries covered can resolve this problem. Figure 6–2 shows the major configurations of Asian trading arrangements that include the nations of ASEAN.

ASEAN + 3

Since ASEAN already has bilateral FTAs with China, Japan, and South Korea, many in the region have been advocating an ASEAN + 3 free trade area, which would be called an East Asia Economic Community.[10] This would require that the stalled negotiations on the Japan–South Korea FTA be completed and that FTA agreements be concluded between China and Japan as well as between China and South Korea.

Figure 6–2. Major Regional Trade Arrangements in the Asia Pacific

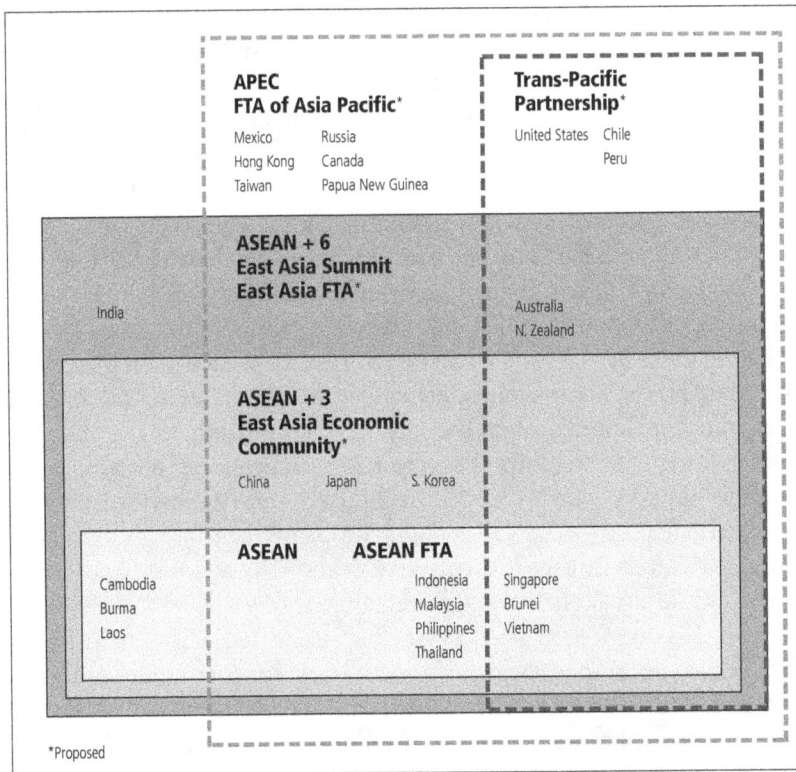

China has been a major force in promoting the ASEAN + 3 process. This apparently has become China's preferred regional forum in which both political/security and economic issues are addressed. The APT provides China with an Asian organization that does not include the United States and gives it opportunities to marginalize U.S. power.

The ASEAN + 3 also addresses a major political deficiency of Asia. The concentration of power in the European Union and in North America allows them to be dominant political forces on the world stage. No comparable trading bloc exists for Asia even though China and Japan have the second- and third-largest national economies in the world. In East Asia, China, Japan, ASEAN, and the United States all are vying for leadership of the region. Traditionally, Japan has led in economics and finance, ASEAN in coordinating regional institutions, and the United States and China in security issues. With China's rise and its increasing clout in political, economic, and security matters, Beijing apparently sees ASEAN + 3 as an institution in which it can take the lead without competition from the United States or Europe or the dilution of East Asian interests by India or Australia.

Currently, the APT is nearly as disjointed and rife with historical rivalries as Europe was before it formed the European Economic Community and then the European Union. However, many hold out the possibility that European-type integration beginning with economics could likewise transform East Asia and bring the countries there closer together.

The APT nations have already established certain cooperative financial arrangements.[11] These have resulted primarily from the adverse effects of the 1997–1998 Asian financial crisis. In particular, in May 2000, the ASEAN + 3 finance ministers agreed to what is called the Chiang Mai initiative (named after the city in Thailand where the meeting took place). The initiative has created a network of bilateral swap arrangements by which short-term liquidity can be provided to support participating ASEAN + 3 countries in need of foreign exchange. The idea is that in times of currency crises, China, Japan, and South Korea would swap their foreign exchange reserves for the currencies of ASEAN countries in need of foreign currencies. This would lessen the need to go to the International Monetary Fund or other lenders to obtain funds in a crisis. This network of bilateral swap arrangements has been formalized among China, Indonesia, Japan, Korea, Malaysia, the Philippines, Singapore, and Thailand—the major countries in

ASEAN + 3. In February 2009, the ASEAN + 3 nations agreed to increase the size of the Chiang Mai initiative from $80 billion to $120 billion and to develop a more robust and effective surveillance mechanism to support its operation. During the 2008–2009 global financial crisis, however, the Chiang Mai initiative arrangements were not used. The APT also has an Asian bond market initiative. [12]

ASEAN + 6

The growing influence of China looms so large over the ASEAN + 3 configuration that Japan and Australia, in particular, worked to expand the core membership of the regional grouping dubbed ASEAN + 6, which brings Australia, India, and New Zealand into ASEAN + 3. The way is open for countries such as the United States, Russia, and Papua New Guinea to join in the future.

In 2006, Japan proposed that the ASEAN + 6 grouping be formalized into an East Asian FTA that would be coordinated by an organization similar to the Organisation for Economic Co-operation and Development. [13] ASEAN and India welcomed the concept, but China and South Korea indicated that their first priority would be the ASEAN + 3 FTA proposal. [14]

The ASEAN + 6 members are not in agreement on whether it or the ASEAN + 3 should take the lead in building an East Asian community. What is evolving is a concentric circle approach that extends the ASEAN FTA to ASEAN + 3 and then to ASEAN + 6.

The ASEAN + 6 configuration coincides with the East Asia Summit, a forum that has been held annually since 2005 by leaders of ASEAN + 6. It mirrors the configuration of the East Asian Economic Caucus proposed in 1991 by former Malaysian Prime Minister Mahathir bin Mohamad. At the time, the summit did not come to fruition partly because it was opposed by the United States for fear that it would develop into an exclusive trading bloc.

Some Americans still argue that American interests in Asia are so deeply ingrained and the American presence so large that U.S. interests need to be represented whenever Asians meet. If the United States is not there, China could assume the leadership mantle and work at cross purposes to American interests. This concern is shared by Japan. In addition, economic interaction among Asia Pacific economies, particularly the United States, China, Japan, and South Korea, has become so extensive that any regional free trade agreement should include countries on both sides of the Pacific Ocean. This has placed emphasis on the Trans-Pacific Partnership and the FTA of the Asia Pacific.

Trans-Pacific Partnership

The TPP was formed by Singapore, New Zealand, Chile, and Brunei in 2006 as a vehicle to liberalize trade in the Asia Pacific region. In March 2008, the United States joined the negotiations to conclude the investment and financial services provisions. On September 22, 2008, President George W. Bush notified Congress of his intention to join with Australia, Peru, and Vietnam in negotiations to gain accession to the agreement, and on December 14, 2009, the U.S. trade representative formally notified Congress of the Obama administration's intent to enter into the TPP negotiations. The goal would be to shape a regional agreement that will have "broad-based membership and the high standards worthy of a 21st-century trade agreement."[15]

The United States already has free trade agreements with TPP members Singapore and Chile and with potential TPP partners Australia and Peru. The inclusion of Vietnam, a socialist country in transition, could be problematic. Given the extent of market liberalization that would be required of Vietnam, it is unclear at this point whether the country will be able to clear hurdles required for its primarily nonmarket economy to come into compliance with free trade requirements or whether the U.S. Congress would approve free trade with it.

It is expected that the Group of 8 countries in the TPP negotiations will aim for an agreement that can be expanded to include other nations. Canada initially refused to join the TPP negotiations because of its dairy interests; in 2010, when the new government in Ottawa sought to join the negotiations, it was told that it was too late.[16] Malaysia also has expressed interest in joining the TPP. Currently, none of the three Northeast Asian economic powerhouses—China, Japan, or South Korea—is a TPP member.

Another aim of the TPP negotiations is to craft a high-standard FTA that can streamline trade and override the profusion of bilateral trade deals that has sprung up in recent years. It could be a way to untangle the spaghetti bowl of bilateral FTAs, each with its different provisions and requirements. The negotiations on a U.S.-Malaysia FTA, for example, have been shelved in favor of Malaysia eventually joining the TPP.[17] As the TPP is enlarged, it could lead to the APEC vision of a Free Trade Area of the Asia Pacific (FTAAP).

Free Trade Area of the Asia Pacific

At the 2006 leaders' meeting of the APEC forum, the members decided to study the possibility of a Free Trade Area of the Asia Pacific. This trans-Pacific FTA was promoted by the United States and Australia, in particular, and would encompass the 21 economies that are in APEC. It would include the ASEAN 6 plus Vietnam, China, Taiwan, Hong Kong, Japan, and South Korea in Asia; the United States, Canada, Mexico, Peru, and Chile in the Americas; Australia, New Zealand, and Papua New Guinea in the Pacific; and Russia.[18] India, a member of the East Asia Summit and the ASEAN 6, is not a member of APEC.

In 1994, APEC declared the so-called Bogor Goal of free and open trade and investment in the Asia Pacific by 2010 for industrialized member economies and 2020 for the rest. The FTAAP would realize the Bogor Goal, but since the possibility of such a large FTA seems remote, the Bogor Goal has become more of a future target than a specific policy end with a timetable for implementation.

Japan hosted the 2010 APEC leaders' meeting in Yokohama, and the United States will do so the following year in Honolulu. Japan has indicated that it hoped to lay the foundation for the FTAAP at the Yokohama meeting and also to push for a shared vision that would allow both industrialized and developing members of APEC to growth together. The Obama administration has not yet laid out its agenda for the 2011 APEC meetings. It is clear, however, that with Japan and the United States leading APEC, in the short term, an opportunity exists for the two countries to use their leadership to establish a new consensus on whether the Bogor goals are to be achieved.

U.S. Interests and China

The creation of a trading bloc based on ASEAN poses little threat to U.S. commercial interests. U.S. companies are well established in ASEAN member economies, particularly in Singapore, the Philippines, Thailand, and Indonesia, and lowered trade barriers within ASEAN tend to benefit both U.S. companies there and U.S. exporters to the region.

The People's Republic of China, however, looms as the large imponderable in the development of the new trade architecture in East Asia. The PRC has taken an aggressive stance toward establishing FTAs with trading partners. In addition to the 2002 FTA (Framework Agreement) with ASEAN, China has FTAs with Hong Kong and Macao and an FTA in cargo trade with Chile. It has discussed FTAs with 27 countries and is negotiating with Canada, Pakistan, Australia, New Zealand, Iceland, and Chile. The PRC also has held discussions on possible FTAs with Japan, Taiwan, South Korea, and India. China also has signed a framework agreement on economic cooperation with the countries of the Gulf Cooperation Council that may lead to FTA negotiations.

FTAs follow trade, and the Chinese economy is beginning to dominate trade in Asia. As shown in table 6–2, China has become the top trading partner for Japan, South Korea, Taiwan, and Australia. It is the second largest trading partner for Singapore and Thailand, and the third largest for Indonesia and the Philippines. With the exception of the Philippines, a former U.S. territory, and Malaysia, the United States ranks below China in the trade rankings for most of East Asia. While the United States still is a major trader there, it is being eclipsed increasingly by China. For China, itself, however, the United States is the top trading partner.

Table 6–2. Major Trading Partners of East Asian Nations and the United States Ranked by Total Exports Plus Imports

Country	Top Partner	Second	Third	Fourth	Fifth
Japan	China	United States	South Korea	Taiwan	Australia
South Korea	China	Japan	United States	Saudi Arabia	Singapore
Taiwan	China	Japan	United States	Hong Kong	South Korea
Australia	China	Japan	United States	South Korea	India
Singapore	Malaysia	China	United States	Indonesia	Japan
Thailand	Japan	China	United States	Malaysia	Singapore
Indonesia	Japan	Singapore	China	United States	South Korea
Philippines	United States	Japan	China	Singapore	Hong Kong
Malaysia	Singapore	United States	Japan	China	Thailand
China	United States	Japan	Hong Kong	South Korea	Taiwan
United States	Canada	China	Mexico	Japan	Germany

Source: Global Trade Atlas.

While the United States does not oppose the creation of regional trading arrangements in Asia, U.S. commercial interests there are huge. Therefore, it seems important for U.S. policy to ensure that any such trading blocs do not work to the disadvantage of exports from the United States or of American companies with a presence there, particularly when competing with China. The danger also exists that security considerations will follow trade and investments. Once China becomes the dominant regional economy, governments may turn to China first in seeking solutions to problems. China then may be able to spread its influence in political, security, and socio-cultural arenas in ways that may or may not be consonant with U.S. interests and values.

The rise of China is posing a dual problem for ASEAN. Many in Southeast Asia fear that the rapidly expanding Chinese economy will draw foreign capital away from their economies. Exports from China also are placing increased competitive pressures on industries throughout the region.

China, moreover, has pursued a "charm offensive" in which it has downplayed traditional areas of dispute, such as territorial claims, and has combined formal trading arrangements with diplomatic initiatives, foreign assistance, and active participation in international organizations to assuage fears of its rising economic and security strength. Beijing increasingly is using soft power and has emphasized the "win-win" aspects of increased economic and political interaction in its relations with Southeast Asian nations. In this respect, it has attempted to create an image as a nonthreatening partner and a stakeholder in regional peace, economic growth, and stability. As compared with the situation several years ago, few Southeast Asian leaders now are heard to question China's rise, although complaints concerning import competition from Chinese goods are common. Chinese businesspeople and policymakers are increasingly given the type of welcome and access in Southeast Asia that once were reserved for American and Japanese elites.[19]

China's quick recovery from the 2008–2009 global financial crisis and vast accumulation of foreign exchange reserves appear to have given Beijing somewhat of a triumphalist attitude. Chinese leaders have become more assertive in diplomatic relations and more confident that their market-oriented socialism is superior to Western free-market capitalism. At some point, China may ride the tide of this national exuberance and attempt to assert control over what it considers to be its sovereign territory—as long as such actions do not threaten its economic growth rate.

China's recent successes, however, should not be overemphasized. The United States still is the world's preeminent economic and military power, and while many global supply chains run through China, many also begin and end in the United States—particularly in product design, technology development, and marketing. Although Southeast Asian nations seek to broaden international options with major powers, they also engage in a continuing round of hedging and maneuvering for advantage and against possible Chinese dominance. In this process, they also are seeking closer ties with each other and also with the United States and Europe.[20]

Effects of the ASEAN FTA

The immediate effects of free trade agreements are to lower the cost of goods originating in member countries and to divert trade toward them (trade diversion). They also may create more opportunities for industries (trade creation) within the free trade area.

For the ASEAN FTA, the trade diversion effect is scarcely apparent. Figure 6–3 shows ASEAN trade (exports plus imports) to other ASEAN countries and to the rest of the world. The data do not include exports from Laos and Burma inasmuch as such data are not reported to the United Nations. The share of trade among ASEAN countries increased from 21 percent in the mid-1990s to around 25 percent in 2003 and has remained at about that level even though total trade is surging. World demand for ASEAN exports apparently is growing as fast as demand within the ASEAN area, and lower internal trade barriers do not appear to be drawing sales away from non-ASEAN export markets.

One cause of the lack of a trade diversion effect is that ASEAN still is far from being a unified free trade area. Countries still compete with each other for foreign direct investment funds and for key industries. Much of the foreign investment in manufacturing in ASEAN countries, moreover, is intended to serve markets primarily in the country where it is located and in non-ASEAN regions of the world. Multinational corporations also are still adjusting their production and marketing plans to account for the various FTAs in the region.

The story is evolving differently, however, for the automobile industry. ASEAN members undertook special measures to rationalize

Figure 6–3. ASEAN Trade within ASEAN and with Rest of World

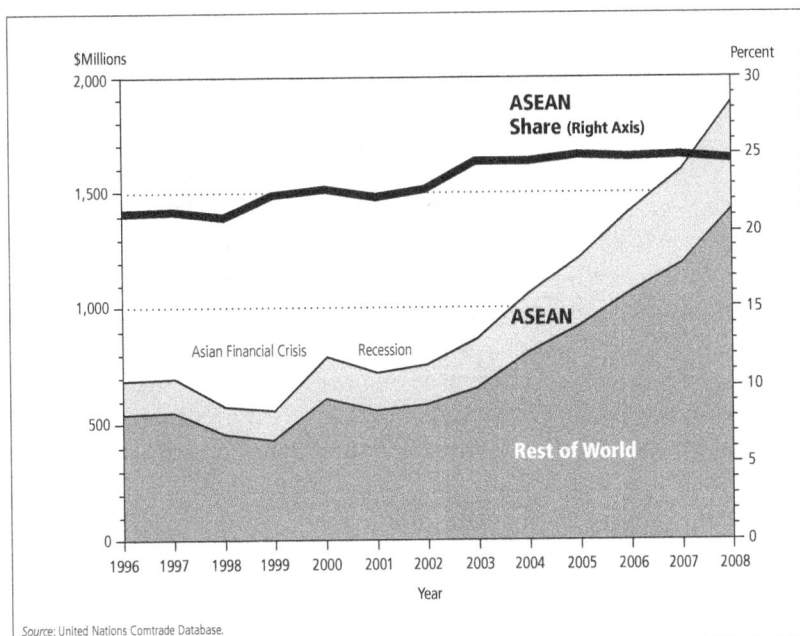

Source: United Nations Comtrade Database.

and regionalize this sector. Motor vehicle manufacturing is a key sector in the industrial strategies of several ASEAN countries. In Thailand, Malaysia, and Indonesia, the industry has been nurtured and protected through local content requirements (40–60 percent of the value contained in the vehicles had to be procured locally in order to escape certain duties or taxes) and high import duties. Under the ASEAN FTA, duties initially dropped to 5 percent or less in the more industrialized ASEAN countries and then to 0 as of January 1, 2010. This has provided a huge advantage to those cars assembled within ASEAN countries when compared with imports. For example, in Thailand, non-ASEAN imports face duties of up to 80 percent for passenger cars and 10–30 percent for auto parts. In Malaysia, non-ASEAN passenger cars are assessed duties of 30 percent plus excise taxes of 80–200 percent.[21]

Japanese automakers, in particular, have been reorienting their automobile parts and assembly plants to take advantage of the liberalized intra-ASEAN automotive trade. Japanese automakers have established production bases for both motor vehicles and parts in Indonesia, Thailand, Malaysia, and Vietnam. Toyota, for example, makes engines in Thailand, Malaysia, and Indonesia and manufactures transmissions and continuous velocity joints in the Philippines for its various assembly plants in the region.[22]

These reductions in tariffs for intra-ASEAN trade in automobiles and parts have begun to divert trade toward other ASEAN countries. Figure 6–4 shows ASEAN exports of automobiles and parts to other ASEAN countries and to the rest of the world. The value of such exports to ASEAN has risen from $1.4 billion in 1996 to $8.6 billion in 2008, but such exports to the rest of the world also have increased from $1.7 billion in 1996 to $19.1 billion in 2008. The share of intra-ASEAN exports of automobiles and parts initially declined from 46 percent in 1996 to 22 percent in 1998, then rose to 36 percent in 2004, but declined somewhat to 31 percent in 2008. What appears to have happened is that the reduction in import restrictions as the ASEAN FTA was implemented caused a surge in intra-ASEAN shipments of automobiles and parts, but as the producers there became more competitive internationally, such exports to the rest of the world also have risen.

Five centers for automotive manufacturing are developing in East Asia: Japan, South Korea, China, the ASEAN countries, and India. In 2008, Japan produced 11.6 million vehicles; South Korea, 3.8 million; China, 9.5 million; ASEAN, 2.4 million; and India, 2.3 million.[23] The auto industry in Japan and South Korea already is mature and depends on exports for additional sales. The competition for new capacity in the region, therefore, tends to be among China, ASEAN, and India. Given that both China and India have populations more than twice the size of ASEAN, and each has unified internal markets, the development of an integrated motor vehicle market in ASEAN becomes all the more imperative.

The ASEAN FTA effect on the automobile industry in ASEAN can be seen more clearly in the exports of motor vehicles and parts from Thailand as shown in figure 6–5. In 2000, Thailand exported more to both the United States and Japan than it did to neighboring Malaysia, Indonesia, or the Philippines. By 2005, it was exporting twice as much to Indonesia as to Japan and nearly four times as much to Indonesia as to the United States. Exports to both the Philippines and Malaysia were roughly comparable to those to Japan and far exceeded those to the United States. Although Thai exports to China are rising, they still were less than those to Laos or Vietnam.

Figure 6–4. ASEAN Country Exports of Automobiles and Parts to ASEAN and to Rest of World

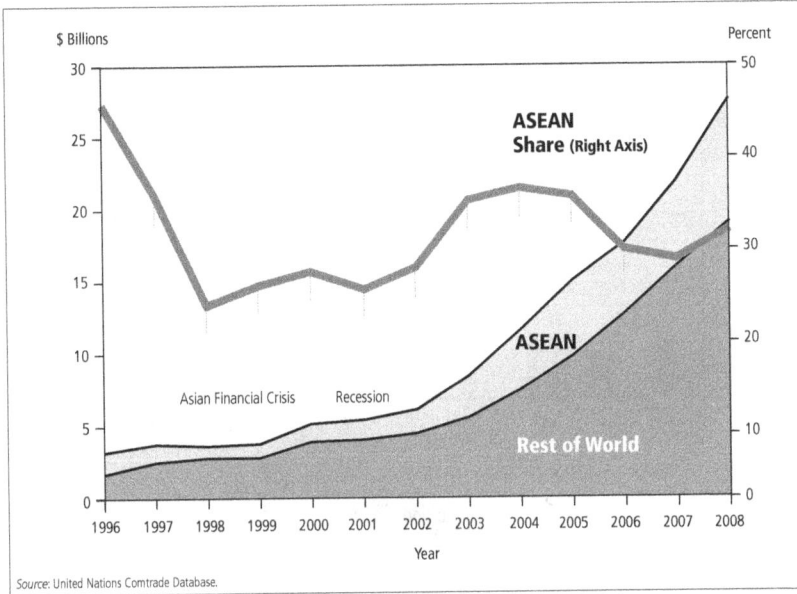

Source: United Nations Comtrade Database.

The crucible of economic interaction for ASEAN nations once circumscribed by their own borders and national tariff barriers now is being enlarged to span fellow ASEAN countries. This larger market not only is creating more sales within ASEAN but also is enhancing the ability of ASEAN nations to compete in global export markets. In exports of motor vehicles and parts, Thailand is exporting more not only to fellow ASEAN countries but also to Japan and the United States.

Multiple forces are enabling this process. First, the larger internal market helps ASEAN national champion companies to become more efficient and more competitive both in their own countries and ASEAN and in world markets. Second, the larger internal market makes ASEAN more attractive for foreign direct investors who plan to export some of the output from their factories in ASEAN to home or other world markets. Third, the larger internal market makes ASEAN more attractive as a hedge against instability in China. ASEAN suppliers can provide an alternative source for products currently made in China. Fourth, the larger internal market increases the incentive for other countries to

Figure 6–5. Exports of Automobiles and Parts from Thailand

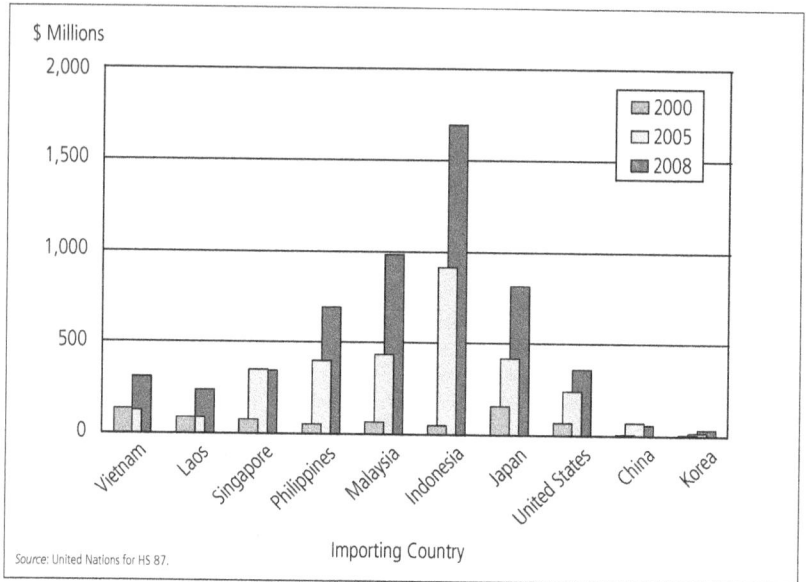

Source: United Nations for HS 87.

link in free trade relationships with ASEAN. This enlarges the market even further.

The proliferation of FTAs and regional trade groupings centered on ASEAN also is having a profound effect on the emerging architecture of East and Southeast Asia. The FTA boundaries coincide with groups of countries joining for political and security purposes. ASEAN forms the center of the various overlapping trade and diplomatic groupings in East Asia.

The final form of the economic and political structure in the anarchic space above the Asian nations is yet to be determined. Whether the ASEAN FTA will morph into an East Asia Community (ASEAN + 3), an East Asia FTA (ASEAN + 6), or extend further into an APEC-based, 21-nation FTA for the Asia Pacific is not yet clear. These economic configurations, however, already are the basis for formal political and security groupings. As has been the experience with the European Union, the economic imperative that drives countries to form an economic community combines with the need for stability and security to invite similar unions to deal with other aspects of international interaction. The end result is a process by which the borders between countries of a community fade while those that separate the community from other states become more distinct. The community also produces interdependence by which the economy of one country becomes intertwined with conditions in another. The integration process among nations begins with trade, and in Asia, the plethora of FTAs clearly are operating as forces for integration. Not only are they drawing those within the groups closer together but also the borders of the groups are stretching to encompass other nations.

Notes

[1] Pew Research Center for the People and the Press, "U.S. Seen as Less Important, China as More Powerful, Isolationist Sentiment Surges to Four-Decade High," *Survey Reports*, December 3, 2009, available at < http://people-press.org/report/569/americas-place-in-the-world>.

[2] U.S. Trade Representative, *2010 Trade Policy Agenda and 2009 Annual Report* (Washington, DC: U.S. Government Printing Office, March 2010), 7, available at <www.ustr.gov/webfm_send/1673>.

[3] Ibid., 8–9.

[4] Men Honghua, "East Asian Order Formation and Sino-Japanese Relations," *Indiana Journal of Global Legal Studies* 17, no. 1 (Winter 2010), 4.

[5] For details on Asian FTAs, see the Asian Development Bank's Regional Integration Center at <http://aric.adb.org/FTAbyCountryAll.php>.

[6] Association of Southeast Asian Nations (ASEAN), "Trade/The ASEAN Free Trade Area (AFTA)," available at <www.aseansec.org/12021.htm>.

[7] ASEAN, Ministerial Declaration on the AFTA–CER Closer Economic Partnership, September 14, 2002; Framework for Comprehensive Economic Partnership between the Association of Southeast Asian Nations and Japan, October 8, 2003; Framework Agreement on Comprehensive Economic Cooperation between the Association of Southeast Asian Nations and the Republic of India, October 8, 2003.

[8] "South Korea Signs Free Trade Pact with ASEAN, Excludes Thailand," *Jakarta Post*, December 13, 2005; ASEAN, "Joint Media Statement of the Third ASEAN Economic Ministers–Republic of Korea Consultations," Makati City, Philippines, May 16, 2006.

[9] *Washington Trade Daily* 17, January 1–4, 2008, 4.

[10] ASEAN, "ASEAN Plus Three Cooperation," available at <www.aseansec.org/16580.htm>.

[11] See David Cowen et al., "Financial Integration in Asia: Recent Developments and Next Steps," International Monetary Fund Working Paper, WP/06/196, August 2006.

[12] See UNESCAP, "Regional Financial Cooperation in East Asia: The Chiang Mai Initiative and Beyond," *Bulletin on Asia-Pacific Perspectives 2002/03*.

[13] "Japan Aims to Launch East Asia FTA Talks in '08: Nikai," Jiji Press English News Service, April 4, 2006.

[14] "S. Korea, China Snub Japan's 16-nation FTA Plan," Organisation of Asia-Pacific News Agencies, August 24, 2006.

[15] Office of the United States Trade Representative, "TPP Statements and Actions to Date," available at <www.ustr.gov/about-us/press-office/fact-sheets/2009/december/tpp-statements-and-actions-date>.

[16] John Ibbitson, "Canada Misses its Chance to Join Major Pacific Free-trade Deal," *Toronto Globe and Mail*, April 11, 2010.

[17] Hong Kong AFP, "Malaysia Studying New Regional Trade Pact with U.S.," March 11, 2010.

[18] "14th APEC Economic Leaders' Meeting, Ha Noi Declaration," Hanoi, Vietnam, November 18–19, 2006.

[19] Men, 36.

[20] Robert Sutter, *China's Rise: Implications for U.S. Leadership in Asia*, East-West Center Policy Studies 21 (Washington, DC: East-West Center Washington, 2006), vii–ix.

[21] U.S. Trade Representative, *2006 National Trade Estimate Report on Foreign Trade Barriers, 2006* (Washington, DC: U.S. Government Printing Office, 2006).

[22] Japan Automobile Manufacturers' Association, Inc., *The Motor Industry of Japan 2006* (Tokyo: Japan Automobile Manufacturers' Association, 2006).

[23] Alan K. Binder, ed., *Ward's Automotive Yearbook 2009* (Detroit: Ward's Reports, Inc., 2009), 6.

Chapter 7

The Environment and Development: Greater Mekong Subregion Dynamics Considered

Richard P. Cronin

In no part of the world are the tensions between the transboundary impacts of globalization and national borders, and between development and the environment, more evident than in the 795,000-square-kilometer basin drained by the Mekong River and its tributaries. The Greater Mekong Subregion (GMS), one of the world's most biologically diverse and productive areas, is comprised of five Southeast Asian countries—Burma, Cambodia, Laos, Thailand, and Vietnam—and China's Yunnan Province and Guangxi Autonomous Zone. The latter technically is not part of the Mekong Basin but has an overland trade relationship with neighboring Vietnam.

After decades of bitter conflict, the people of the Mekong River Basin of Southeast Asia live in peace. The combination of peace and stability and the commitment of governments to bilateral and regional economic cooperation have made the GMS a main destination for global capital and direct investment. However, the people now face new and more fundamental threats to their land, forest, and fishery resources and their traditional livelihoods. The once-war-ravaged Mekong River Basin is under new assault by the powerful economic forces of development and globalization.

Paradoxically, deepening global and regional economic integration have both transcended and reinforced national boundaries. The rapid monetization and integration of natural resources into global markets and production chains have given states new incentives to strengthen their borders and control of their natural resources, but these efforts often are undermined by inadequate local governance, corruption, and the power of well-organized transnational resources cartels.

Globalization in particular has broken down barriers to trade and investment and opened the flow of ideas and people across national boundaries, even to the doorstep of the most remote peasant's hut. It would be bitterly ironic if the peace that followed four decades of ideo-logically based conflict were to be imperiled by a new kind of conflict based on the unrestrained competition for the region's vast but finite natural resources.[1]

The most serious threats to the environment and ecology of the GMS and the human security of some 70 million people stem from the short-term and unsustainable pursuit of rapid economic development. Specific actors in this process include state ministries involved in the promotion of economic development, trade and foreign investment, the multilateral development banks (especially the Asian Development Bank (ADB) and the World Bank), aid donor countries, private companies and investors, corrupt officials, and, in some countries, unsustainable population growth.

The process of development at all costs also has been strongly in-fluenced by China, Japan, and Thailand. Japan has long been the single largest investor in infrastructure and manufacturing investment, while China's fast-growing economy has generated a seemingly insatiable demand for the Mekong Basin's energy, natural resources, and other industrial inputs. China has greatly stepped up its aid and investment in the poorest countries in the Mekong Basin and has become the largest source of infrastructure development in Cambodia.[2]

Large swathes of primary hardwood forests that once covered most of Asia's "last frontier" have fallen to the axe and saw. Overfishing and habitat destruction have pushed local fish populations into severe decline. The Mekong River system itself is being choked, canalized, and polluted in the rush by China and the five Southeast Asian countries that comprise its watershed to capitalize on it to support industrializa-tion and ostensibly lift remote areas out of poverty.

As in other parts of the developing world, the fast-rising global demand for energy, natural resources, and other industrial inputs has both created new state-building opportunities—assuming adequate governance capacity—and potentially destabilizing socioeconomic dislocations. In the least developed parts of the Mekong Basin, the ability of the state to capture growing revenues to make needed social investment and reduce poverty has been undermined by poor plan-ning, corruption, and, in some cases, exploitation by unscrupulous foreign economic interests, often under the rubric of public-private "partnerships." Laws aimed at protecting the environment and the interests of those whose human security depends on access to forests and fisheries are often undercut by close ties between large timber and mining companies. These effects are exacerbated by corrupt dispensers of state licenses and concessions and a weak legal system.

The price of natural resources exploitation generally has been paid by those who historically had used those resources communally or privately to carry out traditional subsistence livelihoods. The alienation of millions of people from their land, forests, and traditional fisheries to make way for hydropower dams, rubber and palm oil plantations, and other forms of commercialized agriculture has swollen the ranks of landless laborers already suffering from scant financial resources, low levels of state capacity, and concomitant high levels of corruption.

Two specific major transboundary development projects have paved the path for the unsustainable exploitation of what some call Asia's last frontier. The first is the multi-billion-dollar GMS cooperative infrastructure development project, conceived and largely financed by the Japanese-led ADB, which has played a key role in opening up the region to the global economy. However well intended, the bank's support of infrastructure development, including an extensive road network and regional electric power grid, has had serious negative environmental and social impacts. These include the expansion of illegal logging, a swelling tide of economic migrants to urban centers, expanded narcotics trade, human trafficking, and the spread of HIV/AIDS and pandemic diseases.

The unconstrained, uncoordinated, and unsustainable development of the region's immense hydroelectric power potential has created another transboundary threat of even more serious proportions. China has completed four dams in a massive cascade of eight dams it is constructing on the upper reaches of the Mekong. These dams will alter the core hydrology of the river that is the key to its almost unequaled bounty of fish and other aquatic life and will destroy valuable wetlands. China's dams will also threaten the viability of Vietnam's Mekong Delta by capturing in their reservoirs a large proportion of the flood-borne silt needed to keep the South China Sea at bay. Meanwhile, Laos and Cambodia have signed agreements with Chinese and other foreign hydropower developers for 11 dams and one non-dam hydroelectric project on the middle and lower reaches of the river between Yunnan and the South China Sea. Together, these dams will threaten the essential hydrological functions and decimate the rich fisheries of the world's most productive and biologically diverse river basins after the Amazon.

The Mekong: An International River That Knows No Boundary

The approximately 4,880-kilometer-long Mekong is the world's 11th or 12th longest river. Its average discharge of 475,000 billion cubic meters into the South China Sea also ranks it among the world's largest rivers, but in full monsoon flood the river's discharge is second only to that of the Amazon, which drains into the Atlantic Ocean and the Brahmaputra River, which debouches into the Bay of Bengal.[3]

Like two other great Asian rivers, the Yangtze and the Salween, the Mekong rises in the snow-capped Tibetan Plateau and cuts its way through China's mountainous Yunnan Province on its way to the sea. In the "Three Parallel Rivers" area of central Yunnan, a breathtakingly beautiful United Nations World Heritage Site, the rivers follow a north-south axis where they are 18 and 66 kilometers apart at their closest point. After running parallel for about 300 kilometers, the rivers diverge. The Yangtze strikes eastward across the center of China to the East China Sea at Shanghai. The Salween turns southwestward to travel the length of Burma to the Andaman Sea of the Bay of Bengal. The Mekong, on the other hand, continues southward from Yunnan and forms the joint borders of or traverses five downstream Southeast Asian countries—Burma, Thailand, Laos, Cambodia, and Vietnam—on its way to the South China Sea.[4]

Among these great Asian rivers, only the Mekong crosses more than one international boundary. The Brahmaputra flows from Tibet/China into India, where it merges with the Ganges and flows into the Bay of Bengal. The Yangtze never leaves Chinese territory, while the Salween remains wholly in Burma after it crosses the border with Yunnan.

The local names for the river reflect its changing character. In Tibet, where it originates, the Mekong is known as *Dza Chu*, or "River of Rock." In Yunnan, the Chinese call it the *Lancang Jiang*, or "Turbulent River." Its biological productivity greatly increases in the middle stretches, where the Thai and Lao call it *Mae Nam Kong*, or "Mother River." The Vietnamese call it the *Song Cuu Long*, or "Nine Dragon River," as it fans out into nine main channels to form the Mekong Delta and disappears into the South China Sea.

The character of the river changes dramatically through upper, middle, and lower segments. In its first segment, wholly in China, the river plunges 4,500 meters from the Tibetan Plateau through Yunnan's high mountain gorges. In its middle reaches, beginning at Yunnan's border with Burma, Laos, and Thailand, the river slows noticeably, and drops less than 500 feet over the next 1,600 kilometers to the foot of the Khone Falls, on the Lao-Cambodian border. From Phnom Penh to the South China Sea, a distance of about 300 kilometers, the river becomes broad and tidal.

The extremes of flood and drought play a major role in making the Mekong second only to the Amazon in its production of fish and other aquatic life. The maximum monsoon flow of the river can be more than 50 times its dry season flow. In comparison, the seasonal differential in the Nile is 30 to 1 and anywhere from 3 to 21 times in the case of the Mississippi River.[5] The annual floods create vast seasonal wetlands in low-lying areas, especially Cambodia's *Tonle Sap* ("Great Lake") and the river by the same name and the Mekong Delta. The Tonle Sap and flooded wetlands of the Lower Mekong serve as the nursery of fish whose spawning grounds are upstream on the main stem of the river and its tributaries.

The Mekong's fisheries directly support tens of millions who depend directly on fishing and in some places aquaculture for their food and livelihoods. The flood plains of Cambodia and the Mekong Delta are some of the most productive rice-growing areas in the world. The delta, which produces 40 to 50 percent of Vietnam's rice crop, makes the country the world's second largest rice producer after Thailand.[6] During the dry season, villagers extensively farm its banks and islands, producing large bounties of vegetables that sustain them when fish are less available.

The river system's high volume of flood-borne suspended silt also plays a key role in annually renewing the fertility of the basin's laterite soil, which is rich in iron but low in essential nutrients, and keeping the sea at bay in the Mekong Delta. While its drainage basin is only about 24 percent of that of the Mississippi, 41 percent of the Yangtze, and 12 percent of the Amazon, the Mekong River's sediment load is about equal to that of the Mississippi, 85 percent of the Yangtze, and 12 percent *greater* than that of the Amazon.[7]

The violence of the flood-drought cycle is both a boon and a bane. The same annual floods that wash away villages carry with them a heavy burden of silt that plays a critical role in the production of rice, especially in Cambodia and Vietnam's Mekong Delta. The biologically rich silt restores the fertility of the soil for lowland rice production and rebuilds the Mekong Delta to hold back the sea.

Not all countries are equally dependent on the river system. While the river defines the borders between Burma, Thailand, and Laos in the "Golden Triangle" region, it remains a remote frontier for Burma, which contributes only 2 percent of its annual flow. Thailand regards the Chao Phraya as the Thai River and the Mekong as the "minorities' river," albeit one that Bangkok depends heavily upon for electric power imports from impoverished but mountainous Laos. The slow-flowing Red River is the principal river in Northern Vietnam, but the rivers of the Central Highlands supply the power for the region's industrialization. Vietnam is only just beginning to realize that it is both an upstream and a downstream country, and that the hydropower dams in the Central Highlands have an important negative impact on the delta, which is rapidly being inundated by rising sea levels and salt water intrusion.

The Mekong is the cradle of mainland Southeast Asian civilization and its defining geographical feature. Its morphology and seasonal hydrological changes have shaped the region's cultures and ways of life. Even in the face of accelerating gross domestic product (GDP) growth and modernization, the river system still constitutes the economic life blood of the vast majority of its inhabitants, who live in a symbiotic relationship with its seasonal variations.

This cycle has shaped the nature of economic activity and fostered a connectedness that transcends national borders. The life ways and cultural differences between the many indigenous minority peoples who live along the higher reaches of the river and its main tributaries, including the Dai (Tai), Khmu, and the Hmong, are much less marked than the differences between themselves and their lowland countrymen.

Historically Contested Territory

A millennium or more of struggle for political control of the region's resources has shaped ethnic, religious, and linguistic patterns of settlement. At one time or another, the ancestors of the Burmese, Khmer, Thai, Viet, and Chinese ethnic groups have controlled significant parts of the Mekong Basin. The modern political boundaries of the five countries and Yunnan Province are largely aligned with the major lowland ethnic groups, but the Hmong and other ethnic minorities predominate in adjacent parts of Burma, Laos, northern Thailand, and Vietnam's Central Highlands.

The natural resources of the Mekong Basin have long beckoned to those with the means to extract them. Historical changes in political boundaries have reflected the ebb and flow of the power of various indigenous kingdoms. The European colonial powers and their chartered companies in the 19th century, and the Japanese Empire in the third decade of the 20th century, carried out resource exploitation on an industrial scale.

From the victory of Mao's Communist forces in China in 1949 to the 1991 Paris Accord on Cambodia, the core of the Mekong region remained largely engulfed by conflict and off limits for development. The United States and its Cold War allies sought to carry out a vast dam-building scheme to turn the Lower Mekong Basin in Cambodia, Laos, Thailand, and then–South Vietnam into a vastly larger version of the Great Depression–era Tennessee Valley Authority (TVA) project. Fortunately, because of the ecological and environmental damage it would have caused, the scheme was cut short by the Vietnam War, but at a high cost.[8]

The damage of more than four decades of conflict remains an obstacle to development. During the Vietnam War, American aircraft dropped 2 million tons of bombs on Laos's Plain of Jars—more than the number dropped on Germany during World War II—in a vain effort to cut North Vietnam's "Ho Chi Minh" supply line to its fighters in the south. The employment of the defoliant Agent Orange in Vietnam, Laos, and Cambodia by American forces created lasting human and ecological damage. The xenophobic and merciless Khmer Rouge killed a generation of Cambodia's urban and educated citizens. The Chinese-backed Khmer Rouge and, to a lesser extent their enemy, Soviet-tilting Vietnam, sowed millions of landmines that continue to kill and maim.

Rise of Important Transboundary Issues

Both the Mekong's status as an international river with six riparians and its unique "flood pulse" hydrology make the river basin an archetype for the clash of national and transboundary interests within the larger context of globalization and regional economic integration. First, while the forces behind rapidly expanding trade, investment, and tourism are largely external, governments continue to view the coveted timber, minerals, fisheries, and hydroelectric power potential as *national* resources. The control of those resources is essential to promoting rapid economic growth and reinforcing the legitimacy of regimes that are mostly nondemocratic.

Second, traditional rules governing upstream and downstream riparian rights are not appropriate to a river system whose enormous biodiversity and bounty depend as much on the timing of water availability as the quantity of water available for cooperative management. In other words, the value of the river to each downstream country depends on the maintenance of the natural hydrology of the river system as a whole.

Dividing the water resources into shares creates an environmental and ecological "tragedy of the commons" that leaves most countries worse off. While river basin agreements based on international watercourse law "have been effective in avoiding conflict between states in the short-term, success at the international scale can, paradoxically, undermine the foundations of ecological and social sustainability at the local scale, thereby threatening long-term stability."[9]

The stakes are very high. The lower Mekong is home to an estimated 1,300 species of fish, about 70 percent of which migrate up and down the river and into tributaries to spawn.[10] Cambodia's Tonle Sap and the river that connects it to the mainstream alone are the world's most productive inland fishery per hectare of surface.[11]

The life-giving role of the river is particularly critical to the alluvial lowlands of Cambodia and the Mekong Delta. Fish, most of it wild-caught, annually provides as much as 80 percent of the animal protein consumed by about 70 million people, mainly in southern Laos, Cambodia, and Vietnam's Mekong Delta. The economic importance of migratory fisheries in Laos, Cambodia, and Vietnam is huge and not replaceable in the short to medium term.

The river system's rich fisheries also play a significant role in global fish production. Its stocks suffer from the same ills of overfishing, the destruction of mangrove forests and other wetlands, and pollution. Research carried out for the Mekong River Commission (MRC) conservatively estimated the first-sale value of the catch throughout the Lower Mekong Basin at U.S. $2 billion. Estimates of the total annual economic contribution of the wild fish catch to the national income of

Mekong countries—including resale, processing, and other value-added activities—range as high as U.S. $9 billion. Wild-caught fish contribute about 12 percent of Cambodia's GDP and 7 percent of Laos, with smaller but still important proportions in Thailand and Vietnam.[12] In Cambodia, whose Tonle Sap River and Great Lake are the nursery of major fish populations in the lower Mekong, the value of the fish catch is greater than that of the rice harvest.[13]

External and Internal Drivers of Change

Beyond globalization, several more specific forces have been at play in the unsustainable rush to develop the Mekong region's natural resources. Rising global demand and prices for natural resources-based commodities and the free flow of capital across national borders have overwhelmed the human and governance capacity of weak governments. States have had a particularly difficult time coping with a fast-growing cast of nonstate actors, including regional and even global cartels. Some unique features of the development environment include the adoption by the former socialist bloc countries, which remain governed by authoritarian communist parties, of market-oriented economic policy reforms.

The main actors include foreign investors, hydropower developers, public-private partnerships backed by the multilateral development banks, corrupt local officials, entrepreneurial migrants—mainly from China—and criminal syndicates. In addition, resources-based economic liberalization has not only pitted development against the environment, but has also strained relations between those who depend on the region's rivers for their livelihoods and the urbanites who benefit from industrialization and market opening. In fact, resources-based economic development in the Mekong Basin has caused massive transfer of resources from the countryside to the cities.

Finally, gross imbalances of national power within the Mekong Basin challenge the ability of the less developed Mekong states to determine their own development paths. China now holds half the voting power of the United States and Japan in the Asian Development Bank and can influence regional development projects that support Beijing's objectives. At the same time, China has emerged as the largest donor of infrastructure development lending in the basin. Its state-owned companies are the leading actors in the illegal destruction of forests for the purposes of establishing rubber, oil palm, and other monoculture plantations.

The State as a Threat to Human Security and Livelihoods

Poor governance and the assumption of state control over land and natural resources have become the two greatest threats to human security in the region. Especially in Laos, Vietnam, and Indonesia, the unscientific and unconstrained exploitation of natural resources, usually by foreign private contractors under the auspices of the state, have displaced tens of millions of people from their lands and traditional sources of livelihood. Many of those have been displaced by forest clearing, the construction of hydroelectric power dams, and mining that has polluted their land and water.

Development in the Mekong region involves the exploitation of rural resources such as timber, minerals, and water to serve the interests of the politically important urban areas. Satisfying the economic aspirations of the growing middle classes, however, is being achieved by a massive rural-urban shift of resources. Because 50 to 80 percent of the populations of Cambodia, Laos, and Vietnam still depend primarily on agriculture for their livelihoods, the imbalance of costs and benefits may become destabilizing, especially if people driven from their villages add to the swelling ranks of underemployed and unemployed urban migrants.

Pinkaew Laungaramsri underscores the inevitability of this process when he writes that "commodifying nature goes hand in hand with the growth of urban middle-class society and its increasingly intense lifestyle in big cities."[14] Despite the rationale that the exploitation of natural resources will give governments more money for antipoverty programs, rural villagers displaced by hydropower projects and other large-scale uses of natural resources are inevitably net losers. However poor their subsistence livelihoods, they almost always end up with insufficient compensation and lands and fisheries that are less productive than those from which they were evicted.

The urban bias of development in the Mekong is also creating the conditions for transborder labor migration, human trafficking, narcotics, and other criminal activity often organized by transborder criminal syndicates. These syndicates in some cases enjoy the support of locally powerful people, indicating that certain areas are returning to a more traditional form of warlordism. In many cases these syndicates and their local political allies are vying with the central governments for control of provinces and districts that lie astride important transportation routes.

Likewise, the race to exploit water resources in the Mekong River Basin threatens in time to create the potential for water conflict. Lower Mekong countries lack the power to challenge China, but their own dams and irrigation projects are creating serious problems for downstream neighbors that may eventually poison relations.

The GMS Cooperative Development Project

The current focal point of development in the Mekong Basin is the GMS cooperative development project led and largely financed by the Manila-based Asian Development Bank. Initiated in 1992 following the end of conflict in Cambodia, the goal of the GMS project is to deepen the economic integration of the Mekong countries with each other and with the global economy.

The core goal of the GMS has been to connect the Southeast Asian countries with each other with navigable roads and with Kunming, the capital of Yunnan, which is a key transportation nodal point from Beijing to its southwest region. The GMS has facilitated China's emergence as the regional core economy with an insatiable appetite for its neighbors' agricultural products, industrial inputs, and energy resources. The emergence of efficient transportation links in the Mekong Basin and beyond to Malaysia and Singapore has also given impetus to the so-called China-ASEAN Free Trade Area.

Initially, the GMS consisted of 11 flagship programs focused on three main economic corridors. More recently, the ADB has revamped the program into nine sector programs—transport, energy, telecommunications, environment, human resource development, tourism, trade, private sector investment, and agriculture—and one multi-sector initiative.[15]

By far the highest priority has been given to the development of three economic corridors: north-south, east-west, and southern. The corridors include the construction of an all-weather regional transportation network and electric power grid. These measures are also designed to facilitate increased trade and tourism, environmental protection, and assistance to health and human resources development. Many of these projects have associated telecommunications components, and border crossings eventually are to be jointly operated to minimize customs delays.

In 2005, the ADB and the GMS countries agreed to expand the number of corridors to nine, but the original three still form the backbone of the regional transportation program. A new feature of the GMS has been the development of subcorridors, a development that appears to be connected to the growing assumption of financing responsibility by China, Japan, and Thailand, the three most important actors in the GMS.[16]

The North-South Economic Corridor includes the construction of a modern, all-weather road linking Kunming to Bangkok, via southern Yunnan, Laos, Burma, and northern Thailand. The project will include a new bridge over the Mae Sai River between Thailand and Burma. The main north-south road between Kunming and Bangkok was completed in 2008, with China assuming responsibility for the last stretch in northern Laos. The lack of a bridge over the river between Chiang Rai Province in northern Thailand and Ban Huoayxay in northern Laos remains a bottleneck. Traffic must still cross the river by ferry.[17] China and Thailand reached an agreement in principle to share the estimated $33 million cost of constructing the bridge, which would be the third international bridge across the Mekong. The North-South road will be Route AH3 of the visionary 141,204-kilometer Asian Highway network connecting 32 countries from Europe to Asia (see map 7–1).[18] A spur from this corridor will connect Kunming to Hanoi and Haiphong. Except for one section, the project will involve limited access roads of four to six lanes. This project will also include a network of urban expressways in and around Hanoi.

The East-West Economic Corridor will link the port of Da Nang, Vietnam, on the South China Sea, to Burma's deep-water port of Mawlamiyne (Moulmein) on the Bay of Bengal, some 1,400 kilometers across the entire width of the GMS. Mawlamiyne, the capital of British Burma from 1827–1852, was made famous in the West by Rudyard Kipling's poem *Road to Mandalay*.[19] Shipping containers overland via this route would take 3,000 miles off the current 4,000-mile sea voyage from Northeast Asia through the Strait of Malacca. The improvement of port facilities and deepening of harbors at the seaward ends of the corridors, when the East-West road link is completed, likely will significantly increase seaborne trade and transit of the region. The cost benefits of

Map 7-1. Greater Mekong Subregion Economic Corridors

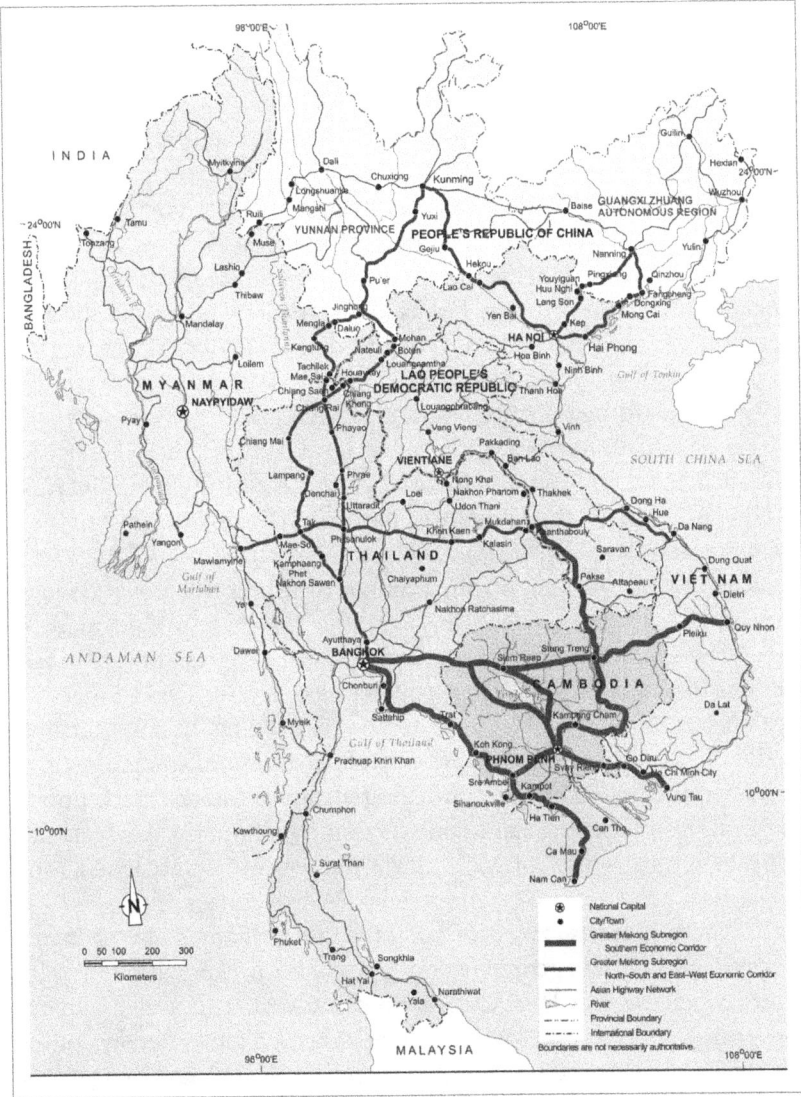

this corridor have been questioned, however, and currently there are major political obstacles to completing the sections in Burma. The Second Mekong International Bridge at Mukdahan-Savannakhet opened in December 2006. Substantial progress has been made on road work in the entire corridor from Da Nang to Mawlamyine.

The Southern Economic Corridor will link the Vietnamese port of Vung Tao to Bangkok, via Ho Chi Minh City and Phnom Penh. Much of this road has been completed. Japan has been active in developing a southern coastal subcorridor to the Southern Corridor, which includes both road and port improvements.[20]

The GMS has wider East Asian implications. For instance, in 2002, the Korean International Cooperation Agency offered to conduct a feasibility study for the Thailand-Burma link of an envisioned Singapore-Kunming railway. The agency's Thailand office and the Thai State Railway signed a memo of record of discussions concerning the proposed study in December 2004.

There are huge issues associated with these projects—environmental degradation, adverse impact on local cultures, the potential for human rights abuses (especially in Burma), an almost certain increase in HIV/AIDS, and actual economic payoff and feasibility. Most of these are being addressed by the ADB with some participation of the World Bank as well, but whether planned countermeasures will prove adequate remains highly questionable.

The GMS has already made significant progress toward transforming the subregion, but its principles of cooperative, environmentally sustainable, and equitable development are being honored mainly in the breach. Major deficiencies include a structural framework that is inadequate to reconcile conflicting national interest perceptions, particularly concerning dam construction by China on the Mekong's upper reaches; insufficient political will and governmental capacity; and disparity of economic power among the GMS countries.

These projects have the potential for fundamentally changing the geoeconomic and geopolitical balance of the Mekong Basin. For instance, when the East-West Corridor is completed, trucks will be able to carry cargo containers across the entire Mekong region, thereby cutting 3,000 miles off the 4,000-mile sea route between Northeast Asia and the Indian Ocean. When the third bridge over the river connecting northern Laos and northern Thailand is completed, the road journey from Kunming to Singapore, via Bangkok, is expected to take 20 hours. Trade and tourism facilitation agreements will deeply integrate mainland Southeast Asia with China, reinforcing the effect of a China-ASEAN agreement to achieve regional free trade by 2010 in the case of the more developed economies, and 2015 in the less developed ones.

Limitations of the GMS Framework

On paper, the GMS project is based on the principles of cooperative, sustainable, and equitable development. In practice, the structure of the GMS does not include an effective mechanism for multinational coordination or decisionmaking. Most enabling agreements on transportation, navigation, and other matters are in fact bilateral ones involving China and its weaker neighbors.

A Basin Development Plan without the River

Most importantly, as a result of Chinese objections, the GMS framework does not include the water of the Mekong Basin. China clearly did not want any constraints placed on its plans to exploit the hydropower potential of the upper Mekong in Yunnan Province. In terms of its national power and international water law, China is free to do almost anything it wants as the upstream riparian. Bringing the Mekong's water under the cooperative, sustainable, and equitable principles of the GMS would unacceptably compromise Beijing's freedom of action.

Thus, China carries on its dam-building and river-deepening operations entirely outside the framework of the GMS without regard for the environment or the interests of its downstream neighbors. China has completed three of at least eight planned dams, which already have interfered with the natural flow of the Mekong.

China's smaller downstream neighbors also make unilateral decisions about building dams on the tributaries of the Mekong that run through their territory. Vietnam's dam on the Se San River at Yali Falls has caused considerable downstream damage, including loss of life and livestock, to Cambodian villages. As a result of negotiations with Cambodia, Vietnam is now constructing a dam and reservoir at the lower end of the Se San cascade whose primary purpose is to "re-regulate" the flow of the river by evening out the frequent rise and fall caused by the responses of upstream dams to changing power load requirements.

Unbalanced Effects

On paper, the concept and principles underlying the GMS are a logical alternative to the unregulated and uncontrolled exploitation of the resources of the Mekong Basin. Certainly, the GMS project and increasing economic regionalism could have a positive impact in the reduction of rural poverty. The project includes considerable funding for technical assistance, human development, and governmental capacity-building, funding that is being supplemented by the World Bank, Japan, and other donors (but not directly, at least, by the United States). Critics of the GMS, however, maintain that the project is overly focused on linking major urban areas with too few projects designed to benefit farmers, such as building feeder roads for getting crops to market. Moreover, the potential negative effects of the GMS, especially the destruction of forests and wildlife habitat, will be largely irreversible. Current GMS programs to counter these consequences are unlikely to achieve the desired results.

In many ways, the GMS constitutes a microcosm of all the most important sources of tension between globalization and its associated transboundary effects in nation-states. These include:

- unsustainable transborder extraction and processing of natural resources, including illegal logging and other environmentally destructive activities
- a dramatic shift of resources and wealth from the rural areas, where the vast majority of the region's people live, to the urban middle classes
- economically driven transborder labor migration, overly rapid rural-urban migration within individual states, and human and drug trafficking
- pandemic diseases
- recent history of conflict, formerly with ideological overtones
- potential for future state-state conflict over scarce resources, especially water.

Geopolitical Consequences of the GMS

The evolution of the GMS is rich in historical irony. The project was launched by the ADB in 1992—the same year that Chinese leader Deng Xiaoping traveled south to Shanghai and proclaimed that to get rich was "glorious." By the mid-1990s, China was a fast-rising economic power, growing at double-digit rates, while post–economic bubble Japan was sinking into its financial and economic "lost decade."

Essentially, a project pushed by Japan with the goal of expanding its regional production network and an economic vector northward into southwest China has become a vector for the southward expansion of Chinese power and influence into an area regarded by Japan as its most important economic hinterland—its "backyard," so to speak.

Upgraded transboundary highways being built with ADB assistance and China's separate blasting of rapids and shoals in the middle reaches of the Mekong will give Yunnan Province and its capital, Kunming, vastly increased access to the global economy. China's own road construction activities will link Kunming to Beijing, while GMS projects will link Yunnan's capital as far as Singapore via Vientiane, Bangkok, and onward. The GMS emphasizes a holistic approach to development that combines measures inherently threatening to more rapid legal and illegal exploitation of the basin's natural resources with programs supporting environmental protection and sustainable development.[21] Unfortunately, the environmental programs receive only a small fraction of the total GMS budget, and most countries lack the institutional infrastructure, capacity, and political will to enforce their own environmental regulations, let alone participate effectively in regional cooperation.[22]

China Takes the Lead in Lower Mekong Hydropower Development

Since about 2005, China increasingly has emerged as the dominant force of hydropower development in the lower Mekong, especially in Burma, Laos, and Cambodia, thereby seriously undercutting the role and influence of the ADB, World Bank, and the MRC. The growing role of China and Chinese banks and companies in numerous downstream projects has both geoeconomic and geopolitical objectives.

China considers the upper Mekong—which it calls the Lancang— in the country's remote and mountainous Yunnan Province to be its national river. A massive project to build a cascade of eight dams on the Lancang is well under way, and the first two moderately sized dams on the main stream have had adverse impacts. Since China began filling the Manwan Dam in 1993, the annual loads of floodborne silt have been reduced and villages downstream have experienced erratic changes in the level of the river. Circumstantial evidence also suggests that China's dams have exacerbated the effects of the multiyear drought.

China's fourth dam in the Lancang cascade, the 4,200-megawatt Xiaowan Dam, will create a quantum increase in the potential for downstream environmental and hydrological damage. The 292-meter-high compound arch dam, the world's highest, would tower 100 meters above the Hoover Dam. The dam's 15-billion-cubic-meter reservoir is designed to allow the cascade's smaller dams to operate in dry weather and also provide power to its six 700-megawatt turbines.

China plans to store and then release 40 to 70 percent more water into the river during the dry season to keep its three lowermost dams operating and to support navigation. The unannounced releases will cause the river to rise and fall between 4 and 10 meters, jeopardizing the lives and property of anyone near it in northern Laos, Thailand, and Burma. Erratic water releases by the first three Chinese dams have already caused serious damage to property and some loss of life far downstream in northern Laos and Thailand.

The increased dry season flow will significantly affect the productivity of Cambodia's Tonle Sap (Great Lake) and river of the same name. Called the "nursery" of the Mekong fishery, the productivity of the Tonle Sap depends on the extremes of flood and drought. Increased dry season flows into the Tonle Sap from China's reservoirs will narrow the band of seasonal wetlands by 5 to 10 percent, which in theory could reduce the productivity of the Tonle Sap comparably.[23]

Chinese dams may capture as much of 80 percent of the sediment flowing from Yunnan, which contributes 40 to 60 percent of the total load. The estimated capture of fine sediment by large storage dams in China and on major tributaries in Southeast Asia could reduce sediment flow to the Mekong Delta by 20 percent and accelerate the already serious loss of land to the sea.[24]

In late 2009, China completed and began filling the Xiaowan Dam, just before the onset of the worst drought to hit the Mekong Basin in half a century. Rightly or wrongly—it cannot be determined because China does not release the necessary data about the operations of its dams—a public outcry ensued in downstream Southeast Asian countries that blamed China for the dire lack of fresh water. Beijing would do well to see this outcry as a harbinger of the future, when its ability to regulate the flow of the river will lead to serious downstream anomalies. A continuation of the pattern of lower than normal rainfall that now has lasted for over a decade could provide insufficient water to make the system work as planned.

Planned Southeast Asian Dams

China's cascade of eight dams in Yunnan will create the most immediate but by no means the only threat to the river. Three had been completed as of mid-2010. Laos, Thailand, and Cambodia also have revealed plans to build up to 11 dams on the lower half of the river, plus one non-dam hydro project. Vietnam itself has no dammable stretch of the river, but Petro Vietnam Power Corporation, a state-owned enterprise, will finance one of the Lao dams.

Both the Yunnan and Lower Mekong dams will have similarly consequential impact, but of differing character. China's eight-dam cascade in Yunnan will fundamentally alter the timing and volume of the river's seasonal changes and capture a significant amount of the silt that normally provides nutrients for the downstream agriculture that is critical to food security. The river's natural rhythm will be significantly altered, narrowing the difference between the peaks of the wet and dry seasons. The Tonle Sap and other wetlands will be affected sufficiently to substantially reduce their productivity of fish and other aquatic life.[25]

Environmental nongovernmental organizations (NGOs), hydrologists, and fisheries experts have singled out the proposed 240-megawatt Don Sahong Dam on the mainstream at Khone Falls, just above the Cambodian border, and the proposed Sambor Dam downstream in Cambodia as the projects most threatening to the lower Mekong fisheries. The Don Sahong dam, which will be undertaken by Malaysia's Mega First Corporation Berhad, would block the single channel (out of 18) that can be traversed by migrating fish during the dry season. At risk are hundreds of species of food fish that migrate between the Cambodian and Lao parts of the river, not to mention the endangered freshwater dolphin and giant Mekong catfish.[26]

In October 2007, the China Southern Power Grid Company and the Cambodian government signed a memorandum of understanding for a feasibility study of a dam at Sambor, just below a major stretch of rapids in Kratie Province. This dam, like the Don Sahong dam, would decimate the lower Mekong fish population.[27]

Geopolitical Implications of Hydropower in the GMS

All of the Mekong countries are determined to exploit their hydropower resources to support economic development. To date, China's highly ambitious program to develop a massive eight-dam cascade in Yunnan and related blasting of the Mekong river floor as far downstream as northern Laos has posed the single greatest threat to the river. Soon, however, scores of large dams planned by Laos, Vietnam, and Cambodia could pose as great a threat to the river's hydrology and ecology as China's, but in different ways.

Most important, if the Lower Mekong countries build the proposed mainstream dams, they will become dependent on China to release the right amount of water at the right time to keep the dams operating through the dry season. Even if China has no desire to harm its neighbors' interests, many variables could affect the operations of its dams in the Yunnan Cascade. Among these are changing power demand, rainfall patterns, and the amount of water behind the Xiaowan Dam at the beginning of the dry season.

Vietnam and Laos are also building smaller dams that are having impacts beyond their borders, but in comparison, the output of the Xiaowan will be three times the combined capacity of all of the dams currently operating or under construction in the lower Mekong. As an example of water usage impacts, filling the reservoir for the Xiaowan will likely consume one-half of the upper Mekong's total flow for 5 to 10 years.

Other Environmental Threats

All of the resources of the Mekong Basin are under severe threat of environmentally destructive exploitation. In most cases, these threats are linked. For instance, exploiting the Lower Mekong's rich mineral deposits, including copper, bauxite, gold, and titanium, requires large amounts of energy. Many of the proposed dams in Laos and Cambodia are intended to generate the power needed for mining and for raising the value of the minerals (such as by smelting copper and turning bauxite into aluminum). The destruction of forests is an unavoidable consequence of dam building and mining. Finally, while global demand is the main driver of unsustainable resources extraction, relatively high population growth rates are a continuing factor, especially among minority groups who occupy the most vulnerable land.

Illegal and Environmentally Unsustainable Logging

The Mekong Basin's large but fast-diminishing stands of tropical hardwoods and other timber are not only a major source of income but also an integral part of the global climate system. The basin's trees remove carbon dioxide, while its wetlands and peat bogs sequester huge amounts of carbon. Because of the largely uncontrolled cutting of timber, the Mekong Basin has lost more than 70 percent of its pre-industrial tree cover, most of that in the last 20 years. The destruction of tree cover has been associated with increased flooding and the degradation of fresh water resources.[28]

In fact, not much primary forest remains. Because primary forests developed over hundreds or even thousands of years, the once-dominant tree species such as teak, mahogany, and other valued hardwoods cannot regenerate in the changed conditions of full sunlight. Secondary forests are dominated by new tree species, usually softer woods that are of lower value even when they reach commercially useful size.

In a very real sense, the current destruction of remaining primary forests and their replacement with rubber, palm oil, and other monoculture plantations is simply completing a process that began during the Western colonial era but that was interrupted by several decades of armed conflict. Extensive commercial-scale logging in Thailand and adjacent areas of Burma started under that pioneer of modern globalization, the British Empire. Commercial-scale logging by British companies began in northwestern Thailand and the ethnic Mon areas of Burma in the late 19th century. Thailand's first railways were built by British and other European interests in the early 20th century to bring teak to Bangkok for milling or to facilitate export of logs.

Efforts by the Kingdom of Siam to regulate logging in the interest of the state began with the establishment of the Royal Forestry Department in 1896, which drew on British and German experience in sustainable harvesting. The British advisors conceptualized the forest as the kingdom's "capital" and the harvested trees as the "interest." For the first three decades, the administrators of the Royal Forestry Department—the conservators of the forest—were British.

The Thai royal government saw several concrete benefits of the foreign logging concessions, especially the collection of taxes on logs and the expansion of central political authority to the farthest extent of the kingdom. Eventually, the goal of sustainable harvesting was overwhelmed by political corruption and a philosophical departure from the original idea of conservation that involved a broader concept of exploiting resources under strict official management for the benefit of the people. Population pressure also resulted in the conversion of clear-cut land from replanting to agriculture. Beginning in the 1960s, authorities began establishing national parks and other protected areas to save some of what was left of Thai forests, especially those that had an alternate economic value for urban middle-class recreation and tourism. At the same time, opposition to cutting in remaining unprotected areas by ethnic highland minority groups and their NGO advocates continued to grow. In 1989, a century after the beginning of large-scale logging, the government banned the cutting of timber.

The loss of tree cover accelerated after the Vietnam War as a result of the rapid growth in the market-oriented industrializing countries in Southeast Asia beginning in the 1970s. Since that period, logging, the expansion of agriculture, dam building, and mining have caused a rapid acceleration of forest loss. The process has slowed down only when most of the easily accessible timber has been cut and/or when governments have become sufficiently alarmed to adopt effective protective measures.

Variables in estimates of deforestation include the survey period, criteria for categorizing tree cover, and completeness of data. These limitations notwithstanding, the studies generally agree that the Mekong Basin has lost about 70 percent of the tree cover that it once had and that remaining natural forest continues to disappear fast. The loss of primary forest has been much greater. As a result, most tree cover is already second-growth timber.

The area of rapid deforestation has moved from Thailand and Vietnam to Cambodia, Laos, and Burma largely because the first two countries have cut so much of their forests in the past. By one account, the countries of the lower Mekong have lost half of their remaining primary forests in the past three decades. Primary old growth forest has been replaced by a mixture of shrubs, grasses, and young trees.[29] Vietnam had 14 million hectares of natural forest in 1955 and only 9.4 million in 1999.[30] Another source gives 12.9 million hectares of forest in 2005, only 85,000 of which is primary forest. In fact, by 2005, Vietnam had lost 77.9 percent of the *primary* forest standing in 1990, which accounts now for only 0.3 percent of the total land area. Thailand, by comparison, has 12.6 percent of its land still under primary forest. Thailand had lost 17.7 percent of its total forest cover between 1990 and 2005, but belated measures have protected the last stands of primary forest.

Cambodia lost 19.3 percent of total forest cover and 58 percent of primary forest during the same period (1990–2005).[31] While Thailand had taken steps to halt cutting of its primary forests, Thai companies connected to the army had been paying the Khmer Rouge, who had retreated to western Cambodia on the border with Thailand, for the right to cut timber.[32]

Currently, the most serious assault on the remaining timber in Cambodia is being carried out by politically connected timber companies such as the giant Pheapimex Group, which operates joint venture logging concessions, pulp mills, and eucalyptus plantations with Chinese and Taiwanese partner companies. Critics in Cambodia charge that Pheapimex's basic modus operandi is to work with highly placed officials in order to gain concessions for establishing plantations on protected forest land. Environmentalists and other supporters of affected villages claim that the operators first cut the larger trees without permits and then have the forests declared "degraded" or "spare forest" so that the rights to develop industrial plantations can be sold without technically violating forest protection laws.[33]

Apart from destroying forests and the livelihoods of Cambodians who depend on them, plantations and pulp mills pollute rivers and pose a special threat to the Tonle Sap. The Great Lake and Tonle Sap River are already being seriously degraded by overfishing and the destruction of wetlands by encroaching farms.

Currently, rubber plantations being established by Chinese companies are transforming northern Laos, destroying remaining stands of timber and polluting the rivers through the destruction of natural watersheds and fertilizer runoff. Chinese commercial operators either gain concessions from local governments or engage Lao farmers in contract production, providing seed, fertilizer, and training. Because the huge demand for latex rubber from China has caused world prices to soar, rubber is far more lucrative than subsistence farming, but the plantations impose a severe environmental cost, and in many cases they have encroached on protected forest land.[34]

Involvement of Regional Militaries in Illegal Logging

Global demand drives illegal logging but only in conjunction with local corruption. One major problem throughout Southeast Asia is that regional militaries generally depend on commercial activities to fully fund themselves, which makes it easy for them to circumvent logging laws.

In the ethnic Shan area, Burma's expanding military presence has had a major impact on river blasting in support of the China, Thailand,

and Laos Mekong Navigational Improvement Project. Overall, the end of fighting between the army and the Shan State army has opened the region to exploitation by "the regime, [Shan] ceasefire leaders and other business elites who have profited from unbridled exploitation of the area's natural resources, with disastrous effects on the environment." It is estimated that eastern Shan State has lost 50 percent of its forest cover since 1988. Wildlife and forest products are also diminishing rapidly.[35] In Burma in particular, the military's involvement in the drug trade has also led to the development of lavish casinos and golf courses.[36]

Reportedly, some Laotian army units are also deeply involved in the illegal timber trade, partly because the Laotian government, like that in Indonesia and some other regional countries, does not fully fund the military's budget. Instead, the military is given timber allotments, allegedly determined by sustainability analysis. By selling the timber, military leaders enrich themselves while the Army supplements its inadequate budget. Although the allotments themselves may be legally assigned, the military can declare timber from any source as coming from the officially allotted tracts.[37]

Mining

The Mekong region's mineral resources have long been an important source of export earnings. Until recently, mining for industrially important minerals has largely been a small-scale activity. This pattern is rapidly changing in concert with the development of numerous hydropower dams, many of them built specifically to provide power for large-scale mining operations. As a consequence, mining has become one of the main sources of water pollution and a major threat to fisheries and human health. To date, mining has been carried out with little or no environmental consideration, and often illegally.

Mining has become a major industry in Vietnam, Laos, and presumably in Burma, and it is taking off in Cambodia as well. Foreign companies—including some of the biggest, such as Oxiana Limited and Rio Tinto in copper and Anglo Gold in that metal—have emerged as the main players in copper, gold, lead, and zinc mining.[38] A number of joint-ventures operations are also involved in mining gemstones, limestone, tin, zinc, and gypsum. Others are making cement to meet the demands of construction activities, including roads, dams, and buildings. In contrast, most domestically operated mines, quarries, and sand dredging operations remain small in scale. Australian companies are by far the biggest operators in Laos, with China in second place. The rapid and largely unregulated expansion of mining in the Mekong region has led to considerable runoff and tailings that pollute the rivers, as well as causing increased deforestation of adjacent land.

Chinese involvement in bauxite mining in Vietnam has become a contentious domestic political issue. A nationalistic outcry followed revelations in 2009 that subsidiaries of the Aluminum Corporation of China had entered into a partnership with Vietnamese companies for extensive bauxite mining in the Central Highlands. Before his death, celebrated Vietnamese military hero General Vo Nguyen Giap raised an unprecedented public outcry against the joint venture over environmental destruction and the presence of Chinese workers at the mine. As evidence of both Vietnam's desire for foreign investment from all quarters as well as the public's neuralgia about China, the presence of Alcoa and other foreign mining companies barely received notice.[39]

Population Growth

Finally, population growth remains a significant threat to the environment and to political stability in some parts of the Mekong Basin, especially in the upland areas, which already are suffering from excessive exploitation. Population growth rates have fallen sharply in much of Mekong Southeast Asia, but high rates continue in some of the poorest countries. Moreover, the comparatively youthful populations in most of the Mekong countries will ensure considerable growth momentum, even after fertility rates have fallen below the natural replacement level.

The population of Laos was growing at an estimated 2.73 percent per year as of 2007, with a very young age structure of 41.2 percent of the population at 14 years and younger. Cambodia is growing more slowly at 1.73 percent per year, and Cambodians 14 and under account for 34 percent of the population. The relevant figures for Vietnam are 1.04 percent growth and 26.3 percent of the population at 14 or under. The Thai population is growing at well under 1 percent per year, and only 21 percent of the population is 14 years or younger.[40] Burma's growth rate has fallen from 2.5 percent in the mid-1970s to below 1 percent in 2008.[41]

Still, demographers estimate that the population of the Mekong Basin will increase from 73 million at present to about 120 million by 2025, an increase of 65 percent.[42] Moreover, some areas are growing far more rapidly and unsustainably. For instance, the population around the Tonle Sap Great Lake is growing 3 percent more quickly than the rest of the Cambodian population.[43]

Expanding populations take their toll on forests, fisheries, and water quality, but small farmers generally are less of a threat than commercial logging interests. Forestry experts have increasingly concluded that swidden agriculture, which involves clear-cutting for crops and then letting the land lie fallow for several years, can be environmentally sustainable. Unfortunately, policies adopted by governments to limit the area of land under swidden agriculture have had the unexpected consequence of forcing communities to reduce the amount of time when the land lies fallow, with negative environmental consequences.[44] The main damage caused by small farmers comes when they migrate into land that has been clear-cut for timber. This pattern prevails whenever the pressure of rising populations coincides with the decimation of the forest by commercial loggers, whether in the Amazon region of Brazil, sub-Saharan Africa, or Southeast Asia.[45]

Prospects

The development juggernaut in the Mekong is unstoppable, but three critical questions remain to be answered. First, will the six GMS countries commit to cooperative and coordinated development, including both water management and other aspects of sustainable development, and if so, will they do it in time to avoid a catastrophe? Second, can regionalism take root without being dominated by China? Finally, will diminishing resources and rising competition for water and energy cause the renewal of regional conflict—not against China but among the lower Mekong countries themselves, which will be competing in an environment of scarcity?

There seems little reason for optimism at present. Most cooperation within the GMS continues to take place on a bilateral or trilateral basis. Many of these agreements now have China at their core.

The GMS has been highly successful in respect to the construction of its transportation corridors and the facilitation of expanded trade and tourism, but it is fighting a losing battle to correct the initial failure to carry out adequate environmental studies. Moreover, improvements in governance and human capacity have lagged far behind the development of economic infrastructure.

The efforts of the ADB and World Bank to promote environmental sustainability have been compromised by at least three developments that are substantially out of their control so long as sustaining themselves as relevant actors remains their foremost interest. First, governments remain suspicious of each other and adamantly opposed to giving up any measure of their sovereignty for the sake of cooperative and sustainable development. Despite the 1995 agreement by Cambodia, Laos, Thailand, and Vietnam to uphold cooperative development of the water resources through the Mekong River Commission, the studies and plans developed by the experts in the commission secretariat are gathering dust. A major problem for the MRC and the banks is that national political leaders and bureaucratic decisionmakers lack the ability to understand the science underlying these studies, even if they were prepared to spend the necessary political capital.

Second, the borrowing countries themselves are shareholders in the banks. China, which gains far more from the banks' infrastructure loans and grant aid for technical studies, now has half the voting power of Japan and the United States on the ADB governing board. China has the ability to mobilize support from other Mekong countries for its projects in return for their support for Chinese projects.

Third, the banks' successful promotion of the concept of private-public partnerships has left them largely in the position of providing risk guarantees for private investors. Moreover, they are offering assistance with environmental mitigation and relocation of those displaced by the projects. Essentially, the multilateral development banks find themselves in a seemingly losing struggle to remain relevant.

Only recognition by the governments themselves that the pursuit of short-term objectives undermines the longer term stability of the region can prevent an environmental and human catastrophe. Unfortunately, the situation will have to get far worse before the dangers are recognized by regional governments. Under current trends, China is fast becoming the dominant economic and political force in the region, but increasingly Beijing will face the prospect of choosing between its "smile" diplomacy and the current narrow calculation of its national interests. There are too many unpredictable forces at work to calculate how and when resistance will grow, thereby forcing China to reconsider its efforts to incorporate the region into its economy, if at all.

Notes

[1] See Richard P. Cronin, "Mekong Dams and the Perils of Peace," *Survival: Global Politics and Strategy* 51, no. 6 (December 2009–January 2010), 147–160.

[2] "Hun Sen Praises China's Aid in Infrastructure Development," *People's Daily Online*, January 27, 2010, available at <http://english.peopledaily.com.cn/90001/90776/90883/6880789.html>.

[3] Fred Pearce, *When the Rivers Run Dry: Water, the Defining Crisis of the 21st Century* (Boston: Beacon Street, 2006), 96.

[4] Two other great Asian rivers rise in Yunnan: the Pearl River, whose delta is the lifeblood of China's dynamic Guangdong Province, on the South China Sea, and the Red River (Yuan Jiang), whose flood plain and delta on the Gulf of Tonkin form the densely populated heartland of northern Vietnam.

[5] Hiroshi Hori, *The Mekong: Environment and Development* (Tokyo, New York, Paris: United Nations University Press, 2000), 31.

[6] Jason Folkmanis and Van Nguyen, "Thailand May Lose Status as World's Top Rice Exporter by 2015, Group Says," Bloomberg.com, available at <www.bloomberg.com/news/2010-06-29/thailand-may-lose-status-as-world-s-top-rice-exporter-by-2015-group-says.html>.

[7] Eric Wolanski and Nguyen Huu Nhan, "Oceanography of the Mekong River Estuary," paper presented at the International Conference on Deltas (Mekong venue): Geological Modeling and Management, Ho Chi Minh City, Vietnam, January 10–16, 2005, available at <www.megadelta.ecnu.edu.cn/main/upload/Eric%20WolanskiExtendedabstract.pdf>.

[8] "Southeast Asia: The Muddied Mekong," *Time*, December 26, 1969; David A. Biggs, "Reclamation Nations: The U.S. Bureau of Reclamation's Role in Water Management and Nation Building in the Mekong Valley, 1945–1975," *Comparative Technology Transfer and Society* 4, no. 3 (December 2006), 225–242.

[9] Colleen Fox and Chris Sneddon, "Flood Pulses, International Watercourse Law, and Common Pool Resources," United Nations University, World Institute for Development Economics Research and Expert Group on Development Issues Research Paper No. 2005/20, April 2005, available at <www.wider.unu.edu/stc/repec/pdfs/rp2005/rp2005-20.pdf>.

[10] David Coates, "Fisheries in the Mekong River," <www.unep.org/bpsp/Fisheries/Fisheries%20Case%20Study%20Summaries/Coates(Summary).pdf>; Chris Barlow et al., "How Much of the Mekong Fish Catch is at Risk from Mainstream Dam Development?" *Catch and Culture* 14, no. 3 (December 2008), available at <www.mrcmekong.org/catch-culture/vol14_3dec08/Mekong-fish-catch.htm>.

[11] "Cambodia," Worldfishing.net, May 1, 2008, available at <www.worldfishing.net/features/new-horizons/Cambodia>.

[12] Mekong River Commission, "The Mekong Fisheries Today," available at <www.mrcmekong.org/programmes/fisheries/fish_ann03.htm>.

[13] Ibid.

[14] Pinkaew Laungaramsri, "On the Politics of Nature Conservation in Thailand," *Kyoto Review of Southeast Asia*, October 2002, available at <http://kyotoreview.cseas.kyoto-u.ac.jp/issue/issue1/article_168.html>.

[15] Asian Development Bank (ADB), "The GMS Program," available at <www.adb.org/GMS/Program/default.asp>.

[16] ADB, summary of proceedings, Greater Mekong Subregion Ninth Meeting of the Subregional Transport Forum, Beijing, June 2005, available at <www.adb.org/Documents/Events/Mekong/Proceedings/STF9-SUMMARY.pdf>.

[17] ADB–Greater Mekong Subregion, Technical Assistance Completion Report, TA 6227–REG: Coordinating the Greater Mekong Subregion North-South Economic Corridor Bridge Project, available at <www.adb.org/Documents/TACRs/REG/37763-02-reg-tcr.pdf>.

[18] Raja M, "Asian Highway Network Gathers Speed," Asia Times Online, June 14, 2006, available at <www.atimes.com/atimes/Asian_Economy/HF14Dk01.html>; "Asia Highway Network: Mainland Southeast Asia," available at <www.atimes.com/atimes/Asian_Economy/images/highways.html>.

[19] The poem begins, "By the old Moulmein Pagoda, lookin' eastward to the sea," which is geographically incorrect or poetic license, as "the sea" would be to the west. Nor would the dawn come up "like thunder outer China 'crost the Bay." But if Kipling had mentally moved Moulmein to the Rangoon side of the Gulf of Martaban, then the rest would make sense, as "China" would likely have been viewed broadly by an illiterate British soldier.

[20] Masami Ishida, "Special Economic Zones and Economic Corridors," Economic Research Institute for ASEAN and East Asia (ERIA) Discussion Paper Series ERIA DP–2009–16, June 2009, available at <www.eria.org/pdf/ERIA-DP-2009-16.pdf>.

[21] Marwaan Macan-Marker, "ADB urges cooperation in Mekong Region, Asia Times Online, April 24, 2004, available at <www.atimes.com/atimes/Southeast_Asia/FD23Ae01.html>.

[22] Jorn Dosch, "Environmental Issues in Trade and Investment Policy Deliberations in the Mekong Subregion," in *Balancing Trade Growth and Environmental Protection in ASEAN*, Policy Report 2, 2010, available at <www.tradeknowledgenetwork.net/pdf/balancing_trade_growth_asean.pdf>.

[23] Discussion Draft, Impacts Assessment, MRC Strategic Environmental Assessment, May 14, 2010, 80. The draft notes that more research is required to reliably estimate the impact. The theoretical projection is based on the extrapolation of other research, not the discussion draft; available at <www.mrcmekong.org/ISH/SEA-Baseline/SEA_impacts_assessment_report_Discussion_Draft-15May.pdf>.

[24] Ibid., 24.

[25] Richard Cronin and Timothy Hamlin, "Mekong Tipping Point: Hydropower Dams, Human Security and Regional Stability," Henry L. Stimson Center, 2010, 4.

[26] Eric Baran and Blake Ratner, "The Don Sahong Dam and Mekong Fisheries," World Fish Center, June 2007, available at <www.worldfishcenter.org/resource_centre/DonSahong-final.pdf>.

[27] "Sambor Dam, Kratie Province, Cambodia," *Terrapaper*, September 2007, available at <www.terraper.org/articles/Sambor-TERRA%20Sept07.pdf>.

[28] "Asian/Indomalayan Realm," Mongabay.com, available at <http://rainforests.mongabay.com/20asian.htm>.

[29] Andrew J. Mittelman, "Secondary Forests in the Lower Mekong Subregion: An Overview of their Extent, Roles and Importance," *Journal of Tropical Forest Science* 13, no. 4 (2001), 691–690, available at <www.cifor.cgiar.org/publications/pdf_files/SecondaryForest/Andrew.pdf>.

[30] Center for International Forestry Research, "Vietnam," available at <www.cifor.cgiar.org/rehab/_ref/countries/Vietnam/Brief.htm>.

[31] "Asian/Indomalayan Realm."

[32] "Sustainable development and Environmental Awareness: Unsustainable Practices in the Mekong River Basin," *MRCS Environment Training Program Case Studies*, available at <www.mrcmekong.org/envir_training_kit/English/Course%20A%20-%20Sustainable%20Development%20and%20Environmental%20Awareness/Operational/Readings/PDF/Reading%2002-Unsustainable%20Practices%20in%20the%20MRB.pdf >.

[33] Chris Lang, "Cambodia: Eucalyptus Plantations and Pulp Production Threaten Forests and Rivers," *World Rainforest Movement Bulletin* 44 (March 2001), available at <www.wrm.org.uy/bulletin/44/Cambodia.html>.

[34] Brian McCartan, "China Rubber Demand Stretches Laos," Asia Times Online, December 19, 2007, available at <www.atimes.com/atimes/China_Business/IL19Cb01.html>.

[35] "Aftershocks along Burma's Mekong, The Lahu National Development Organization," available at <www.ibiblio.org/obl/docs/Aftershocks.html>.

[36] Ibid.

[37] Conversation with a part-time timber dealer in Laos, 2005.

[38] Florence Chong, "Laos Hits Gold in Copper Exports—Buyers Are Virtually Standing at the Front Gate," Asia Today Online, March 21, 2005, available at <www.asiatoday.com.au/feature_reports.php?id=163>.

[39] Martha Ann Overland, "In Vietnam, New Fears of a Chinese 'Invasion,'" Time Online, April 16, 2009, available at <www.time.com/time/world/article/0,8599,1891668,00.html>.

[40] Central Intelligence Agency World Factbook, available at <https://www.cia.gov/library/publications/the-world-factbook/geos/vm.html>.

[41] World Bank, World Development Indicators, last updated June 15, 2010, available at <www.google.com/publicdata?ds=wb-wdi&met=sp_pop_grow&idim=country:MMR&dl=en&hl=en&q=burma+population+growth>.

[42] J. Christenson, "Food Security and Development in the Lower Mekong River Basin: A Challenge for the Mekong River Commission," conference paper, Asian Development Bank, February 2001.

[43] Ulla Heinonen, "Environmental Impact on Migration in Cambodia: Water-related Migration from the Tonle Sap Lake Region," *Water Resources Development* 22, no. 3 (September 2006), 449–462.

[44] Mittelman.

[45] Ibid.

Chapter 8

Displaced Populations in Burma's Borderlands: When Are Borders a Significant Barrier or Means of Protection?

Rhoda Margesson

The changes brought about by globalization—in particular, the flow of goods and money—raise the possibility that borders are becoming less relevant. While this may hold true for certain shifts taking place in the global economy, borders remain critical in the relationships between states—particularly with regard to the movement of people, where they often serve as either a barrier or a means of protection for those who are forced to leave their homes or flee their country.

The impact of globalization on population movements, the links between globalization and migration, and the implications of mixed migratory patterns that may include migrants, refugees and asylum seekers traveling together (yet having very different assistance and protection needs) are topics of growing interest and study. The issue is made more pressing by the increasing numbers of people on the move, and the degree to which crossing borders has become more rather than less critical in terms of protection and the expected opportunities on the other side. Furthermore, modern borders do not always coincide with historical links of culture and identity, daily working patterns, and the network of relationships that may exist between people living in communities on either side of what to them is an otherwise artificial line.

Borders do not necessarily allow the free movement of people. The problem of human displacement, which often occurs involuntarily during international disasters and conflicts, presents many challenges for the international community. Often, those in flight will cluster at the border of their own country or cross over into neighboring countries, which then become hosts to the displaced, sometimes for long periods. Difficult operating environments often accompany these situations. Some of the global challenges created by displacement at borders include asylum-migration questions, the problem of long-term refugees, and increasing numbers of internally displaced persons (IDPs).

In the case of Burma, the drivers of its population displacement have been primarily conflict, human rights violations, and oppression.[1] Globalization may have exacerbated the contrast between Burma's elite and its citizens, and between the economic growth within Burma and regional development outside its borders. It may also have contributed to the opportunities for other criminal activities, such as human trafficking, illicit trade in timber, wildlife, and gems, money laundering, arms dealing, and a robust drug trade.[2] But globalization did not cause the longstanding political situation in Burma or create the reasons Burmese continue to flee the country. It remains to be seen if the broad reach of globalization may eventually have a positive impact on Burma and, in time, help bring about part of a solution to its current crisis.[3]

Amid an atmosphere of continuing tensions over the Burmese military's suppression of antiregime protests in August and September 2007, the potential for worsening humanitarian conditions and a possible increase in Burmese fleeing the country became clearly evident. The situation raised questions about what more, if anything, could and should be done by members of the international community not only to focus attention on the abuses of the regime, but also to alleviate the suffering of the people. Increasingly, some argue it is the suffering of ordinary Burmese that brings into sharp relief the continuing violation of fundamental rights—rights pertaining to food security, refugee and IDP status, and individual freedoms—and raises questions about how those rights should be protected and by whom. State sovereignty, defined in part by the borders of a country, remains critical to the answer.

To illustrate the complex issues surrounding displaced populations, this chapter focuses on refugees who have fled the eastern part of Burma for Thailand and those who have been displaced within Burma. It does not address other issues, such as Burmese refugees in Bangladesh (or elsewhere in the region) or the religious and ethnic identities of certain populations, such as the Rohingyas, many of whom are not recognized by Burma as Burmese nationals and are considered stateless.[4] This chapter was written before Cyclone Nargis struck Burma in May 2008 and examines the situation for refugees and IDPs prior to the impact of this natural disaster.

Overview: Humanitarian Crises, Population Displacement, and Borders

Humanitarian emergencies occur worldwide and stem mainly from natural disasters or conflicts. Each year, they affect millions of people who often require prolonged urgent assistance. Natural disasters (like the 2004 tsunami, 2005 earthquake in South Asia, and 2010 earthquake in Haiti) typically require a multilateral response and are less likely to be hindered by the politics of the situation. In many political crises, such as war or civil conflicts—where groups within a country are fighting and a political solution is not forthcoming—the response often cannot be separated from broader foreign policy developments. Factors that may impact outside states' decision to intervene include the severity of the situation, the type of humanitarian assistance required, the impact of conflict and refugee flows on stability in the region, and the role of neighboring countries in contributing to the relief effort. The broader international response—coordination of assistance, sharing the cost of an international recovery effort, and donor fatigue—are significant issues and may impact levels of funding and support available. Assistance may last for many years and can require delivery of supplies in areas of open conflict. In cases like these, refugees may be stranded in camps for decades, and those displaced within their own country may be separated from their homes for long periods.

As a result of different types of crises, forced population movements often occur within the affected country or flow across borders to countries in close proximity. Definitions of status are assigned to various groups and may include refugees, IDPs, stateless persons, asylum seekers, returnees, and other vulnerable populations (those who might have difficulty moving, such as women, children, and the elderly).

A *refugee* is a person fleeing across the border from his or her country. Unlike refugees who seek asylum outside their country of citizenship, *IDPs* have not crossed an international border but are displaced inside their own country. *Asylum seekers* are people who flee their home country and seek sanctuary in another state where they apply for asylum—which is the right to be recognized as a refugee—and may receive legal protection and material assistance until their formal status has been determined. *Stateless persons* are individuals who are not considered as citizens of any state under national laws. *Returnees* are refugees who return to their home countries. All can emerge as groups requiring particular protection, the basis of which for some may be found in international humanitarian law, and needing emergency assistance, which is typically provided by a host of national and international actors.

International Protection Mechanisms for Refugees

The United Nations High Commissioner for Refugees (UNHCR) is the UN agency dedicated to the protection of refugees and other populations displaced by conflict and natural disasters, and it is mandated to lead and coordinate international action to protect refugees and resolve refugee problems worldwide.[5] It is also the institutional mechanism for the implementation of the 1951 UN Convention Relating to the Status of Refugees (Refugee Convention) and the 1967 protocol to that convention.[6] A *refugee* is defined as a person who has fled his or her country because of persecution or "owing to well-founded fear of being persecuted for reasons of race, religion, nationality, membership of a particular social group or political opinion, is outside the country of his nationality and is unable or, owing to such fear, is unwilling to avail himself of the protection of that country."[7] Parties to the Refugee Convention have an obligation to abide by the principle of "non-refoulement," which means that "no contracting State shall expel or return (*refouler*) a refugee in any manner whatsoever to the frontiers of territories where his life or freedom would be threatened on account of his race, religion, nationality, membership of a particular social group, or political opinion."[8] Refugees are granted special status under international law. Once someone is considered a refugee, that individual automatically has certain rights, and states that are parties to the Refugee Convention and its 1967 protocol are obligated to provide certain resources and protection. UNHCR ensures those rights, works to find permanent, long-term solutions for refugees, and helps coordinate emergency humanitarian assistance for refugees. Increasingly, UNHCR assists other persons of concern, including IDPs.[9]

Under UNHCR's mandate, refugees may have several solutions available—voluntary repatriation, local integration in the country of first asylum, or resettlement in a third country. Finding durable solutions for refugees is receiving renewed interest, particularly in the context of Development Assistance for Refugees.[10] The so-called 4Rs— repatriation, reintegration, rehabilitation, and reconstruction—in addition to resettlement, focus on ways that the burden of sustainability can be shared with the state involved and the actors providing assistance on the ground.

Protection and Assistance for Internally Displaced Persons

The plight of the IDP has gained international recognition as a critical challenge to be addressed.[11] In 1992, the UN Secretary General defined *IDPs* as "persons who have been forced to flee their homes suddenly or unexpectedly in large numbers as a result of armed conflict, internal strife, systematic violation of human rights or natural or man-made disasters, and also who are within the territory of their country." By the end of 2009, there were an estimated 27.1 million IDPs worldwide in more than 40 countries. Most were displaced as a result of conflict or human rights violations. The number of IDPs grew dramatically with the outbreak of low-intensity internal conflict at the end of the Cold War. As those displaced in past conflicts return to their places of origin, emerging conflicts often create newly displaced populations. Access to those displaced within the borders of a particular country often is not possible, thus denying them provision of protection and assistance. IDPs face some issues and problems similar to those that challenge refugees, but they face other unique problems as well. For example, if displacement is a result of conflict, IDPs often flee to areas near or around the conflict, which makes protection and vulnerability an issue.[12]

The international community is not under the same obligation to protect and assist IDPs, who, unlike refugees, have not crossed an international border.[13] National governments have the primary responsibility for all displaced people in their territory. In many cases, however, they are unable or unwilling to fulfill this obligation. Moreover, governments themselves may be the primary perpetrators of violence and persecution and may not allow aid organizations access to displaced populations. Donors often lack the political will to fund projects that may be interpreted by national governments as intervening in internal affairs or where assistance provided may not reach the persons for whom it was originally intended. Lack of security often poses a threat to humanitarian staff.[14]

In the 1990s, the international community began to recognize the complexity of the IDP issue and to grapple with its responsibilities in situations where governments do not fulfill their obligations to protect their citizens. In 1992, the UN Commission on Human Rights asked the UN Secretary-General to appoint a representative on IDPs. A 1998 collaborative effort produced the UN Guiding Principles on Internal Displacement, which have since gained recognition and international support.[15] In the absence of a single agency dedicated to helping IDPs, the international community tries to work together with governments to address the needs of the internally displaced on a case-by-case basis. But the numbers are staggering. And even when a political agreement is reached, it can take a long time for IDPs to be able to return home.

Why Displacement Occurs

People cross borders for many different reasons—some do so voluntarily, while others are forced to flee as a matter of life or death. A key consideration is whether the movement is voluntary or involuntary. On the one hand, the impact of globalization influences the movement of people. For example, migrants often seek better opportunities—and do this legally or illegally, for the long term or on a temporary basis. There are many potential risks for migrants, such as falling victim to trafficking, smuggling, abuse, and discrimination. Migrants present both potential benefits (usually in the form of labor) and burdens (security, impact on social services, local neighborhoods, and so forth) to host countries. Although migrants seeking opportunities elsewhere face great hardship, many are seeking a new life, not fleeing their existing one. In theory, should they decide to return to their country, they would continue to receive the protection of their government. According to UNHCR, there were approximately 407,000 refugees and over 22,000 asylum seekers from Burma as of the end of 2009. Most of Burma's refugees are from one of the country's ethnic minorities that have been subjected to discriminatory and repressive treatment by the State Peace and Development Council (SPDC) and the Burmese military. Following a military offensive against separatist militias in 1984, an estimated 140,000 Karen, Karenni, and Mon people from eastern Burma fled into Thailand. Many of these refugees are now living in nine camps along the Burma-Thailand border. In 1991 and again in 2000, military assaults in southwestern Burma pushed about 250,000 Rohingyas into Bangladesh and to a lesser degree into India to escape the violence. In August 2009, an estimated 37,000 Kokang, the Burmese term for ethnic Chinese, crossed the border into Yunnan Province in China due to a military attack on the Myanmar National Democratic Alliance Army and the United Wa State Army. According to UNHCR, there are over 150,000 Burmese refugees and asylum seekers in Thailand, over 80,000 in Malaysia, approximately 200,000 in Bangladesh (mostly living outside the camps), up to 100,000 in India, and an unknown number in China.[16]

On the other hand, refugees and others displaced involuntarily face a different set of circumstances. Instead of choosing to leave and cross borders, they may be forced to leave their place of origin for a host of reasons, such as conflict, ethnic strife, human rights violations, large development projects, environmental hazards, or natural disasters.[17] The terms *push factor* and *pull factor* are often used to explain why people move. As in many refugee situations, there are push and pull factors that influence certain people to leave their country. The reasons Burmese seek refuge in Thailand (or elsewhere in the region) may vary based on individual circumstances, but despite limited access and information, it is clear that two key elements driving Burmese across the border into Thailand or out of their homes include deteriorating humanitarian conditions/increasing human rights violations and abuses perpetrated against minorities and ethnic groups.

But transborder movements are highly complex. Some also argue that political economic conditions within Burma and the economic opportunities in Thailand benefit the local Burmese military commanders, many of whom are poor and ill equipped. Furthermore, the migrants send money home to their families, bribes may keep local officers in power, and goods exported from Thailand support not only local economies but the military as well. While border crossing is considered illegal, as is cross-border illicit trade by the Thai and Burmese authorities, "it is the illegal border crossing that keeps the Burmese people from starvation and the Burmese officers from poverty or in fact staying in power."[18]

An emerging trend involves mixed migration where different groups are on the move together or where a person may change his or her status en route. Here, issues of protection and determination of status may overlap and be more problematic and complicated. In recent years, the lines of distinction between and among refugees, asylum seekers, and migrants have caused confusion and raised questions about the principles of protection for those seeking assistance and the degree of impartiality in the provision of that assistance. UNHCR describes this as a gray zone, where "people . . . are leaving a country where persecution and discrimination are unquestionably occurring and the economy is also dire. Are people leaving such countries for refugee reasons, or economic ones—or do both sets of reason fuse into one that is, in many cases, almost impossible to unravel?"[19] States concerned about the economic burden of those seeking help and the potential security issues resulting from uncontrolled migration (and raised in part because of the threat of terrorism) insist on stricter enforcement of asylum and immigration policies. Human trafficking is another means individuals may use to enter another country, either as a refugee or migrant, and could increase the risk of detention, exclusion, and lack of due process. In some instances, these problems lead to a more restrictive interpretation of the Refugee Convention and its 1967 protocol.

As populations are displaced, the issue of borders becomes hugely significant. Host countries may accommodate up to a certain threshold, and then set limits. This "push-down" effect may create a "pop-up" effect elsewhere, unless the flow eases. With no resolution to some of these situations, the displaced may end up in temporary residences for a long time. *Warehousing* has become a term of reference to describe the plight of refugees forced to remain in camps over decades. Reportedly, more than half the world's refugees have been in camps for 10 years or more. Advocates argue that for refugees, "situations of restricted mobility, enforced idleness, and dependency—their lives on indefinite hold—[are] in violation of their basic rights under the 1951 UN Refugee Convention."[20] Although UNHCR and others want to find durable solutions, protracted situations do not necessarily create the conditions for this to happen. The movement of people is therefore very much a product of conditions in the country of origin and protections available on either side of the border.

Global Displacement

UNHCR reports that by the end of 2009, the total number of forcibly displaced people worldwide was the highest since the mid-1990s: 43.3 million, which included 15.2 million refugees, 983,000 asylum seekers, and 27.1 million IDPs. About 26 million of these people (10.4 million refugees and 15.6 million IDPs) were receiving some form of protection or assistance from UNHCR. In addition, UNHCR identified 6.6 million stateless persons, although it is estimated that the overall number worldwide may be closer to 12 million. The number of new claims for asylum and refugee status registered in 2009 totaled 922,000.[21] Approximately 251,500 refugees voluntarily repatriated in 2009, which is the lowest number since 1990, whereas 2.2 million IDPs returned to their homes, representing the highest number of IDP returns in a decade.

Humanitarian crises are numerous and as varied in profile as in the causes that bring them about—some gain attention that is sustained for a period of time in the eyes of the international community; others remain the so-called forgotten crises and never reach the world stage. Still others mediate between the two, rising and falling with a spike in events or deteriorating conditions, but usually becoming victim to fatigue in world attention.

Displacement Trends in Southern Asia

Migration has historically been significant in South and Southeast Asia and remains a complex issue. As practically all regional states became independent after 1947, millions of people moved to avoid persecution, escape war, or meet basic needs through opportunities for work. In South Asia alone, the number in the past half-century is thought to be about 30 million people.[22] With well-established networks in the region, people have continued to move out of economic necessity, because of natural disasters, or to escape conflict and civil unrest either within their country or internationally across borders. Some move for temporary, seasonal migration, while others move for more long-term, permanent settlement. Recent trends have been influenced by globalization and trade, growth in communication technology, and other factors related to economic need and employment opportunities, and increasingly, environmental degradation, land scarcity, and population growth. Trafficking in persons has become a significant problem, although underreporting makes it difficult to assess the full extent and impact:

> The emergence of nation-states in 1947 also resulted in the beginning of impositions of various procedures on people's mobility in South Asia for the first time. However, these could not altogether stop the flow of people within and outside the sub-continent. The "natural integrated labour market" of South Asia on the one hand, and limited, state capacity to monitor and control borders effectively on the other, remained as major factors in the management of population movement in the region, with far-reaching consequences on the economies and societies.[23]

Irregular migration, in the absence of policies that allow regular temporary migration for work, such as seasonal employment, has also become a significant issue. Forced migration due to natural disasters, large-scale development projects, and conflict remains a problem. Newly emerging trends see more women joining those on the move and more circular migration, where people who leave eventually return to their countries, often with new skills. Internal displacement in South Asia in general is an enormous problem.[24] Francis Deng, Representative of the UN Secretary-General on Internally Displaced Persons from 1992 to 2004, stated that:

> Asia's list of problems calling for urgent attention must place internal conflicts highest in the order of priorities, followed by human rights violations, dictatorial or authoritarian systems of governance, and flawed economic policies, all of which are closely interconnected in a chain of cause and effect. These factors and the related issues of responsibility are all germane to the crisis of internal displacement. . . . overwhelmingly, the main cause of displacement is civil wars or armed insurgencies, which force large numbers to leave their homes or areas of residence.[25]

It is estimated that more than half of the 4 to 5 million internally displaced in Asia are displaced in Southeast Asia.

Southwest China, northern Burma, Thailand, and northeast India and Bangladesh all have borderland communities that impact and define the identity, culture, economy, and status of the people living there. With the fixed and well-defined boundaries captured in modern lines of delineation, the communities that existed within the borderlands for centuries are now divided among different states. But borderland communities continue to thrive; in some places, borders remain fluid or at least permeable, and transnational linkages continue. For the populations on the borders between Burma and Thailand, a complex web of interrelationships is also at play.

Burma's Displaced Populations

Conflict and migration among the many diverse peoples in Burma have punctuated the country's history. Multiparty elections to the National Assembly in 1990 resulted in a decisive victory for the main opposition party, the National League for Democracy (NLD). However, the SPDC, which had been in power since 1988, refused to accept the results of the election. The opposition leader, Aung San Suu Kyi, was under house arrest for much of the time since the elections. Throughout the reign of the SPDC, hundreds of her supporters were arrested. According to a range of sources, including the U.S. Government, human rights groups, relief organizations, and news reports, the SPDC has conducted a campaign of persecution against Burmese minorities, causing many to flee its acts of repression and persecution. Violations include acts of religious persecution, sexual violence against women, human trafficking, forced labor, development-induced relocation, and forced relocation as an instrument of control. Military expenditures have continued to be a priority, with little support given to public services. According to the World Health Organization, one-third of children under 5 suffer from malnutrition. Armed opposition is confined to the three ethnic groups that operate along Burma's border with Thailand: the Shan State Army, the Karen National Union, and the Karenni National Progressive Party. The situation in Burma has triggered a flow of refugees over the eastern border into Thailand and elsewhere in the region. According to UNHCR, in 2009 Burma produced one of the largest numbers of refugees (206,650) and people in refugee-like situations (200,019) in Southeast Asia, but the actual number could be much higher.[26] This chapter looks at two aspects of Burma's displaced population prior to Cyclone Nargis: Burmese refugees in Thailand and Burmese IDPs.

Profile of Burmese Refugees in Thailand

Representing one of the largest groups of refugees in East Asia, refugees of Burmese origin in Thailand (as well as in Bangladesh) come from a variety of ethnic groups that have fled attacks on their villages by Burma's army and warlords. These ethnic groups have reportedly been subjected to forced labor, use as human mine sweepers and bullet shields, forced relocation, conscription into the army as porters or soldiers, rape, mass killing, extortion, and denial of basic human needs, which has led to a large internally displaced population as well. Although some experts estimated that there are more than 100 ethnic groups in Burma, 7 groups—the Shan, Karen, Karenni, Mon, Chin, Arakan, and Kachin—have been reportedly targeted by SPDC troops, in part because they continue to seek a measure of autonomy.[27]

In a move to consolidate power, the SPDC periodically has signed ceasefire agreements with armed insurgent groups associated with several of the ethnic groups demanding some autonomy, creating a mini-border within a border. The homelands of non-Burman ethnic groups are mostly along Burma's borders, described as forming a horse-shoe around the central part of the country. This idea of a center and periphery within a country, which may be more of an Asian concept (compared with the Western idea of a frontier), also translates into social and economic status. Poverty exists throughout the country, but those in the border areas are most vulnerable. Ongoing Burmese military offensives against Karen insurgents highlight the ongoing struggle within and across Burma's internal borders. Burma's population is estimated to be 52 million.[28] It is believed that there are possibly 500,000 to 1 million IDPs within Burma, mostly as result of ethnic fighting, poor economic policies, deteriorating economic conditions, or forced relocation. These people can be thought of as crossing internal "frontiers" that may have greater significance to them than international borders.[29]

UNHCR estimates that around 3 million asylum seekers have sought refuge in Thailand in the past three decades. Burma presents the largest source: Based on official registration numbers compiled in 2007, 140,000 to 155,000 refugees were estimated to be in the nine refugee camps recognized by the Thai government on the Thai-Burma border, which extends for 2,401 kilometers (see map 8–1).[30] Approximately 128,500 were registered as refugees, and the rest were pending a decision on their status by Thailand's Provincial Admissions Boards. Some refugees have been in camps for 20 years.[31] Other asylum seekers are thought to be in urban areas. In addition, refugees and asylum seekers representing groups (mostly from other bordering states) live elsewhere in the country.[32]

The Thailand Burma Border Consortium (TBBC), a registered charity in the United Kingdom, is a nonprofit nongovernmental organization (NGO) that is the umbrella for nine international NGOs that provide humanitarian relief. TBBC estimates that the Burmese state of origin of the registered refugee population breaks down as follows: 62 percent Karen, 13 percent Karenni, 9 percent Tenasserim, 5 percent Mon, 5 percent Pegu, 4 percent unknown, and 2 percent other (including Chin, Kachin, Irrawaddy, Magwe, Mandalay, Rakhine, Rangoon, Sagaing, and Shan).

Map 8–1. Refugee and Resettlement Sites along Thai-Burma Border

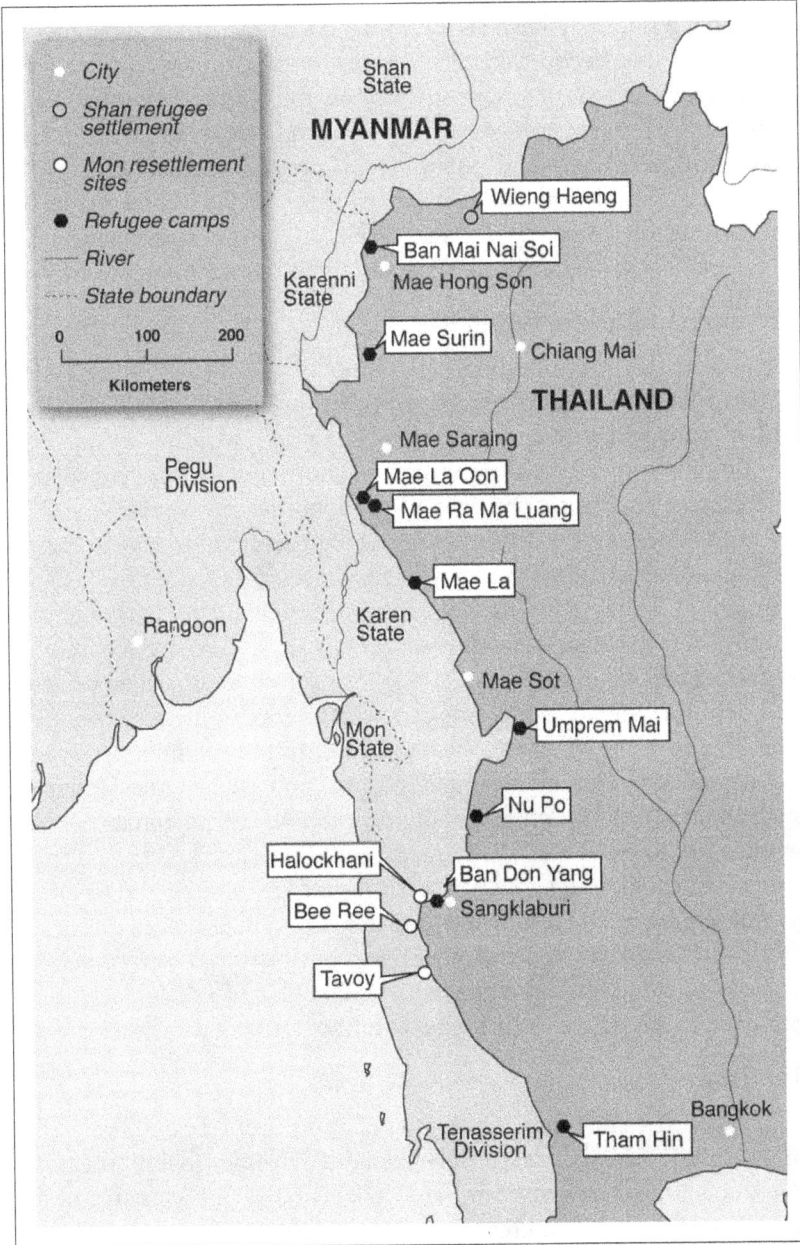

In addition to the registered refugees, another 1 million or more Burmese may be illegal migrants in Thailand.[33] It is unclear how many from this group may have valid claims to asylum. Other Burmese are thought to have become illegal migrant workers in Bangladesh, India, China, and Malaysia. It is also unclear how many may have valid claims to asylum. Humanitarian needs include food, water, sanitation, basic household assistance, and public health programs. According to the European Commission's Humanitarian Office, the situation for refugees fleeing outside Burma and those displaced within Burma itself is a "silent crisis" that demonstrates increasing humanitarian needs.[34]

Urban versus Border Refugees

In addition to questions of autonomy and displacement within Burma, distinctions about status must be made in Thailand as well, which again points to the question of boundaries within borders that can directly impact the degree of protection and assistance available. There are two distinct refugee groups: border refugees and urban refugees. The border refugees are typically permitted to stay in camps for humanitarian reasons. The urban refugees are thought by the government of Thailand to include many political dissidents, although this group also has refugees who did not feel safe at the border. For a number of years, Thailand has been tightening the restrictions on urban refugees and defining anyone living outside the camps as an illegal immigrant. The Thai government has also wanted to control the number of refugees in Bangkok and their involvement in illegal political activities or crimes such as drug dealing. With the support of UNHCR, an agreement was worked out to move some urban refugees to the camps. If considered a "person of concern" by UNHCR, then the refugee is supposed to return to and register at one of the refugee camps. UNHCR divides this urban group into two subcategories: those refugees who would have protection at the border and those refugees who flee because of a secondary fear of persecution from Thai security forces at the border itself.

Thailand's Response to Burmese Refugees

Countries that host refugee populations over an extended period of time argue that refugees must be contained in order to limit the negative impact they may have on the local economy. Governments of developing countries are increasingly worried that they are burdened with a disproportionate share of refugees, which they view as flooding the labor market and placing pressure on already strained social services. Critics contend that confining refugees to camps leads to increased crime and illicit market activities. Still others suggest that allowing refugees to participate in local markets is advantageous to local economies.

Thailand has long been a "pull" for economic and political refugees, particularly from the neighboring countries of Laos, Cambodia, and, most prominently, Burma. Displaced populations of ethnic minorities from Southeast Asia have sought refuge across Thailand's long borders, often attracted by relatively loose immigration controls and lenient treatment by Thai authorities. Thailand is not a signatory to the 1951 UN Convention Relating to the Status of Refugees or the 1967 protocol, and the term *refugee* and the protection mandates recognized under international law are therefore not formally recognized in Thailand. A strong network of international humanitarian organizations exists in Thailand to assist these populations.

Thailand has responded to the population flows in different ways over time, with give and take occurring between the government, UNHCR, and human rights organizations over the criteria for determining refugee status, areas of protection, and provision of services. Successive Thai governments have expressed frustration with this continuing presence and periodically have clamped down on the incoming asylum seekers. Often, this response relates to Bangkok's wish to maintain strong political relationships with other regional governments. Asylum seekers are technically viewed as illegal immigrants, although the legal issues are often circumvented through the use of informal references—*temporary shelters* instead of *refugee camps* or *displaced persons fleeing fighting* rather than *refugees*.

With no access to Burma, UNHCR is limited in its repatriation efforts. It has three field offices in Thailand and has worked with the Thai government since 1998 to register and protect those in refugee camps along the Burmese border, which were first established in Thailand in 1984. The camps were intended for temporary use and are not considered suitable for permanent habitation. According to UNHCR, refugee status in the camps is regulated by ad hoc administrative procedures, although the Thai government maintains ultimate authority. Provincial Admission Boards administer admission to the camps using criteria similar to the 1951 Refugee Convention.

Thailand has been generally cooperative in helping refugees, but does not want to become an indefinite host, nor does it want to absorb those Burmese who do not qualify as refugees. The Thai government views Burma as presenting the most immediate source of refugee problems and at different times has cooperated with the resettlement of large numbers of Burmese in third countries.[35] Until an agreement can be reached with Burma and it is safe for the Burmese to return, Thailand has basically accepted the influx of refugees on humanitarian grounds. Reportedly, the Thai government takes pride in its humanitarian response to refugees fleeing neighboring countries. However, it is also feeling the strain from the increasing numbers of refugees and migrants, which raises concerns about whether it has the capacity to continue to accommodate new arrivals. The United States has been encouraging the Thai government to permit UNHCR to continue its work with refugees or to establish a Thai-managed screening mechanism in consultation with UNHCR.

Internally Displaced Persons in Burma

In Asia, the problem of IDPs is considered an internal, domestic matter. In most cases, states are committed to the principle of sovereignty, and thus IDPs are not thought to be a matter of regional concern.[36] There is much that is not known about the plight of IDPs in Burma, but the situation is apparently one of the worst in Asia. Lack of access has been a barrier to adequate information on needs and a barrier to the delivery of assistance. It is believed the situation continues to worsen. While humanitarian needs of the displaced vary, most people in Burma live in poverty and lack adequate health care and education. Many struggle to meet their daily needs. The Internal Displacement Monitoring Centre and others report that the largest group of IDPs is found in eastern Burma in the border states with Thailand, primarily among the Karen, but also including the Karenni, Shan, and Mon. Total numbers of displaced range from 500,000 to 1 million, but an accurate figure is not known. IDPs live in temporary sites, in hiding, or in relocation sites. The government's strategy of social control is to use forced assimilation and repression of movements of autonomy and independence through displacement of populations, burning of fields and crops, destruction of villages, and perpetration of human rights abuses and atrocities. Displacement by development is also increasingly a factor. Lack of food, shelter, and medical care is common, while protection and assistance are inadequate or not available. And the military junta continues to deny there is any sort of humanitarian crisis or need.

Present Outlook on International Assistance

When responding to humanitarian crises, international assistance efforts vary in size but are typically complex because they require coordination among different actors. Those responding to humanitarian crises include UN agencies, international organizations, intergovernmental entities, NGOs, private voluntary organizations, and bilateral donors. The operational environment is another critical factor that greatly affects the provision and effectiveness of humanitarian assistance. Lack of security and political instability often pose challenges in the response to these crises. When conditions on the ground limit access, the delivery of humanitarian assistance and protection monitoring is also substantially reduced. Difficult conditions also considerably increase the safety risk and expense of a relief operation. In addition to situations involving escalating conflicts, border disputes, and heightened tensions, natural disasters also contribute to major population movements. These same conditions may hamper the sustainable return and reintegration of returnees where inadequate services and poor development options limit the number who can be repatriated.

In cases such as Burma, without consideration of the response to Cyclone Nargis, international assistance has maintained certain services over time, many informally, but this by itself cannot create conditions for a long-term solution.[37] For example, the United States has been providing assistance for refugees along the Burmese border since the 1990s. It does not provide any bilateral assistance to Burma, and sanctions against the junta continue. U.S. contributions to assist with the Burmese refugee situation come from both the U.S. Agency for International Development and the State Department's Bureau for Population, Refugees and Migration. This U.S. Government funding provides support for programs such as humanitarian assistance, food security, health care (including support to combat infectious disease), and education to Burmese refugees, refugees not in camps, migrants, IDPs along the border but within Burma, and ethnic minorities. U.S.

funding is also provided to international organizations, principally UNHCR and the International Committee of the Red Cross, to support their programs in East Asia, some of which include activities focused on Burmese refugees and IDPs. In the past, its activities in Thailand have included helping to provide access to asylum seekers in border camps and ensuring that procedures of admittance and registration by the Thai government comply with international standards. Other activities are related to antitrafficking in persons, migrant rights, HIV/AIDS prevention, and democracy-building.

Some have called for increasing aid to those providing emergency relief for both IDPs and refugees, despite hesitation by governments and donors over the actions of the Burmese government. A number of experts have articulated concerns that once aid agencies are operating in Burma, they will be reluctant to criticize the government in order to protect access. Others are concerned that humanitarian assistance could improve living conditions and mask the Burmese government's policies or enable it to take credit for improvements in living conditions. Still others fear that without adequate monitoring and enforcement, resources could be diverted (perhaps to the military) and not provided to those for whom they were intended. Discussions with the Burmese government ebb and flow. In late December 2007, Charles Petrie, the former UN resident and humanitarian coordinator, was asked by the Burmese government to leave his post, in part because he publicly linked the September 2007 protests with frustration of deteriorating daily living conditions.

Formulating policy toward Burma that goes beyond the band-aid of humanitarian assistance can be characterized as deciding among a range of poor options. Future policies will likely have to integrate a combination of approaches—from the role of intergovernmental organizations such as the European Union and a call for a clearer common position on Burma with particular sanctions on investment, to the role of the Security Council and its potential impact on humanitarian and human rights crisis in Burma, to the part the UN Human Rights Special Envoy could play.[38] Regional frameworks, such as initiatives to address migration management, trafficking, and forced displacement, and international agreements such as the Refugee Convention, Guidelines on IDPs, Trafficking Convention, and Human Rights Conventions, all can play a part when productive communication is possible and when the international community is prepared to stand together to denounce the policies of a particular government or to enforce the consequences. But political will has not stood the test of time so far on Burma, and the citizens caught within its borders have little recourse but the one millions have already tried: move or flee.

Borders and the Responsibility to Protect

While the UN Charter obligates members to promote respect for human rights and asserts as a primary purpose the promotion of human rights and fundamental freedoms for all, it also recognizes the doctrine of nonintervention. Thus, article 2, paragraph 7, of the UN Charter states that "nothing in the Charter authorizes the United Nations to interfere in matters which are essentially within the domestic jurisdiction of any state." Because of the traditional approach toward human rights as a matter exclusively within the domestic jurisdiction of sovereign states, Article 2 (7) has been viewed by some as an obstacle to the implementation of the human rights provisions of the charter. States accused of human rights violations frequently cite this provision in response to criticisms by other states (or international organizations) relating to human rights conditions within their borders.

However, many advocates argue that there is substantial justification for state responsibility for the protection of the human rights of individuals and for some level of "interference" by the international community on behalf of those whose rights have been infringed. Activity for the protection of human rights has been constantly subjected to tension between state sovereignty as protected by the doctrine of nonintervention and state obligations to protect human rights and fundamental freedoms. Increasingly, protection of populations affected by conflict within a country is seen as partly the responsibility of the international community. For example, some might argue that the Burmese government is a threat to its own people and that Burma has violated its responsibility to protect its own citizens, thus warranting action by the international community and the UN Security Council.

At the 2005 UN World Summit, the "Responsibility to Protect" concept was introduced, putting forward the idea that each state has a responsibility to protect its people from genocide, war crimes, ethnic cleansing, and crimes against humanity, and that human rights violations committed in one state are the concern of all states.[39] It is an agreement in principle that speaks to the obligations of a state to protect its own people and the obligations of all states when that fails, but it does not make action easy or even probable. Lee Feinstein, senior fellow for U.S. foreign policy and international law at the Council on Foreign Relations, observed that:

> Adoption of the responsibility to protect begins to resolve the historic tension between human rights and states' rights in favor of the individual. Where the state had been erected to protect the individual from outsiders, the responsibility to protect erects a fallback where individuals have a claim to seek assistance from outsiders in order to substitute for or protect them from the state.[40]

Still, translating principle into action remains an enormous challenge, as the case of Burma so aptly demonstrates.

Conclusion

In a discussion paper on dealing with Burma's sovereignty, Jack Dunford, director of the Thailand Burmese Border Consortium, stated:

> It is all too little and too slow in terms of the immediate situation. There are enormous unmet humanitarian needs. Hundreds of thousands of people are suffering. Social fabric is being destroyed. Hatred is being fueled. Land is being laid waste. People are becoming refugees. The damage being done today will take years to undo and will cost an enormous amount of money even when change comes. The Guiding Principles seem to offer no guidance for emergency humanitarian situations such as this where the Sovereign State refuses to cooperate and is seemingly impervious to all pressure.[41]

It remains the case that the feasibility of any sustainable and voluntary return of Burmese refugees and IDPs must be based on the reality of conditions on the ground, which so far have not changed.

In an increasingly globalized world, some have argued that borders are becoming less significant, and that in the future, they may be irrelevant. But this view denies the plight and the often critical circumstances of those who are displaced. For individuals or groups who are fleeing their country of origin and trying to cross borders to potentially safer surroundings, nothing is further from the truth. Globalization has not changed the significance of borders when it comes to the movement of people. Borders may provide protection if the host country is willing or the protection of a refugee camp offers safe haven. But as the Burma case demonstrates, borders can also be a barrier—to protection, to escape, often to life. Those caught within the boundaries of conflict or at the hands of a repressive regime with no means of crossing into another country may face a rigid, unforgiving, perilous journey, and many go into hiding to avoid a worse outcome. Internal displacement in these circumstances offers no protection, only barriers. And the very walls of protection in safe havens such as refugee camps may over time feel like barriers of a different kind—barriers to acceptance in a new country and the possibility of a better life. Refugee camps are not meant to be permanent solutions, but when they become that by default—as in the case of Burmese living in Thailand—they can also be seen as temporary barriers that cannot be changed until the countries that control the borders provide options to ensure protection and freedom.

Movement of people is a complex issue with many implications. Those who are forced to move face unique challenges. Borders by definition are significant because they so clearly mark the place where one country ends and another begins. As is the case for hundreds of thousands of Burmese, borders mark the place that for some may be a barrier, and for others, a possible step toward protection.[42]

Notes

[1] In July 1989, the State Law and Order Restoration Council changed Burma's name to Myanmar. The United Nations and others recognized the change, while the United States, Australia, and some European countries did not. The opposition boycotts the name change as a form of protest against human rights abuses.

[2] Burma is the largest producer of methamphetamines in the world and also trades opium, the production of which jumped almost 50 percent in 2007 over previous years.

[3] There are some experts who hold the view that globalization will only continue to benefit and strengthen the ruling junta. China, for example, invests in Burma's natural resources and reportedly supplies the regime with arms and international political protection.

[4] United Nations High Commissioner on Refugees (UNHCR), "Refugee or Migrant? Why it Matters," *Refugees* 4, no. 148 (2007), 31. The Rohingyas are a largely Muslim minority from Burma's Arakan state (now renamed Bakhine state) and have been considered stateless since 1948, when the Burmese government claimed this group of people were recent migrants from the Indian subcontinent and did not qualify for citizenship under the constitution. Many have fled to Bangladesh in different cycles of mass departures over the past several decades. As of 2007, in Bangladesh there were 27,000 Rohingyas in two UNHCR-run camps and an estimated 200,000 more Rohingyas of undetermined status living among the local population.

[5] UNHCR was established by UN General Assembly Resolution 428 (V) of December 14, 1950, and made operational in 1951.

[6] UNHCR was established to help resettle European refugees after World War II. The 1951 convention limits the definition of *refugees* to those created by events occurring prior to 1951. In response to the emergence of large refugee movements since 1951, the 1967 protocol incorporates the measures included in the 1951 convention but imposes no time or geographical limits. For texts, see <www.unhcr.org/protect/3c0762ea4.html>.

[7] Text of the 1951 United Nations Convention Relating to the Status of Refugees, chapter 1, article 1 (A) 2.

[8] Ibid., article 33.1. The issue of non-refoulement is also considered part of customary international law.

[9] Enforcement of the Refugee Convention can present challenges. For example, the national laws of a state may not be developed sufficiently to allow full implementation of its provisions. Often, becoming a party to the convention is a first step, and UNHCR serves as an important resource. Sometimes, the convention may contradict bilateral agreements between states. From UNHCR's point of view, international law overrides other bilateral agreements, but governments may not agree. UNHCR may try to assist in creating a solution, or states may use ad hoc procedures to determine whether an individual has a well-grounded fear of persecution and thus is protected from deportation. UNHCR often works with governments behind the scenes in asylum cases to push for application of the principles of the Refugee Convention and protection of the rights of the individual, even though there may not be agreement on legal jurisdiction.

[10] This UNHCR concept is discussed in "Rethinking Durable Solutions," in *The State of the World's Refugees 2006: Human Displacement in the New Millennium*, April 19, 2006, available at <www.unhcr.org/4444afcc0.html>.

[11] Francis M. Deng and Roberta Cohen, *Masses in Flight: The Global Crisis of Internal Displacement* (Washington, DC: Brookings Institution Press, 1998).

[12] For more information, see Khalid Koser, "Addressing Internally Displaced Persons in a Peace Process: Why and How?" Brookings Institution, December 14, 2007, available at <www.brookings.edu/speeches/2007/1214_peace_koser.aspx?rssid=koserk>.

[13] UN agencies and the UN Secretary-General have looked to UNHCR to provide assistance to certain displaced populations, though they do not fall within UNHCR's original mandate. By default, UNHCR has provided assistance and some protection to internally displaced persons (IDPs), but it has argued that it lacks the capacity and resources to cope systematically with the needs of IDPs in addition to its refugee caseload. As of 2009, UNHCR offered assistance to more than 15 million IDPs throughout the world. Already under critical budgetary pressure in providing assistance and protection to refugees, UNHCR and other international entities face a significant challenge in addressing the global IDP situation. For background, see "Internally Displaced Persons: Questions and Answers," UNHCR, 2005.

[14] Ibid.

[15] How the global IDP situation will be addressed remains to be seen. Even as states reportedly accept broader interpretations of international law, such as the 1951 convention and the 1967 protocol, through an interagency collaborative approach, UNHCR will likely play a leading role in addressing the plight of this large and vulnerable population, along with other UN agencies that will be assigned specific sectoral responsibilities. See "Internally Displaced Persons: Institutional Arrangements: the 'collaborative approach,'" in *State of the World's Refugees 2006*.

[16] Refugee statistics are from conversation with UNHCR officials and UNHCR's Web site, available at <www.unhcr.org>.

[17] It should be noted that some individuals may be uprooted and move due to severe hardship and lack of resources and for this reason are perhaps considered migrants, but could technically be IDPs.

[18] Niti Pawakapan, "Crossing is Illegal, Money is Not: Intertwined Linkage of Burmese Migrants, Burmese Military Officers and Thai Traders," Social Science Research Council, accessed at <http://programs.ssrc.org/southasia/researchnetworks/borderlands/pawakapan/printable.html>.

[19] "Refugee or Migrant? Why it Matters," 2. See also UNHCR's Ten Point Plan of Action that addresses some of the difficulties that emerge with overlaps in migration and refugee movements at <www.unhcr.org>.

[20] Reportedly, more than half of the world's refugees fell into the warehousing category and are being denied what some argue are the basic rights afforded them by the 1951 Convention Relating to the Status of Refugees. Such rights include freedom to be gainfully employed, freedom of movement, due process, and access to certain public services, such as health and education. See for example, Merrill Smith, "Warehousing Refugees: A Denial of Rights, a Waste of Humanity," *World Refugee Survey*, 2004, 38–56.

[21] UNHCR, Division of Programme Support and Management, 2009 Global Trends, Refugees, Asylum-seekers, Returnees, Internally Displaced and Stateless Persons, June 15, 2010.

[22] For information on UNHCR's role in relief operations in Asia, see "Rupture in South Asia," in the *State of the World's Refugees 2006*. See also "Refugee or Migrant? Why it Matters."

[23] Md. Shahidul Haque, "Migration Trends and Patterns in South Asia and Management Approaches and Initiatives," Regional Seminar on the Social Implications of International Migration, August 24–26, 2005, Bangkok, Thailand, 3.

[24] See Paula Banerjee et al., eds., *Internal Displacement in South Asia* (New Delhi: Sage Publications, 2005).

[25] Francis M. Deng, "Internal Displacement: A Global Overview," *Refugee Survey Quarterly* 19, no. 2 (2000).

[26] "Refugee or Migrant? Why It Matters," 31.

[27] According to the Internal Displacement Monitoring Centre, many ethnic groups originally fought for independence but now want autonomy under a new federal structure.

[28] Estimates of Burma's population range from 47 million to 53 million. The figure cited was used by the United Nations Office for the Coordination of Humanitarian Affairs in December 2007. According to Refugees International, no census has been taken since 1983. All displacement figures must be taken as estimates due to poor security, lack of access, and ongoing movement of people. The exact numbers cannot be verified as independent monitoring has not been authorized.

[29] In many cases, internal displacement may also have other impacts on the populations affected. For example, in Burma, crossing from one ethnic, linguistic, cultural, or religious region to another within the state may seem more significant than crossing an international border. Conversely, physically crossing an international border, if groups on either side share ethnicity, language, culture, or religion and have more in common, may have less of an impact in terms of group identity and sense of belonging.

[30] Based on registration completed by UNHCR in 2007. This range draws on estimates from UNHCR's registration and figures provided by the Thailand Burma Border Consortium, July 2007. In 2010, the number of refugees is still estimated to be approximately 140,000.

[31] This chapter does not address the issues that arise in protracted refugee situations, such as the citizenship status of children born in camps.

[32] UNHCR, "Analysis of Gaps in Protection Capacity: Thailand," November 2006.

[33] In 2010, it is estimated that 2 million vulnerable Burmese may be residing elsewhere in Thailand.

[34] European Commission's Humanitarian Aid Department, "Burma-Myanmar: A Silent Crisis," 2004, available at <ec.europa.eu/echo/pdf_files/leaflets/burma_en.pdf>.

[35] Approximately 5,000 Burmese from camps were resettled in 2006, mainly to the United States, Canada, Australia, Sweden, the Netherlands, or Finland.

[36] For useful background information, see UNHCR, Centre for Documentation and Research, "Internal Displacement in Asia," *Refugee Survey Quarterly* 19, no. 2 (2000).

[37] UN Office for the Coordination of Humanitarian Affairs, "Myanmar: Aid in a Tight Space," December 18, 2007.

[38] On December 16, 2005, the UN Security Council had its first briefing on the situation in Burma and the impact of the situation on the region.

[39] General Assembly Resolution 60/1 and confirmed by the Security Council Resolution 1674 (2006).

[40] Lee Feinstein, "Darfur and Beyond: What is Needed to Prevent Mass Atrocities," Council on Foreign Relations Special Report, No. 22, January 2007.

[41] Jack Dunford, "Principles Relating to Humanitarian Assistance: Dealing with Sovereignty: Burma," *Refugee Survey Quarterly* 19, no. 2 (2000), 163.

Chapter 9

Center-Periphery Relations and Borders in Western New Guinea

Patricia O'Brien and Bruce Vaughn

Border dynamics both within the region of Western New Guinea and between this peripheral region and its center in Jakarta are particularly interesting for several reasons. Borders drawn by the Dutch and the Republic of Indonesia have defined the region of Western New Guinea as part of larger political units of very different ethnic/linguistic/social and political character. Internal borders have been created within Western New Guinea to facilitate rule from Jakarta, and further subdivisions of the territory are being contemplated. Many in Western New Guinea continue to prefer greater autonomy despite efforts by Indonesia to integrate the territory more closely into the Republic of Indonesia, while a minority has fought for secession from Indonesia. An assessment of the importance of borders to the people of Western New Guinea as well as to the political powers that have asserted their control over the territory concludes that the borders, which delineate political and military control, have been, and remain, extremely important in this peripheral region. The peripheral nature, both geographically and politically, of the territory's position relative to Jakarta is also instrumental to understanding its relative underdevelopment and the condition of its people.

Introduction

The region of Western New Guinea exists on the eastern periphery of the state of Indonesia. It is inhabited by a Melanesian people similar to the people of Papua New Guinea (PNG) and is situated on the western half of the island of New Guinea. New Guinea's tribal groups are thought to speak some 15 percent of the world's languages. The indigenous Melanesian people have a culture dating back, by some estimates, 40,000 years. This background differs significantly from the Malay character found on the rest of the Indonesian archipelago.

Western New Guinea at a Glance

Population: 2.3 million people, or approximately 1 percent of the total population of Indonesia

Racial/ethnic backgrounds: Approximately 1.2 million people are Melanesian with the balance having transmigrated from Malay and parts of Indonesia

Religion: Christian, Muslim, and Animist

Languages: With over 245 different tribal peoples, the inhabitants of the island of New Guinea speak approximately 15 percent of the world's languages

Area: Some 422,000 square kilometers, which represents 21 percent of the land mass of Indonesia

Location: Between the Equator and 10 degrees south latitude

Topography: Coastal forests and swamps, central mountains, and highlands

Key resources: Gold, silver, copper, natural gas, oil, timber, and marine resources

Administrative units: Currently divided into the two main provinces of Papua and West Papua, with plans contemplated to further divide the province of Papua into two additional provinces, establishing a total of four provinces

Western New Guinea has wide-ranging topography. A central mountain chain contains peaks as high as 4,884 meters as well as permanent glaciers, though these are melting because of climate change. The region also has vast northern and southern coastal lowlands consisting of rainforests and wetlands that contain some of the world's largest mangrove forests. Research has shown that coastal West Papua was incorporated into a pre-European world of archipelagic East Indies. In addition to significant trade relationships, "wars, depopulation, migration and the exchange of great numbers of prisoners of war and slaves by eastern Indonesian and local traders and dignitaries" took place, as well as the transmittance of a wide variety of trade goods into the interior of Papua.[1]

A discussion of the region of Western New Guinea necessitates a definition of how this term is used.[2] It is used here in a geographic sense to refer to the western half of the island of New Guinea, which is the world's second largest island. This term for the region is less commonly used than the Republic of Indonesia's former name for the territory, Irian Jaya, or West Papua. West Papua has generally become the preferred term used by activists sympathetic to the condition of Papuans inhabiting Western New Guinea, many of whom are thought to seek increased autonomy from central rule from Jakarta. To further complicate the issue, the government of Indonesia has divided the territory into two provinces now known as Papua and West Papua.[3] This chapter employs the term Western New Guinea because it is geographically neutral and is not associated with either the government or advocate positions regarding the territory.

The Borders of Western New Guinea

Cartographic representations of the borders of Western New Guinea have gone through several phases. The Dutch extended their political and economic influence over much of what was to be known as Netherlands New Guinea during the period 1895 to 1962. During a brief United Nations (UN) transition period from 1962 to 1963, it was known as West New Guinea. The area was known as West Irian and was initially under Indonesian control from 1963 to 1973 and later was known as Irian Jaya from 1973 to 2000. In 2003, then-President Megawati Sukarnoputri directed that the province be subdivided into Papua, Central Irian Jaya, and West Irian Jaya provinces. A government for West Irian Jaya, the name of which was changed to West Papua on April 18, 2007, was installed in 2003, but the Indonesian courts stopped any further subdivision of the Papua province into Papua and Central Irian Jaya at that time due to the controversial nature of the proposal and its contravention of the Special Autonomy Law for the region. The creation of West Irian Jaya, now known as West Papua, by Megawati's government was allowed to stand. Manokwari is the provincial capital of West Papua, while Jayapura is the capital of Papua.

The change in name for the territory and increasing attempts to subdivide the region are likely due to a combination of factors. Some are motivated by a desire to more firmly assert Indonesia's political control over this vast and diverse area. To others, it represents a peripheral region rich in natural resources with few people, most of whom are not viewed in the same light as the majority Malay populations who inhabit the rest of the Indonesian archipelago. The fact that this mineral-and timber-rich region constitutes 21 percent of the land mass and approximately 1 percent of the population of Indonesia demonstrates the potential development opportunities of Western New Guinea for the state of Indonesia.

Internal borders now divide the territory of Western New Guinea into smaller administrative units to facilitate rule from the center in Jakarta. Many indigenous Papuans reportedly view the division of Western New Guinea as a divide-and-rule tactic aimed at thwarting efforts by Papuan separatists. The split also casts doubt over whether the Special Autonomy Law would pertain to West Papua.[4]

The Indonesian house of representatives initiated legislation in early 2008 to divide Papua into South Papua, Central Papua, and Barat Daya provinces and to recognize West Papua. This would have divided the region into four administrative provinces as opposed to the current two provinces. Such moves would cost the state money and have yet to demonstrate a benefit to the people. They have reportedly been opposed by President Susilo Bambang Yudhoyono for these reasons. Governor Barnabas Suebu was thought to oppose such initiatives on the basis that Western New Guinea does not have the resources to staff new administrative units.[5] The recently proposed administrative units would appear to separate the central highlands—the area of greatest concern for security forces—from other parts of Western New Guinea where lucrative mining and hydrocarbon projects are under way.

Maintaining the territorial integrity of the Republic of Indonesia as the successor state of the Dutch East Indies is of considerable importance, and Jakarta has been sensitive to any move that might encourage the secession of Western New Guinea. Secession might lead to a further breakup of the Indonesian state, a diverse nation comprising thousands of islands and much ethnic and linguistic diversity. The Indonesian archipelago has over 17,000 islands, spans an area of ocean 5,000 kilometers across, and is strategically located between the Indian Ocean and the Southwest Pacific. Concerns about secession and state instability were heightened in the period after the financial crisis of 1997. The successful breakaway of East Timor beginning in 1999, a former Portuguese colony that had been incorporated into Indonesia in 1975, made this issue even more sensitive. The relative weakness of the center in the period of Reformasi (reform) following former President

Suharto's rule also added to fears of secession. The growing strength of the increasingly democratic state of Indonesia, particularly after the elections of 2004, could provide the basis for a more inclusive approach to Western New Guinea.

While most border concerns relative to Western New Guinea pertain to assertions of control over the territory by either the Dutch or the Indonesians, there are some international dimensions to the region's external frontier as well. The region shares a land border only with Papua New Guinea to the east. In the mid-1980s, Australian Defence Minister Kim Beazley was reportedly concerned that Indonesia would launch an invasion across the PNG border.[6] At times, the Organisasi Papua Merdeka (OPM), or Free Papua Movement, was thought to have operated out of sanctuaries on the PNG side of the border with Indonesia.[7] Problems remain over the disposition of Indonesian Papuan refugees living in and around Papua New Guinea's national capital, Port Moresby, some of whom arrived in PNG over 30 years ago.[8] There have also been claims that forces in Jakarta have sponsored Islamic militia groups in Papua and that they have been placed along the border of PNG.[9] This could be destabilizing to inter-communal harmony between the largely Muslim Malay transmigrants and the indigenous Melanesian Christians and animists.[10]

Dutch New Guinea Colonial Borders

The division of the island of New Guinea into separate colonial entities dates to the early 19th century. In 1828, the Netherlands expanded its colonial entity of the Dutch East Indies to encompass the western half of the imperially unclaimed island of New Guinea, though its eastern boundary was not fixed by the Dutch at the 141st meridian until the entry of imperial competitors in the 1880s.[11] The colonial presence in Dutch New Guinea remained limited to missionary work and small-scale commercial relations until the end of the 19th century. The Dutch presence was formalized by the establishment of administrative posts in Fak Fak and Manokwari in 1898 as a result of European claims over eastern New Guinea.[12]

Britain laid claim to southeastern New Guinea in 1884 as a British protectorate, and 4 years later the area was annexed as British New Guinea. In 1906, the territory was handed over to Australian control,

Table 9–1. Chronology of Key Events in Western New Guinea

1545	Spanish sail to the north coast of New Guinea and claim the territory for the Spanish Crown, naming it Nueva Guinea.
1828	The Dutch claim the southwest coast of New Guinea.
1848	Dutch claims extend to the northwest coast.
1898	The Dutch assert control over what becomes the Netherlands New Guinea.
1945	Sukarno declares independence for Indonesia following the surrender of Japan.
1947	The Dutch launch a police action with 100,000 troops to reassert their authority.
1948	International opposition to a second Dutch police action mounts.
1949	The Dutch cede sovereignty over Netherlands East Indies to the new Indonesian Republic but retain control over Western New Guinea.
1961	Armed Indonesian infiltrators are captured by the Dutch.
1962	The Dutch agree to transfer authority over Netherlands New Guinea to the United Nations Temporary Executive Authority (UNTEA).
1962	Indonesian and Dutch naval forces clash. The United States facilitates discussions between the Netherlands and Indonesia. Indonesia drops paratroopers into Western New Guinea. In August, the New York Agreement is signed by Indonesia and the Netherlands and a ceasefire is enforced. The UNTEA begins in October and the last Dutch troops leave in November. Indonesian security forces assert control over the territory.
1963	In May, the UNTEA transfers administration of the territory to Indonesia.
1965	OPM established. The first counterinsurgency operation against the OPM is conducted by Indonesian military forces.
1965–1998	Indonesia led by President Suharto.

1967–1969 Armed rebellion by Papuans against Indonesian rule occurs across the region.

1969 Indonesian troops cross the Papua New Guinea frontier in pursuit of rebels.

1969 "Act of Free Choice" leads to Indonesia's annexation of Western New Guinea.

1980s Transmigration program leads to large numbers of non-Melanesian Indonesians moving to Western New Guinea from elsewhere in Indonesia.

1998–2001 Reformasi period begins in Indonesia.

2001 Special Autonomy Law grants special provisions to Western New Guinea, but the provisions are not fully implemented.

2003 A plan by President Megawati Sukarnoputri divides Western New Guinea into two provinces—Papua and West Irian Jaya. Her plan to further divide Papua in two does not go forward.

2004 Susilo Bambang Yudhoyono becomes Indonesia's first directly elected president in free and fair elections.

2007 West Irian Jaya becomes known as West Papua. Legislation to divide Papua into three separate provinces is put forward.

and with the passage of the Papua Act it was thereafter known as the Territory of Papua.[13] This initial British claim was followed within weeks by the German claim to the northeast quarter of the island and the Bismarck Archipelago. The main part of German New Guinea, established as a German protectorate from 1884 until 1914, was known as Kaiser Wilhelmsland. The borders of these territories were solidified to ensure "equitable divisions" between Britain and Germany.[14]

German New Guinea fell to Australia in 1914, and until the outbreak of World War II the northeast quarter of the island continued to be administered by Australia, passing from military occupation to the League of Nations Mandated Territory of New Guinea in 1921. During World War II, when the northern half of New Guinea was occupied by Japanese forces, the two eastern regions were administered together and were combined in 1949 by Australia as the Territory of Papua and New Guinea. After the war they were administered as a UN trusteeship until both territories were granted full independence by Australia in 1975 and named Papua New Guinea. Despite the shifts in administrative control and the political flux caused by World War II, the borders of the eastern regions of Papua and New Guinea were roughly reestablished, though smaller administrative units were created within them, as was the division of the island into its eastern and western halves at the 141st meridian. These borders have had more meaning as administrative units than as barriers to traditional human currents until more recent, contested times.[15]

The United Nations, the New York Agreement, and Handover to Indonesian Control

Through the 1950s, former President Sukarno agitated for the "reunification" of Dutch New Guinea with the Republic of Indonesia. In 1959, Sukarno bedeviled the Dutch with small military incursions into Western New Guinea that resulted in skirmishes between Dutch and Indonesian forces. Diplomatically, Sukarno's call for the incorporation of Western New Guinea into Indonesia, as opposed to Dutch pledges to guide the territory toward its own independence, rested upon the doctrine of *uti possidetis juris,* or the belief that the "territorial boundaries of a postcolonial state should match those of the colonial territories they replaced."[16] Ironically, this doctrine swayed numerous newly independent African nations more than Dutch and Australian calls for Papuan self-determination. This support for Sukarno was solidified in 1960 when a border dispute erupted within days of the independence of the Congo. The secession of the resource-rich Katanga province, believed to be supported by Belgium and other Western interests, provided a mirror for Sukarno's West New Guinea scenario that not only swayed the United Nations against independence for West New Guinea but also convinced the newly elected U.S. President John F. Kennedy.[17]

Kennedy differed on this issue from Dwight D. Eisenhower, whose policy had been to keep out of a negotiated settlement. By the beginning of 1962, the United States and Australia no longer supported the Dutch plan and instead shifted policy toward a handover of Papua to Indonesia. Australia's sudden shift away from the Dutch reflected the absence of any international support, most notably from the United States, in the event of armed conflict with Indonesia over the territory.[18] With this drastically altered international climate, talks ensued throughout 1962 without any Papuan representation at them, though they were suspended in August following the dropping of large contingents of Indonesian paratroopers into Western New Guinea.[19]

The New York Agreement, signed on August 15, 1962, included a ceasefire agreement as well as an arrangement in which the Netherlands would transfer control of West New Guinea to the United Nations Temporary Executive Authority (UNTEA) that administered the area from October 1, 1962 to May 1, 1963. From May 1, 1963, control of Western New Guinea was transferred to Indonesia; the UN was supposed to continue to monitor the area and ensure compliance with the New York Agreement.

Dissenting Papuan political organizations were banned by Indonesia, and the OPM was founded in the mid-1960s. Indonesian military presence was stepped up by President Suharto to meet the rising number of Papuan rebellions as well as to assure success in the "Indonesian-organized act of Papuan self-determination" known as the "Act of Free Choice," a staged plebiscite scheduled for 1969 in which 1,022 tribal elders (or fewer than 1 percent of the population) were selected to vote on the question of independence or integration into Indonesia.[20] The predetermined result—to integrate with Indonesia—was endorsed by the UN and has served as the basis for conflict in the region.[21]

The years that succeeded the "Act of Free Choice" have been characterized by increased rebel activity, an Indonesian military presence, the Indonesian government–sponsored program of transmigration of non-Papuans to the region, urbanization, and a considerable number of Papuan refugees fleeing across the border to the Australian-administered territory of Papua and New Guinea and then-independent Papua New Guinea because of Indonesian army (Tentara Nasional Indonesia, or TNI) violence.[22] Some estimates put the numbers of Papuans killed since the beginning of Indonesian rule at over 100,000.[23] Others claim this number to be greatly exaggerated. Accurate data are very difficult to come by, in part because of the relative inaccessibility of the region to foreign journalists and researchers. The increased repression of Papuans from 1969 has also been exacerbated by the dramatic upsurge in the exploitation of Papuan resources. In 1973, the Freeport McMoRan–run Grasberg mine near Timika commenced operating what would become the biggest gold mine in the world, and it became a leading player in the politics of the territory.[24] Along with Freeport McMoRan, other multinational operations likewise significantly contributed to the litany of grievances of indigenous Papuans since 1969, particularly the gross disparity between the massive revenues being generated by Papuan resources and the grinding poverty experienced by the Papuan people.

Special Autonomy Law

Poor relations between Papuans, the Indonesian government, and the TNI made Western New Guinea one of the three main "troubled" areas of Indonesia—along with East Timor and Aceh—that became a focal point of world attention after the fall of President Suharto in 1998 and the accompanying democratization of Indonesia promping the transitional Reformasi era from 1998 to 2001. For Western New Guinea, post-Suharto Reformasi resulted in a recognition for "the need for special autonomy" for the region "given the diversity of Papua and the dictates of participatory democracy in the newly emerging Indonesia."[25] Despite this, the benefits of the Special Autonomy Law have not reached the average Papuan. Some observers feel that "the Papuan political elite are too distracted by the fight over resources to implement real changes in the standard of living for Papuans."[26] Others assert that "while the Special Autonomy process has been marred by long delays and wavering commitment on the part of the Indonesian government, the latter cannot be blamed for all of Papua's continuing problems, and an increasing portion of responsibility must rest with Papuan maladministration."[27]

Law No. 21 on the Special Autonomy of Papua granting greater autonomy to the Papuan Province of 2001 acknowledged, among other things, that development in the Papuan Province:

> [has] not completely fulfilled the sense of justice, enabled the attainment of prosperity for the people, supported the upholding of the law, nor shown respect for human rights in the Papuan Province, in particular those of the Papuan community . . . [and] that the management and utilization of the natural wealth of the Papuan Province have not been optimally utilized for improving the standards of living of the native community, thereby causing the formation of the gap between the Papuan Province and the other

regions, and constituting a neglect of the fundamental human rights of the native inhabitants of Papua.[28]

Given these premises, the Law on Special Autonomy made generous concessions in terms of governance; political, religious, and cultural protections; freedoms and human rights for Papuans; as well as an immense redistribution of Papua's wealth generated from exploitation of natural resources back into the province. For instance, it allowed for 80 percent of forestry, fishing, and general mining and 70 percent of oil and gas revenue to be channeled back into provincial revenues.[29]

Papuan living standards continue to lag well behind the rest of Indonesia. According to a 2007 World Bank report, "Forty percent of Papuans still live below the poverty line, more than double the national average . . . one third of Papua's children do not go to school . . . [and] nine out of ten villages do not have basic health services with a health center, doctor or midwife."[30] President Yudhoyono has acknowledged the continuing problems in Papua despite the new autonomy legal framework. In February 2007, he stated, "the improvement of peoples' [sic] prosperity in the two Papua provinces is slow. Special autonomy has not been implemented in a good way." He undertook to "issue a presidential decree to accelerate the development in the two Papuan provinces. Funds will come from the region and the central government."[31] The division of Western New Guinea into two provinces—West Papua and Papua—has been widely perceived as contravening the freedoms and protections dimensions of the new law. This division is symptomatic of the continuing abuses of Papuan human rights despite recognition of the problem by the Indonesian government.

The announcement by President Yudhoyono in May 2010 that Indonesia would institute a moratorium on logging of natural forests may have positive implications for Western New Guinea. Yudhoyono's efforts are part of a larger commitment to reduce Indonesia's carbon emissions by 26 percent by the year 2020. Norway signed a $1 billion deal with Indonesia to help Indonesia preserve its forests. Indonesia is the world's third largest emitter of greenhouse gases, 85 percent of which come from deforestation. This commitment with Norway places the massive food development estate in Merauke, Papua, in question. In 2008, the government had released over a million hectares of land for agricultural development near Merauke. Much of this land is peat swamp, which when burned releases even more carbon. It was thought that such a massive project would prove to be alienating for local Papuans, as such projects can lead to the migration of non–Papuan Indonesians to the area to take up new jobs.

TNI and Conflict in Western New Guinea

The Indonesian military continues to exert considerable influence in Western New Guinea. There was reportedly a plan in 2006 to deploy 35,000 additional troops along Indonesia's border with Papua New Guinea. These would be in addition to the 6,000 to 7,000 troops who were already thought to be stationed in Papua. At the end of 2007, it was estimated that there were some 12,000 Indonesian troops and 2,000 to 2,500 paramilitary police in the region.[32] While this level of deployment is low when one considers the length of the land border with PNG, and that Papua and West Papua constitute 21 percent of the land area of Indonesia, it does raise questions given the poor state of relations between the TNI and indigenous Melanesian peoples in Papua and West Papua. There is concern as to what effect this will have on illegal logging and intercommunal harmony in these two eastern provinces.[33]

Some officers who have been sent to Western New Guinea played a role in events in East Timor in the leadup to and wake of the 1999 referendum on independence.[34] Colonel Burhanuddin Siagan, who was indicted in 2003 by UN investigators for murder and torture in East Timor and who was based in Papua in 2007, has stated, "In the interests of the Republic of Indonesia we are not afraid of human rights. . . . [A]nyone who tends towards separatism will be crushed."[35] In August 2007, there were reports that Indonesian military operations had destroyed houses and crops in the remote Jamo Valley in Puncak Jaya. This led to the starvation of local inhabitants who had fled the security forces operations.[36]

An International Crisis Group report on Radicalization and Dialogue in Papua, released in March 2010, found that there was an increase in political violence in 2009 and 2010 that was leading to increased radicalization of militants and formerly peaceful activists. Apparently, some activists have taken the view that dialogue with the Indonesian government should only take place within an international context. Such an internationalization of the conflict is not what the government in Jakarta wishes. Some militants have been increasingly drawn to the view that the East Timor experience has lessons on how the internationalization of the conflict can help their cause. A 2010 book by John Braithwaite and others at the Australian National University, *Anomie and Violence: Non-Truth and Reconciliation in Indonesian Peace Building*, has concluded that Papua is a "case with both high risks of escalation to more serious conflict and prospects for harnessing" peace initiatives.

Human Rights in Western New Guinea

In this era of globalized media, Western New Guinea remains one of the most remote areas of the planet, one where information is not easily disseminated and journalists have limited and controlled access to media. The region's remoteness means that the operations of security forces there are not subject to the scrutiny they would experience were they closer to the core of Indonesia on Java. As a result, the increased openness of the media elsewhere in Indonesia that has occurred since the period of Reformasi has not similarly constrained security forces' abuses in remote areas. Security operations in Papua and West Papua are viewed by human rights advocates as operating with a large degree with impunity. Some go so far as describing the operations as genocide. Others characterize the situation as one where "chronic low level abuse on the part of security forces [is a] fact."[37]

The catalyst for human rights abuses of the indigenous Papuan people of the Indonesian provinces of Papua and West Papua, and particularly in the central highlands, is apparently related to security sweeps by police and security forces. These sweep operations have the objective of capturing or destroying cells of the pro-independence OPM. Other key political actors include the Papuan Presidium Council and the Papuan People's Council. These operations "typically involve looting, destruction of property, and in some cases harm to civilians and displacement" and are probably related to perceptions by security forces of popular support by Papuans for OPM groups. Human Rights Watch has found that security forces "continue to engage in largely indiscriminate sweeping operations in pursuit of suspected militants, using excessive, often brutal, and at sometimes lethal force against civilians." According to one OPM fighter interviewed in April 2010, OPM is now seeking to provoke a Santa Cruz–type response by the TNI to mounting violence by the OPM. Santa Cruz was the site of a massacre by the TNI in East Timor in 1991. It has been reported that at least some OPM fighters are considering expelling transmigrants and seeking a merger with Papua New Guinea.[38]

This problem of human rights abuses came to wider international attention in March 2006 when 42 refugees from Western New Guinea were granted temporary protection visas by the Australian government. Indonesia responded by withdrawing its ambassador from Canberra. President Yudhoyono also made direct calls to then–Prime Minister John Howard to return the asylum-seekers to Indonesia. Australia responded by passing a new migration bill "that would deter Papuan asylum seekers from coming to Australia."[39]

Mineral, Natural Gas, and Timber Extraction in Western New Guinea

The Indonesian military and political elites have vested interests in reaping benefits from resource extraction industries. The wealth generated from these projects flows overwhelmingly to foreign multinational companies, the central government in Jakarta, and allegedly to Indonesian individuals in government and in the military who are in a position to gain financially from the process of production. Local communities that overwhelmingly bear the costs of production, such as environmental degradation, increased rates of HIV/AIDS transmission, and radical changes to their traditional way of life, reap little relative long-term economic advantage for their people. In many cases, these communities become politically and/or economically marginalized either from direct rule from the center or through the transmigration of Indonesians from other parts of the archipelago.

In Western New Guinea, the nexus between conflict, corruption, and environmental exploitation is clear. The struggle for control of Papua's abundant natural resources has contributed significantly to the conflict. Concessions given to mining companies without consideration for the rights of local people, and the involvement of state security forces in guarding mining sites, have provided fertile ground for conflict. The direct involvement of senior members of the police and army in resource extraction—such as where members of the military hold logging concessions themselves or receive payment from mining companies for security services—combined with the lucrative taxes that flow to the Indonesian state provides powerful motives for the state to retain tight control.[40]

One of the most exploited natural resources of Western New Guinea is its forests. Deforestation is threatening to eliminate Indonesia's remaining forests, which are to a large extent found in

Western New Guinea. About 10 percent of the world's remaining tropical forests, a total forested area of some 225 million acres, are found in Indonesia, a country that has already lost over 72 percent of its forests. This process of deforestation has made Indonesia the world's third largest emitter of greenhouse gases, which contribute to global warming. Illegal logging in Indonesia is estimated to fell some 5.2 million acres of forest each year with an estimated value of $4 billion.[41] Ironically, rainforest clearing is also being carried out to establish palm plantations for biofuel projects ostensibly aimed at cleaner sources of energy. Such projects, which can displace local people, have been associated with human rights abuses.[42] Palm oil projects are also associated with the influx of transmigrants who take the jobs the projects create away from the locals.[43]

Global initiatives to address climate change may lead to increased international attention regarding the forests of Western New Guinea that could help end illegal logging and mitigate intercommunal strife. Such plans could also lead to payments to help protect the forests. There were negotiations under way in late 2007 to implement a Reduced Emissions from Deforestation scheme as part of the Kyoto Protocol that could earn Indonesia $10 billion a year for preserving its forests by selling carbon credits.[44]

The vast mineral riches of Western Papua were suspected by the Dutch as early as the 1930s, but their exploitation did not commence in earnest until after World War II. By 1961, some 7.4 million guilders' worth of oil was exported but the more inaccessibly located mineral resources of the region were not tapped. The economy of Dutch New Guinea was primarily structured around agricultural products. Under Indonesian rule, interest in tapping the natural wealth of the region grew exponentially as did the revenues from oil and mineral extraction, particularly from the 1970s.[45]

Extracting the immense natural resources of Western New Guinea is intimately intertwined with the expansion of Indonesian control, secured by the TNI, and the accompanying upsurge in human rights abuses. This history is also shaped by the significant roles played by multinational companies, though only one of a number of corporate players in Papua—U.S.-based Freeport McMoRan Copper and Gold, Inc.—has had a colossal impact on the history of Papua since it began investing in mining operations in 1967. Its main operation, the Grasberg deposit, became the "largest gold and most profitable copper mine in the world" in the 1990s, thereby making the company the largest taxpayer in Indonesia. Freeport McMoRan has paid the TNI to provide security for the mine. The military's large presence around the mine has reportedly exacerbated conflict with local populations. The relationship between Freeport McMoRan and the TNI gained international attention in August 2002 when two U.S. citizens and an Indonesian employee of the mine were killed in an ambush near Timika. While many suspected TNI involvement, Anthonius Wamang, who is believed to have been an OPM operational commander as well as an informant for the TNI, was arrested for the crime in January 2006 along with 11 others.[46]

The excessive costs borne by local Papuans for Freeport's mining operations can also be measured in company employment practices, where only 20 to 26 percent of workers are Papuan, and even fewer come from the Amungme and Kamoro groups, the traditional land owners in the area. The mine has been a major driver of transmigration to Papua, mostly from Java. In addition to the disruptive impact of this transmigration for Papuan rights, the Grasberg mine has also had a fundamental impact on the spread of HIV/AIDS. The nearby town of Timika is the service town and residence for approximately 12,000 male employees of the mine. Timika also has the second highest rate of HIV/AIDS in West Papua, the province with the highest rate in the nation of Indonesia. Along with the social and political dimensions of Freeport McMoRan's operations, the mine has led to a massive degradation of the ecosystem of the highlands, river systems, and distant coastal areas where tailings are piped. The company's favored status with the TNI and the Indonesian government has resulted in widespread accusations that it circumvents the existing environmental protection laws of Indonesia, which are far weaker than those enforced in the United States, the company's home country.[47]

International Support for Independence or Autonomy in Western New Guinea

Respect for the borders and territorial integrity of Indonesia has been a key objective of Indonesian foreign relations, particularly with Australia and the United States. Indonesia's sensitivity on the issue is understandable given the pivotal role that Australia played in assisting East Timor achieve its independence, and because of the support by

Australia for the Papuan people. Support by some Members of Congress for the plight of the people of Western New Guinea as well as past U.S. Government support for secession elsewhere in the Indonesian archipelago may also contribute to Indonesian concerns.[48] Indonesian sensitivities over Western New Guinea are strong, as is their sense that it is an integral part of Indonesia because of the territory's common control under the Dutch. This differs somewhat from Indonesia's perceptions of East Timor, which was controlled by the Portuguese until 1975.

In 2006, Indonesian Foreign Minister Hassan Wirajuda and Australian Foreign Minister Alexander Downer signed a security treaty on the island of Lombok that replaced a previous treaty between Prime Minister Paul Keating and Indonesian President Suharto that was abandoned as a result of Australia's support of East Timor's independence. The new treaty binds both states in an agreement not to support separatists in each country. The clause was reportedly included at the urging of Indonesia following the previously mentioned diplomatic controversy surrounding Australia's granting of temporary protection visas to the group of 42 Western New Guinean asylum seekers who entered Australia in January 2006. The new security treaty addresses border protection, defense, counterterror cooperation, law enforcement, and other issues.[49] Critics of the treaty in Australia have felt that the document will facilitate the suppression of the Papuan independence movement.[50] There is a tendency in strategic circles in Australia to focus first on establishing and maintaining good bilateral relations with Indonesia. Many who hold this view would argue that it is the most effective way to help positively influence the situation in Western New Guinea.[51]

Australia has been a center of support for Western New Guinean human rights activists. This is not surprising, given that some 77 percent of Australians support an act of self-determination for Western New Guinea[52] and that Australia has a long historical relationship with Western New Guinea's eastern neighbor, Papua New Guinea. In March 2007, the University of Sydney's Centre for Peace and Conflict Studies produced a report prepared by the Western New Guinea Project that describes Western New Guinea as a "humanitarian emergency," where the "outlook for the Western New Guinean People is worsening." The report, authored by Jim Elmslie, Peter King, and Jake Lynch, was critical of the security treaty between Australia and Indonesia and viewed that document as tantamount to a decision by Australia "to take sides with the corrupt Indonesian military against the Western New Guinean people."[53] While some have criticized this conclusion on the basis of a lack of evidence of deliberate intent, there is a general view that a "systematic pattern of rights violations by Indonesian security forces" has occurred.[54]

Attention to Papua and West Papua by the U.S. Congress has caused concern for the government of Indonesia. It has perceived congressional attention in the form of proposed legislation as a challenge to Indonesian sovereignty over the area. Such sensitivity is understandable on the part of the Indonesians, given past Central Intelligence Agency covert operations in Indonesia that sought to destabilize or overthrow the regime of former President Sukarno by providing support to separatist military elements in the outer islands of Sumatra and Sulawezi.[55] Congressman Eni Faleomavaega, who was born on American Samoa and is chairman of the House Foreign Affairs Subcommittee on Asia, the Pacific, and the Global Environment, spoke out on behalf of the Papuan people at a time when the administration of President George W. Bush had focused on establishing closer relations with Indonesia.[56] Other Members of Congress have taken the view that Indonesia's importance to the United States in the struggle against violent Islamist militants and its increasing geopolitical importance in the region outweigh concerns over Papua and West Papua. Following a brief visit to the region in November 2007, Faleomavaega stated, "Clearly the Papuans in these two provinces are still being intimidated, harassed, and abused by the TNI."[57]

At the request of President Yudhoyono, Congressman Faleomavaega and Congressman Donald Payne reportedly suspended their support for Papua's and West Papua's right to self-determination in 2005 in order to give President Yudhoyono time to implement Special Autonomy legislation for the two provinces. After 3 years, they wrote to President Yudhoyono to say that "continued refusal by your military to allow our access to Jayapura and other parts of Indonesia will inevitably call into question the seriousness of your government's assurances to us regarding your intent to implement Special Autonomy and to end unreasonable restrictions on international access to West Papua."[58]

The development of a Comprehensive Partnership between the United States and Indonesia, which was expected when President Obama visited Indonesia in November 2010, may provide a dialogue framework within which the two nations can develop confidence in their dealings with one another. This could potentially provide a venue to discuss constructive ways for the United States and the international community to assist Indonesia in fostering peaceful and sustainable development in Western New Guinea. Such development could defuse mounting conflict by bringing together various stakeholders to focus on forest preservation and the empowerment of indigenous people while reaffirming Indonesian sovereignty and developing intercommunal dialogue between Papuans, transmigrants, the TNI, police, and other state actors.

Conclusion and Recommendations

Based on an analysis of the history of borders in Western New Guinea, one can conclude that the salience of national and subnational borders remains central to the course of political, cultural, demographic, and economic developments in the territory. Borders have become the focus of those seeking greater autonomy, or independence, as well as those from the center who seek to more firmly extend central state control, whether for reasons of national sovereignty or less noble aims. The situation of the people of Western New Guinea is very much dependent on the manner in which the extension of central government control takes place. If it is simply to install a new tier of elites who will be better positioned to exploit the people and the ample natural resources of the region, then these new borders will work to the detriment of the people. If they can bring new levels of government that can provide new services, such as health and education, then they could be a positive factor. The extreme power differential between the Papuan people and the Malay people of the rest of the Indonesian Archipelago means that the course of political development of Western New Guinea depends principally on the larger democratic development of Indonesia. If graft and corruption can be minimized and the rule of law and respect for minority peoples can be extended, the plight of the Papuan people may be alleviated by increased political involvement by Jakarta in the affairs of Papua. That said, there is the very real fear that the region will be used by elites and the military for little more than exploitation for personal gain. Such an outcome would be to the detriment of the people, the environment of Western New Guinea in particular, and to the world at large because of the role that the world's great forests play in carbon sequestration.

The following recommendations are put forward based on the above analysis. They are made with the knowledge that the general trend in Indonesian governance since the democratic elections of 2004, which brought President Yudhoyono to power, is positive. That said, abuses continue, and much remains to be done to improve the condition of the Melanesian Papuan people living in Western New Guinea.[59]

- Continue to encourage a peaceful resolution of the conflict with respect for the territorial integrity of Indonesia and understanding of the plight of the Papuan people.
- Stop the transmigration of people from elsewhere in Indonesia to Western New Guinea.
- Continue the positive trend of increasing openness of the media in Indonesia to include Papua and West Papua by allowing unrestricted access to Western New Guinea by Indonesian and foreign journalists and academics.
- Continue the positive trend of getting the military and police out of the business of protecting businesses, including multinational corporations.
- Fully implement the Special Autonomy Law of 2001.
- Place special emphasis on improving local health, job training, and education opportunities.
- Continue the positive current trend toward increasingly democratic government at the national level in Indonesia to the local level in Papua and West Papua.
- Place renewed emphasis on local customs and culture and observe past commitments to do so.
- Work to minimize the negative impact of corrupt practices at the national, provincial, and local levels.
- Ensure that a reasonable amount of wealth generated by mineral and other resource extraction industries remains in Western New Guinea and flows to local communities.
- Implement programs to mitigate detrimental effects of resource extraction industries and move quickly to preserve intact forests and fisheries and to develop sustainable development strategies.
- Partner with the international community to preserve Western New Guinea forests.

Notes

[1] Jan Pouwer, "The Colonisation, Decolonisation and Recolonisation of West New Guinea," *Journal of Pacific History* 34, no. 2 (1999), 160–161.

[2] John McBeth, "Two Papuas Too Many," *The Straits Times*, February 14, 2007.

[3] Bruce Vaughn, "Papua, Indonesia: Issues for Congress," Congressional Research Service Report RL33260, January 19, 2006.

[4] For a text of the law and the Indonesian government's view on Papua, see *Questioning the Unquestionable: An Overview of the Restoration of Papua into the Republic of Indonesia* (New York: Permanent Mission of the Republic of Indonesia to the United Nations, 2004).

[5] John McBeth, "The Slicing and Dicing of Indonesia," *The Straits Times*, February 16, 2008.

[6] Geoffrey Barker, "Revealed: The Day Australia Planned to Bomb Indonesia," *Australian Financial Review*, December 1, 2007.

[7] Hall Greenland, "Rumble in the Jungle," *The Bulletin*, November 13, 2007.

[8] Maureen Gerawa, "Refugees Neglected," *PNG Post Courier*, January 3, 2008.

[9] "Indonesian Papuan Students 'Terrorized' by Islamic Militia," BBC News, July 11, 2007.

[10] "PNG to Partner with Indonesian Province to Prevent the Spread of HIV Along Border," Kaiser Network, April 3, 2008.

[11] Clive Moore, *New Guinea: Crossing Boundaries and History* (Honolulu: University of Hawaii Press, 2003), 150. See also Paul W. Van der Veur, *Search for New Guinea's Boundaries* (Canberra: Australian National University Press, 1966).

[12] Pouwer, 161.

[13] Donald Craigie Gordon, *The Australian Frontier in New Guinea 1870–1885* (New York: Columbia University Press, 1951).

[14] Moore, 151.

[15] Ibid., 152, 196; Ben Scott, *Re-Imagining Papua: Culture Democracy and Australia's Role* (Sydney: Lowy Institute for International Policy, 2005), 10.

[16] John Saltford, *The United Nations and the Indonesian Takeover of West Papua, 1962–1969: The Anatomy of Betrayal* (London: RoutledgeCurzon, 2003), 8.

[17] Ibid., 9; United Nations Security Council Resolution (S/5002) of November 24, 1961.

[18] Ibid., 14; David Palmer, "Between a Rock and a Hard Place: The Case of Papuan Asylum-Seekers," *Australian Journal of Politics and History* 52, no. 4 (2006), 577–578.

[19] Saltford, xix; "Autonomy for Papua: Opportunity or Illusion?" (Berlin: Friedrich Ebert Foundation et al., 2003), 122.

[20] Saltford, 2; Moore, 200. Moore cites the number of 1,025 "representatives."

[21] Rodd McGibbon, *Pitfalls of Papua: Understanding the Conflict and Its Place in Australia-Indonesia Relations* (Sydney: The Lowy Institute, 2006), 1–12; Jason Macleod, "Gagged," *Arena Magazine* 68 (December 2003–January 2004), 30.

[22] "PNG Currently Hosts up to 10,000 Papuan Refugees Although the Overall Number to Have Sought Asylum in PNG since 1973 May Number 20,000," Palmer, 597.

[23] Palmer, 584; McGibbon, 95.

[24] Peter King, *West Papua and Indonesia Since Suharto: Independence, Autonomy or Chaos?* (Sydney: University of New South Wales Press, 2004), 22–23; Denise Leith, *Politics of Power: Freeport in Suharto's Indonesia* (Honolulu: University of Hawaii Press, 2003).

[25] *Questioning the Unquestionable: An Overview of the Restoration of Papua into the Republic of Indonesia*, Permanent Mission of the Republic of Indonesia to the United Nations (New York, 2004), 70.

[26] Erica Vowles, "West Papua: Special Treatment," *New Matilda*, August 22, 2007.

[27] "West Papua's Cultural Identity," BBC News, available at <www.bbc.co.uk/worldservice/people/features/ihavearightto/four_b/casestudy_art27.shtml>; Human Rights Watch, "Out of Sight: Endemic Abuse and Impunity in Papua's Central Highlands," New York, July 2007.

[28] Annex VIII, Law No. 21 on the Special Autonomy of Papua granting greater autonomy to the Papuan Province, "considering" points f and g in *Questioning the Unquestionable*, 105.

[29] Article 34 b and c, Law No. 21 on the Special Autonomy of Papua granting greater autonomy to the Papuan Province in *Questioning the Unquestionable*, 119.

[30] World Bank, "Spending for Development: Making the Most of Indonesia's New Opportunities: Indonesia Public Expenditure Review 2007," Jakarta, 2007.

[31] "Indonesian President Urges Faster Papua Development," Reuters, February 16, 2007.

[32] "Papua: Answers to Frequently Asked Questions," Crisis Group Asia Briefing No. 53, International Crisis Group, September 5, 2006; "Indonesia Exploiting Prejudices to Stay in Papua—Academic," Australian Associated Press, December 3, 2007.

[33] Evi Mariani, "Alternatives Sought to Papua Border Militarization," *The Jakarta Post*, November 22, 2006.

[34] "Lack of Support Helped in Cover-up of Indonesian Atrocities," *The Canberra Times*, July 23, 2007.

[35] Tom Hyland, "Mysterious Killings Seek to Silence Papuan Voices," *The Sunday Age*, August 26, 2007.

[36] "Indonesian Military Operation Causes Starvation," *Institute for Papuan Advocacy*, August 29, 2007.

[37] "Papua: Answers to Frequently Asked Questions," Crisis Group Asia Briefing No. 53, International Crisis Group, September 5, 2006.

[38] Tom Allard, "Papua Ready to Explode," *The Age*, April 11, 2010; "Indonesia's Last Frontier," *The Economist*, June 5, 2010; Human Rights Watch.

[39] Tom Allard and Craig Skehan, "Visa Ruling Puts Jakarta Ties at Risk," *Sydney Morning Herald*, March 24, 2006; "Jakarta Rage Over Visas," *The Age*, March 24, 2006; McGibbon, 85.

[40] "Indonesia: Resources and Conflict in Papua," International Crisis Group, September 2002; "Out of Sight," BBC, July 2007, 13.

[41] "Indonesia's Aceh, Papua Pledge to Protect Forests," Reuters, April 26, 2007.

[42] "Man Dying After Kostrad Beating and Torture," *Scoop News*, July 31, 2007.

[43] "West Papua Rainforests on Fragile Edge," *The Canberra Times*, December 8, 2007; Juliet Eilperin and Steven Mufson, "Trees Are at Heart of Talks on Climate," *The Washington Post*, December 9, 2007.

[44] "Cutting to the Real Root of the Problem," *Asiamoney*, December 28, 2007.

[45] Pouwer, 177–178; Denise Leith, "Freeport and the Suharto Regime 1965–1998," *The Contemporary Pacific* 14, no. 1 (Spring 2002), 69–70.

[46] In 1995, Anglo-Australian mining giant Rio Tinto began a joint venture with Freeport McMoRan. King, 22–23; Leith, *Politics of Power*; and Damien Kingsbury, *Power, Politics and the Indonesian Military* (New York: RoutledgeCurzon, 2003), 195.

[47] WALHI—Indonesian Forum for Environment, "The Environmental Impacts of Freeport-Rio Tinto's Copper and Gold Mining Operation in Papua," Jakarta, 2006; "Indonesia Commission: Peace and Progress in Papua" (New York: Council on Foreign Relations, Inc., 2003), 52–53; Nurlan Silitonga, A. Ruddick, and F.S. Wignall, "Mining, HIV/AIDS, and Women: Timika, Papua Province, Indonesia," in *Tunnel Vision: Women, Mining and Communities*, ed. Ingrid MacDonald and Claire Rowland (Melbourne: Oxfam Community Aid Abroad, 2002), available at <www.caa.org.au/campaigns/mining>.

[48] Audrey R. Kahin and George McT. Kahin, *Subversion as Foreign Policy: The Secret Eisenhower and Dulles Debacle in Indonesia* (New York: The New Press, 1995).

[49] "Treaty Will Not Silence Western New Guinean Activists," *The Canberra Times*, November 13, 2006.

[50] Ross Peake, "New Treaty Won't Affect Human Rights," *The Canberra Times,* November 9, 2006.

[51] McGibbon.

[52] Noel Pearson, "Uses of Layered Identity," *The Australian,* November 18, 2006.

[53] Jim Elmslie, Peter King, and Jake Lynch, *Blundering In? The Australia-Indonesia Security Treaty and the Humanitarian Crisis in Western New Guinea,* Western New Guinea Project at the Centre for Peace and Conflict Studies, The University of Sydney, March 2007.

[54] Rodd McGibbon as quoted in Paul Kelly, "A New Diplomacy over Papua," *The Australian,* October 7, 2006.

[55] Robert McMahon, review of Kenneth Conboy and James Morrison, *Feet to the Fire: CIA Covert Operations in Indonesia, 1957–1958* (Annapolis, MD: U.S. Naval Institute Press, 1999), in *The Journal of Military History* 64, no. 3, 903.

[56] M. Taufiqurrahman, "Papuan Movement Part of Democracy," *The Jakarta Post,* July 6, 2007.

[57] "Faleomavaega Disappointed with Visit to Biak and Manokwari Papua," *States News Service,* December 17, 2007.

[58] "House Foreign Affairs Subcommittee Chairman Call Upon Indonesia to End Unreasonable Restrictions on International Access to West Papua," *US Fed News,* March 10, 2008; Abdul Khalik, "U.S. Congressman in Papua to Assess Condition," *The Jakarta Post,* November 28, 2007; "DPR Considers U.S. Congressman Insult RI," *Kompass,* March 25, 2008.

[59] For an additional and more detailed list of recommendations, see Blair King, *Peace in Papua: Widening a Window of Opportunity,* Council on Foreign Relations Special Report No. 14, March 2006.

Chapter 10

China and Southeast Asia: A Shifting Zone of Interaction

Carlyle A. Thayer

China's relations with Southeast Asia may be viewed historically as a shifting zone of interaction. One constant that has governed interstate relations throughout history has been the adjustment and accommodation of smaller and weaker states to China's preeminent power. As Southeast Asian states gradually developed a regional identity, this zone took on a more structured and institutional nature. The formation of the Association of Southeast Asian Nations (ASEAN) and the ASEAN Regional Forum (ARF) provided a multilateral framework for structuring interstate relations. Nonetheless, Southeast Asia remains a shifting zone of interaction due to contestation over sovereignty claims in the South China Sea between China and littoral states and also because of pressures to expand the boundaries beyond the region to a wider East Asian setting.

Beijing views Southeast Asia—particularly the South China Sea—as China's traditional sphere of influence and has worked hard to develop bilateral ties with all regional states across the spectrum of economic, social, political, security, and military relations. China's reliance on imported energy resources has given it a strategic interest in promoting political stability in those countries where these resources are found. In addition, China also has a strategic interest in maintaining the security of sea lines of communications, especially through Southeast Asia.[1] Therefore, China has sought to bolster a stable and secure region in order to maintain access to regional energy resources and raw materials, protect maritime trade routes across the region, and develop wide-ranging relations for economic, defense, and political purposes, including isolating Taiwan and countering U.S. influence. In sum, the shifting zone of interaction between China and the ASEAN states has been expanded to the entire Southeast Asia region through the development of bilateral and multilateral relations. As this zone of interaction is consolidated, it will become a permanent feature of the regional security architecture.

There can be no doubt that the most significant future development over the next two decades that will reshape Southeast Asia as a zone of interaction will be the rise of China and its influence in all spheres—economic, political-diplomatic, social-cultural, and military.[2] China's "peaceful development" has already stimulated trade and investment with its neighbors and become a catalyst for their growth.[3] Its early rebound from the current global financial crisis is also assisting Southeast Asia to recover. China's economic rise will continue to spur increased demand for energy resources and other raw materials. Its energy needs already have been a boon to Indonesia's oil, gas, and mining sectors.

Evolution of China's Shifting Zone of Interaction

During the precolonial era, China interacted with the states of Southeast Asia through the framework of the "tributary system."[4] This was a hierarchical pattern of interaction that placed China at the center of regional affairs. China's role as paramount power was displaced during the colonial era when the countries of Southeast Asia (with the exception of Thailand) lost their independence and relations with China were conducted by the major European powers.

The rise of Japan and World War II fatally weakened the colonial system and ushered in the era of decolonization that followed. On October 1, 1949, the Chinese Communist Party declared the founding of the People's Republic of China (PRC). China then breached the partition erected during the colonial period and opened diplomatic relations in 1950 with the Democratic Republic of Vietnam and the newly independent states of Indonesia and Burma.

China's attempt to regain some semblance of its prewar regional preeminence was stalled by the outbreak of conflict on the Korean Peninsula (1950–1953) and the U.S.-led policy of containment. Nonetheless, China's regional importance was acknowledged by the major European powers when they sought Beijing's assistance in ending the first Indochina War (1946–1954). China played a major diplomatic role at the 1954 Geneva Conference and made its debut on the Southeast Asian stage at the Bandung Conference of Afro-Asian countries in April 1955.

As a result of Beijing's support for regional communist parties and a U.S. strategy of containment, China's zone of interaction with

Southeast Asia was largely restricted for the next two decades. The boundary demarcating it shifted twice during this period. China expanded its zone of interaction when it established diplomatic relations with two regional states that adopted a policy of neutrality, Cambodia (1958) and Laos (1961). However, these gains were offset in 1967 when Indonesia severed diplomatic relations in response to China's support for the Indonesian communist party.

In the late 1960s, the structure of international relations began to alter as the United States extricated itself from the Vietnam conflict. In 1971–1972, the United States and China began a phase of strategic collaboration to contain the Soviet Union. In January 1973, a peace settlement ended America's military involvement in Vietnam. This set the stage for a dramatic enlargement of China's zone of interaction with Southeast Asia as Beijing terminated its support for regional communist parties. On May 31, 1974, China and Malaysia formally established diplomatic relations; the following year, China opened diplomatic relations with two staunch U.S. allies, the Philippines and Thailand.

The pattern of China's interaction with Southeast Asia was again transformed by the emergence of rival communist regimes in Cambodia (Khmer Rouge) and a reunified Vietnam. As tensions mounted, China sided with Cambodia, and the Soviet Union backed Vietnam. When Vietnam invaded Cambodia, China responded by punitively attacking Vietnam's northern border provinces. Overnight, Thailand became a frontline state and therefore forged an alliance of convenience with China to resist Vietnamese occupation of Cambodia. This alignment lasted for a decade until a comprehensive settlement of the Cambodian conflict was reached at the end of the Cold War. After Vietnam withdrew from Cambodia in September 1989, the stage was set for the enlargement of China's zone of interaction to embrace all of Southeast Asia. In 1990, Beijing and Jakarta restored their ties and for the first time diplomatic relations were opened between China and Singapore and Brunei. The following year, Beijing and Hanoi normalized their relations. China was the first country to recognize the newly independent state of Timor-Leste in 2002.

In the early 1990s, China's ability to expand its zone of interaction with Southeast Asia beyond formal diplomatic relations into more substantial forms of cooperation was constrained by latent fears of "the China threat."[5] This chapter examines how China overcame these concerns by developing a series of policies that resulted in close diplomatic and political relations, economic interdependence and nascent integration, and, most recently, international security and defense cooperation.[6] Next, the chapter considers the mechanisms that structure China's relations with Southeast Asia. Then, it highlights China's bilateral security and defense cooperation with individual states of Southeast Asia. The chapter concludes with an assessment of China's "peaceful development" and its implications for regional security.

China's "New Security Concept"

Chinese security thinking underwent a change with the end of the Cold War and the collapse of the Soviet Union. According to Wu Baiyi, China's policy planners and academics began to revise the country's national security strategy in 1993.[7] This resulted in an expanded definition of security to include political, defense, diplomatic, and economic considerations. Two major changes were especially significant: economic security was elevated on a par with "high politics," and greater emphasis was given to the interrelationship between internal and external security challenges.

The result of Chinese rethinking of its security policy was embodied in what Beijing called its "new security concept."[8] Significantly, this new orientation was first introduced by Chinese officials at a conference on confidence-building measures hosted by the ASEAN Regional Forum held in Beijing in March 1997. In July of that year, Chinese Foreign Minister Qian Qichen formally presented the new security concept to the fourth ARF meeting in Malaysia.[9]

An authoritative exposition of China's new security concept appeared in its Defence White Paper released in July 1998.[10] This document stressed China's support for "regional-security dialogue and cooperation at different levels, through various channels and in different forms" including the ARF and the Council for Security Cooperation in Asia and the Pacific.[11] The white paper also endorsed "the ARF's creative explorations for the promotion of confidence-building measures" in such nonsensitive areas as military medicine and law, and multilateral cooperation on conversion of military technologies and facilities for civilian use.

China's emphasis on regional multilateral institutions and confidence-building measures was two-pronged. First, China sought to win support in Southeast Asia by "talking the talk" by endorsing proposals that already had widespread support among ASEAN members. Second, China sought to undermine support for the U.S. alliance structure. For example, President Jiang Zemin asserted in a major speech delivered in Bangkok in September 1999:

> Hegemonism and power politics still exist and have even developed in the international political, economic, and security fields. The new "Gunboat Policy" and the economic neo-colonialism pursued by some big powers have severely undermined the sovereign independence and the development interests of many small- and medium-sized countries, and have threatened world peace and international security.[12]

A similar theme was presented by Vice President Hu Jintao in July 2000 in a speech delivered in Jakarta to the Indonesian Council on World Affairs. Hu argued:

> A new security concept that embraces the principles of equality, dialogue, trust and cooperation, and a new security order should be established to ensure genuine mutual respect, mutual cooperation, consensus through consultation and peaceful settlement of disputes, rather than bullying, confrontation, and imposition of one's own will upon others. Only in that way can countries coexist in amity and secure their development.[13]

Two close observers of Southeast Asia's security scene concluded their assessment of China's new security concept with these observations:

> China has made it official policy to gain influence in Southeast Asia by contrasting its behavior in the region with that of the U.S. The implication was clear: Not only can China be a good neighbor, but Southeast Asia would benefit from partnering with Beijing rather than the U.S.,

which typically sees political and economic reform as prerequisites for amicable relations. While China has long inferred as much, Hu's speech marked the first time that the message was framed as a formal policy.[14]

Two years later, Foreign Minister Tang Jiaxuan asserted that China's new security concept should supplant Cold War bilateral alliances as the basis of regional security order.[15] However, in light of the terrorist attacks on the World Trade Center in New York and the Pentagon in Washington, DC, in September 2001, China's criticism of the U.S. alliance system fell on deaf ears. But China's advocacy of cooperative security through regional multilateral institutions slowly gained traction. The China threat of the early 1990s dissipated as Beijing repackaged its new security concept with such expressions as *peaceful rise* (2003), *peaceful development* (2004), and most recently, *harmonious world* (2005).[16]

China's Multilateral Relations with Southeast Asia

ASEAN

China's relations with Southeast Asia are structured on both a bilateral basis, through long-term cooperative framework agreements with each of ASEAN's 10 members (Brunei, Burma, Cambodia, Indonesia, Laos, Malaysia, the Philippines, Singapore, Thailand, and Vietnam) and a multilateral basis between ASEAN and China. Formal linkages between China and ASEAN date to 1991 when Qian Qichen attended the 24th ASEAN ministerial meeting in Kuala Lumpur as a guest of the Malaysian government. Qian expressed China's interest in developing cooperation with ASEAN in the field of science and technology. ASEAN responded positively.

In September 1993, ASEAN Secretary General Dato Ajit Singh led a delegation to China for talks with Vice Foreign Minister Tang Jiaxuan to follow up on Qian's proposal. This resulted in a formal agreement in July 1994 to establish two joint committees—one on science and technology cooperation and the other on economic and trade cooperation. China and ASEAN also agreed to open consultations on political and security issues at the senior official level. The first China-ASEAN senior officials meeting was held in Hangzhou in April 1995.

In 1996, China was accorded official dialogue partner status by ASEAN, and in February of the following year, ASEAN and China formalized their cooperation by establishing the ASEAN-China Joint Cooperation Committee. The committee first met in Beijing where it was agreed that it would "act as the coordinator for all the ASEAN-China mechanisms at the working level."[17] As an ASEAN dialogue partner, China regularly participates in the annual ASEAN postministerial conference consultation process. This takes the form of a meeting between ASEAN and its 10 dialogue partners (ASEAN 10 + 10), and a separate meeting between ASEAN members and each of its dialogue partners (ASEAN 10 + 1).

China-ASEAN relations advanced in November 2002 with the signing of three major documents: the Framework Agreement on Comprehensive Economic Cooperation between ASEAN Nations and the People's Republic of China, the Joint Declaration between China and ASEAN on Cooperation in Non-Traditional Security Fields, and the Declaration on the Conduct of Parties in the South China Sea (DOC). The first agreement laid the foundations for the China-ASEAN Free Trade Area. A major advance toward the free trade area was made in January 2007 when China and ASEAN signed the Agreement on Trade in Services at their tenth summit in Cebu, the Philippines. The free trade agreement came into force in January 2010 for the original five founding members of ASEAN and Brunei. It will come into effect for the newer, less-developed ASEAN members in 2015.

In April 2003, ASEAN and China convened a special meeting to discuss joint responses to deal with the Severe Acute Respiratory Syndrome epidemic.[18] Cooperation in this area led to a memorandum of understanding (MOU) in January 2004 to implement the ASEAN-China joint declaration on nontraditional security. In 2005 and 2007, China was invited to attend informal ministerial consultations with ASEAN on transitional crime held in Vietnam and Brunei respectively. In November 2009, the informal meeting was upgraded when the First ASEAN Ministerial Meeting on Transnational Crime Plus China was held in Phnom Penh.

Originally, ASEAN sought to negotiate a code of conduct for the South China Sea. China resisted ASEAN diplomatic pressure to agree to a formal, legally binding code. Early in 2004, 13 months after the DOC was signed, China and ASEAN agreed to set up a joint working group to consider ways to implement the DOC and to submit its recommendations to the first ASEAN-China senior officials meeting on the implementation of the DOC, which was held in Kuala Lumpur in December. ASEAN implementation meetings have since been held in May 2006 in Cambodia and in April 2010 in Hanoi.

Strategic Partnership for Peace and Prosperity

In October 2003, China's zone of interaction with ASEAN was enhanced when China acceded to the ASEAN Treaty of Amity and Cooperation, and China issued a joint declaration with ASEAN establishing a strategic partnership. The joint declaration was the first formal agreement of this type between China and a regional organization, as well as a first for ASEAN itself. The joint declaration was wide-ranging and included a provision for the initiation of a new security dialogue as well as general cooperation in political matters.[19]

In July of the following year, state councilor Tang Jiaxuan raised the prospect of developing "enhanced strategic relations" with ASEAN in his discussions with Secretary General Ong Keng Yong in Beijing. As a result, China and ASEAN drafted a 5-year plan of action (2005–2010) in late 2004. This plan included, inter alia, a joint commitment to increase regular high-level bilateral visits, cooperation in the field of nontraditional security, security dialogue, and military exchanges and cooperation.[20] The plan set out the following objectives:

- promote mutual confidence and trust in defense and military fields with a view to maintaining peace and stability in the region
- conduct dialogues, consultations, and seminars on security and defense issues
- strengthen cooperation on military personnel training
- consider observing each other's military exercises and explore the possibility of conducting bilateral or multilateral joint military exercises
- explore and enhance cooperation in the field of peacekeeping.

ASEAN has been reluctant to advance military cooperation with China too quickly. In May 2004, during the course of a visit to Beijing by Malaysia's newly installed Prime Minister, Abdullah Badawi, his Chinese counterpart, Premier Wen Jiabao, suggested they consider a joint undertaking to maintain the security of sea lines of communication through the Malacca Strait. This proposal was pressed the following month by Senior Colonel Wang Zhongchun from the People's Liberation Army (PLA) National Defense University. In a paper presented to the China-ASEAN forum in Singapore, Wang proposed joint naval exercises and patrols as well as intelligence exchanges on terrorism. According to one analyst, Wang's proposal was received coolly and with considerable skepticism by the audience.[21]

In 2004, China and the ASEAN states became charter members of the Regional Cooperation Agreement on Combating Piracy and Armed Robbery against Ships in Asia, a Japanese initiative that also included South Korea, India, Bangladesh, and Sri Lanka. China later offered modest assistance to build antipiracy capacity among states bordering the Malacca Strait.

In September 2003, Wu Bangguo, chairman of the Standing Committee of the National People's Congress, proposed joint oil exploration and development in areas of overlapping claims in the South China Sea. A year later, premier Wen Jiabao reiterated this proposal at the eighth China-ASEAN summit. Wen called for shelving of disputes "while going for joint development." This led to a major breakthrough in March 2004, when the national oil companies of China, the Philippines, and Vietnam signed a 3-year agreement to conduct joint seismic testing in the South China Sea.[22] The agreement was not renewed in 2008 when it expired.

In July 2005, Hu Jintao reiterated China's call for joint development during the course of state visits to Brunei, Indonesia, and the Philippines.[23] That month, China and ASEAN set up a joint working group on the Declaration on the Conduct of Parties in the South China Sea to recommend measures to implement the agreement. The working group held its second meeting in Hainan in February 2006. In light of deadly pirate attacks on Chinese fishing vessels, in May 2006, China, the Philippines, and Vietnam agreed to strengthen security cooperation in the South China Sea.[24] But few tangible results appeared to follow.

As a measure of the progress in consolidating the China-ASEAN strategic partnership, the first workshop on regional security between officials representing their respective defense departments was held in Beijing in July 2006. China and ASEAN also held a heads of government commemorative summit in Nanning in 2006 to mark the 15th anniversary of China's status as a dialogue partner. By the end of 2006, China and ASEAN had concluded 28 "cooperation framework mechanisms," including regular consultations between senior officials on strategic and political security cooperation, a yearly conference of foreign ministers, and an annual summit meeting of government leaders.[25] These developments provided a foundation for the development of security and defense cooperation.

ASEAN Regional Forum

When China first joined the ARF, it was suspicious of multilateral activities that might curtail its national sovereignty. Over time, however, China has come to embrace multilateral security cooperation under the forum's auspices.[26] China has taken a particularly active role in the ARF's intersessional work program related to confidence-building measures, hosting the group's meetings in March 1997 and November 2003.

In 1997, China sent representatives to the ARF meeting of heads of defense colleges and hosted the meeting in September 2000. The meeting was opened by Defense Minister Chi Haotian, who argued that the ARF's stress on dialogue and consultation represented a "new security concept" and the trend of "multi-polarization" in the region. Chi noted that regional flashpoints still existed, "hegemonism and power politics have shown new traces of development," "democracy and human rights" were being used as pretexts for intervention, and "separatism was gaining ground. All these will endanger or jeopardize the security and stability of the region. That's why we advocate that all countries adopt the new security concept built upon equality, dialogue, mutual confidence and cooperation."[27] In 2000, China also contributed for the first time to the ARF's *Annual Security Outlook* and began providing voluntary briefings on regional security.

While China's participation in the ARF's program of confidence-building measures has evolved over time, its endorsement of preventive diplomacy has been more circumscribed. In a defense white paper issued in late 2000, China provided this cautious assessment:

> China holds that the ARF should continue to focus on confidence-building measures, explore new security concepts and methods, and discuss the question of preventive

diplomacy. At the same time, it believes that the parties concerned should have a full discussion first on the concept, definition, principles and scope of preventive diplomacy in the Asia-Pacific region and reach consensus in this regard.[28]

According to one China analyst, "Two of the defining features of that document [the 2000 Defence White Paper] were the emphasis on the dominance of peace and development as forces driving global development and a corollary imperative toward implementing external policies based upon multilateral cooperative approaches."[29] Since 2000, China has consistently promoted its new security concept as the preferred framework for multilateral cooperation. For example, in July 2002, China presented a position paper outlining its new security concept to the annual ARF ministerial meeting. And in August 2007, at the 14th ARF meeting, China once again pressed its new security concept.

In 2003, China launched a major initiative to further its new concept of security. At the annual ARF ministerial meeting in Phnom Penh, China proposed the creation of a security policy conference comprised of senior military and civilian officials (at vice ministerial level) drawn from all ARF members. The objective of this new security mechanism would be to draft a treaty to promote "peace, stability and prosperity" in the region. Chinese officials said the new treaty would give equal attention to the concerns of all ARF members and guarantee security through united action rather than seeking "absolute security for oneself and threaten[ing] other parties' security."[30] China drafted and circulated a concept paper prior to hosting the first ARF Security Policy Conference in November 2004.[31] Due to reservations by some ASEAN members, no security treaty has been approved.

At the 11th ARF ministerial meeting in 2004, China tabled a series of proposals for the future development of the ARF. These were later summarized as follows:

> To maintain its forum nature and adhere to the basic principles of decision-making through consensus, taking an incremental approach, and moving at a pace comfortable to all member so as to encourage the initiative and active participation of all members; to continuously strengthen and consolidate confidence-building measures

(CBMs) while actively addressing the issue of preventive diplomacy, so as to gradually find out cooperative methods and approaches for preventive diplomacy that are suitable to the region and fitting the current needs; to increase participation of defense officials, promote exchanges and cooperation among militaries of the countries concerned, and give full play to the important role of the militaries in enhancing mutual trust; to highlight cooperation in non-traditional security fields such as counter-terrorism and combating transnational crimes.[32]

China's 2004 defense white paper identified five main areas of international security cooperation: strategic consultation and dialogue, regional security cooperation, cooperation in nontraditional security fields, participation in United Nations peacekeeping operations, and military exchanges. The white paper also set out Beijing's policy on international cooperation in the area of defense-related science, technology, and industry, including the export of military products and related technologies. According to this document, China's exports in this sensitive area were governed by three principles: "It should only serve the purpose of helping the recipient state enhance its capability for legitimate self-defense; it must not impair peace, security, and stability of the relevant region and the world as a whole; and it must not be used to interfere in the recipient state's internal affairs."[33]

The 2008 defense white paper declared, "China attaches great importance to the ASEAN Regional Forum" and noted that in 2007 and 2008, China co-hosted with Indonesia and Thailand, respectively, the ARF roundtable discussion on stocktaking on maritime security issues and the ARF seminar on narcotics control.[34] The white paper also noted with pride that China's draft of the general guidelines for disaster relief cooperation had been adopted by the 14th ARF ministerial meeting. In March 2008, China hosted the first China-ASEAN dialogue between senior defense scholars.

China has also expanded its zone of interaction with Southeast Asia through the ASEAN + 3 (China, Japan, and South Korea) process. In June 2007, China, ASEAN member countries, Japan, and South

Korea held a 5-day workshop on disaster relief by their armed forces in Shijazhuang, capital of Hubei Province.

At the ASEAN + 3 summit in November 2007, China proposed a number of initiatives in the field of nontraditional security cooperation and pressed for institutionalized defense cooperation and military exchanges among its members. In June 2008, China hosted the second ASEAN + 3 workshop on the role of armed forces in disaster relief.

Bilateral Security Cooperation with Southeast Asia

Between February 1999 and December 2000, China negotiated long-term cooperative framework arrangements, generally in the form of joint statements signed by foreign ministers or vice premiers, with all 10 ASEAN members.[35] In the case of Vietnam, an additional agreement was signed between the leaders of the Chinese and Vietnamese communist parties.

Subsequently, several of these long-term cooperative framework agreements have been enhanced through additional joint declarations and/or memoranda of understanding. For example, in April 2005, bilateral relations between China and Indonesia took a dramatic step forward when Presidents Sisilo Bambang Yudhoyono and Hu Jintao issued a joint declaration on building a strategic partnership in Jakarta.[36] At a summit meeting in Kuala Lumpur at the end of the year, China and Malaysia issued a joint communiqué pledging to expand strategic cooperation by promoting the exchange of information in nontraditional security areas, consultation and cooperation in defense and security areas, and military exchanges between the two countries.[37] In April 2006, China and Cambodia issued an agreement on comprehensive partnership for cooperation. In May 2007, China and Thailand signed a joint action plan for strategic cooperation to flesh out their 1999 cooperation agreement. In June 2007, Wen Jiabao told visiting Indonesian Vice President Yusuf Kalla that he hoped the two countries would adopt an action plan on their strategic partnership "at an early date."[38] But it was not until January 2010 that China and Indonesia finally agreed to sign a plan of action.

Key Aspects of China's Security and Defense Arrangements

The following section reviews key aspects of China's bilateral security and defense cooperation arrangements with individual members of ASEAN, including high-level visits, naval port calls, defense MOU, and weapons and technology sales.

Cooperative framework arrangements. Seven of China's long-term cooperative framework agreements (with Thailand, Malaysia, Vietnam, Brunei, Singapore, the Philippines, and Laos) include a reference to security cooperation. The Sino-Thai agreement declared:

> The two sides agree to strengthen security cooperation through confidence-building measures. This will include enhanced cooperation between their strategic and security research institutes, strengthened consultations between their military personnel and diplomatic officials on security issues, exchange between their armed forces of experience in humanitarian rescue and assistance and disaster reduction and exchanges of military science and technology as well as information of all kinds.[39]

In 2004, China dispatched a team of landmine clearance specialists to give a 6-week training course to Thai military personnel and then jointly work with the Thai military in mine clearance along the Thai-Cambodia border.[40]

Security and defense cooperation between China and Malaysia included an exchange program of high-level visits, study tours, seminars, and ship visits. In addition, the two sides pledged to cooperate in training, research and development, and intelligence sharing. Finally, the joint statement made provision for cooperation between national defense industries to include reciprocal visits, exhibitions, and seminars and workshops "to explore the possibility of identifying joint or co-production projects."[41] China and Singapore agreed that "both sides will promote security cooperation by facilitating exchange of high-level visits, dialogue between defense institutions, cooperation between their strategic security research institutes, exchanges between professional groups of their armed forces and exchange of port calls."[42]

The joint statement between China and the Philippines pledged that:

> The two sides agree to make further exchanges and cooperation in the defense and military fields, strengthen consultations between their military and defense personnel

and diplomatic officials on security issues, to include exchanges between their military establishments on matters relating to humanitarian rescue and assistance, disaster relief and mitigation, and enhance cooperation between their respective strategic and security research institutes.[43]

China also offered to fund a Chinese language center in the Philippines and provide five places for Filipino military officers in courses run by the PLA. In September 2002, during the course of a visit by Defense Minister Chi Haotian, China offered to cooperate with the Philippines in "all fields of defense and the armed forces which facilitate stability and development of the region and the world at large."[44] General Chi specifically proposed bilateral military cooperation in training, personnel exchanges, information sharing on counterterrorism, and the provision of military equipment.

The relatively detailed programs of security and defense cooperation just discussed contrast with the Sino-Brunei joint statement that merely expressed "mutual interest in exploring possible cooperation in science and technology and defense."[45] The Sino-Vietnamese joint statement provided for multilevel military exchanges. The 2000 Sino-Lao statement declared that both sides would "further strengthen the friendly exchange and cooperation between the defense institutions and armed forces of the two countries through maintaining high-level exchange of visits and expanding exchanges of experts."[46] In furtherance of the China-Indonesia strategic partnership, in February 2007, China provided Indonesia's Sea Security Coordinating Agency technical assistance (computers, laptops, and printers) for a satellite-linked information early warning system.

High-level visits. China and the 10 ASEAN members conducted 124 high-level defense visits from 2002 to 2008, including 25 at ministerial level. Reciprocal visits by defense ministers were conducted by China with Indonesia, Malaysia, the Philippines, Singapore, Thailand, and Vietnam. China also hosted defense ministers from Cambodia and Laos, while Brunei hosted a visit by the Chinese defense minister.

China conducted its most intense high-level contacts with Thailand. Defense ministers made 3 reciprocal visits in addition to 15 other high-level exchanges for a total of 21. Vietnam ranked second with 18 two-way high-level visits, including 3 ministerial exchanges. Indonesia and the Philippines both exchanged 14 high-level delegations with China, followed by Cambodia with 12. Laos, Singapore, and Burma each exchanged 10 delegations with China, followed by Malaysia (8) and Brunei (7).

Classifying the exchange of high-level military delegations between China and Burma is problematic because members of Burma's government, the State Peace and Development Council, are also field-grade military officers. Their visits have been included in the total. In August 2003, during the visit of army commander Senior General Maung Aye, Guo Boxiong, vice chairman of the central military commission, stated that China viewed military-to-military relations with Burma as a major component of the bilateral relationship.[47] Both Cambodia and Singapore have a marked imbalance in high-level exchanges with China. Cambodia sent three times as many delegations as it received; Singapore sent twice as many high-level officials to China as it received (Chinese participants at the Shangri-la Dialogue were not included in the total). It will be recalled that the joint China-Cambodia statement on long-term relations omitted any reference to security cooperation.[48] Cambodia's exchanges with China picked up markedly after 2006 when the two countries signed an agreement on Comprehensive Partnership for Cooperation.

Naval ship visits and combined exercises. Between 2001 and 2009, China and 9 of the 10 ASEAN states (Laos is landlocked) conducted 21 naval goodwill visits. Chinese warships visited Vietnam (on three occasions), Singapore and Thailand (twice each), and Brunei, Cambodia, Indonesia, Malaysia, and the Philippines. In turn, China hosted port visits from Malaysia, Singapore, and Thailand (twice each), and Indonesia, the Philippines, and Vietnam.

In a new development, China has begun to conduct joint exercises with regional states and has participated in multilateral naval exercises in Southeast Asia. As early as 2002, China invited the Philippines to participate in a naval exercise. This suggestion was reiterated in May 2005 at the first China-Philippines defense and security dialogue. China proposed that the Philippines conduct joint maritime security exercises with the PLA Navy (PLAN) focusing on search and rescue. As of May 2010, Manila had not taken up the offer.

At the invitation of Thailand, in 2002 PLA observers began attending the annual Cobra Gold exercise co-hosted by Thailand and the United States. In June 2005, China proposed extending PLAN port visits to include bilateral exercises. Thailand responded by suggesting it would prefer to participate in a multilateral exercise that included other ASEAN states. Nevertheless, in December of that year, the Royal Thai Navy conducted its first combined exercise with the PLAN involving search and rescue and escort. In July 2007, Thailand and China initiated an annual combined small-scale antiterrorism training exercise involving Special Forces.[49] China and Thailand alternate as hosts. The first Strike 2007 Special Forces exercise was held in Guangzhou.

In April 2006, China and Vietnam commenced biannual joint naval patrols in the Gulf of Tonkin. This was a first for the Chinese navy. In August 2006, after party leaders Nong Duc Manh and Hu Jintao met in Beijing, they issued a joint communiqué noting that "both sides spoke positively of . . . the joint patrol conducted by the navies of the two countries in the Tonkin Gulf."[50] Seven additional joint naval patrols were conducted in the Gulf of Tonkin by late 2009. After a gap of 17 years, PLAN vessels resumed goodwill port visits to Vietnam in November 2008 and December 2009. Vietnam made its first port call to China in June 2009.

In late 2006, China approached individual ASEAN states to suggest combined multilateral naval exercises. In April 2007, defense circles reported that this proposal was under "active consideration."[51] The following month, the PLAN participated in the second multilateral maritime combined exercise under the sponsorship of the Western Pacific Naval Symposium in waters off Singapore.

Southeast Asian attitudes toward Chinese involvement in antipiracy have begun to thaw. In October 2005, for example, during a visit to Beijing, Singapore's Prime Minister Lee Hsien Loong and Premier Wen Jiabao agreed to work closely to meet the threat of terrorism and piracy in the Strait of Malacca.[52] At the China-Malaysia summit held later that year, Malaysia welcomed China's role in enhancing the security of the strait.[53] China offered support in the form of training opportunities, equipment, and information exchanges to build capacity to fight piracy. For example, in July 2007, Indonesia and China announced that they would conduct joint maritime navigation and security operations aimed at security of the Malacca Strait.[54] China later donated computer equipment to Indonesia's Maritime Security Coordinating Agency and invited Indonesian naval personnel to undertake training in China.

Security consultations. China has initiated defense and security consultations with 6 of ASEAN's 10 members. The Sino-Thai defense security consultations are the oldest, having commenced in

December 2001. In November 2004, China and the Philippines inaugurated an annual dialogue in Beijing on defense and security. In 2005, China expanded its circle of defense dialogue partners, beginning defense and security consultations with Vietnam in April and inaugurating a consultative mechanism for defense and security officials with Indonesia in July.[55] China-Malaysia defense consultations commenced in April 2006. At the end of 2005, China reached agreement with Singapore to hold an annual defense policy dialogue at permanent secretary level. However, the first meeting was not held until January 2008.

MOUs on defense cooperation. Between 2002 and 2009, China signed five memoranda of understanding with individual ASEAN members: Cambodia (November 2003), the Philippines (November 2004), Thailand (May 2005), Indonesia (July 2005), and Malaysia (September 2005).

China provided Cambodia with a $10 million loan in late 1997 after Western nations imposed sanctions following the violent political upheaval in July. Cambodia drew on U.S. $2.8 million to purchase Chinese military vehicles. Under the Sino-Cambodian MOU, China agreed to provide military training and equipment for the Royal Cambodian Armed Forces. China also financed the upgrade of an airfield and construction of barracks and officers' quarters. Between 2005 and 2007, Cambodia took delivery of 15 Chinese patrol boats for use by Cambodia's interior ministry in maritime security operations. In a major development, in May 2010 Prime Minister Hun Sen held discussions with President Hu Jintao at the Shanghai World Expo and elicited a Chinese pledge to provide 255 military trucks and 50,000 military uniforms in a package valued at U.S. $14 million.[56] Earlier, in April, the United States suspended its offer to provide Cambodia with 200 military vehicles in protest of Phnom Penh's decision to deport Uygur asylum seekers back to China.

In September 2005, China and Malaysia signed an MOU on defense cooperation covering personnel exchanges and training and an annual security dialogue. Under the terms of the Sino-Filipino MOU, China proposed stepping up military exchanges and cooperation against terrorism, creating a consultation mechanism, and conducting joint military exercises.[57] Members of the armed forces of the Philippines subsequently attended a variety of courses in China including language training, military security management, command, and special operations.

In November 2007, the Chinese and Indonesian defense ministers signed a defense cooperation agreement that included provisions on defense technology sharing, exchange of military students, and arms sales. China also offered billets for Indonesian military personnel in over 20 training courses.

Weapons sales and technology transfer. China's most substantial military relations in the region have been with Burma. In the 1990s, China provided U.S. $1.6 billion in military assistance and trained substantial numbers of military personnel. In particular, China assisted with the modernization of Burma's navy, provided assistance for the construction of naval facilities in Hainggik and Great Cocos Islands, and helped to upgrade the Mergui naval base.[58]

In September 2003, China offered Thailand a loan valued at U.S. $600 million for the purchase of weapons and spare parts. In 2004, it was announced that China would supply Thailand with 96 Chinese armored vehicles in exchange for agricultural produce.[59] In May 2005, the two sides signed an MOU formally outlining the terms of a 3-year barter exchange.[60] In May 2007, China and Thailand signed a joint action plan on strategic cooperation in 15 areas, including defense industry cooperation. In September, Thailand placed an order valued at U.S. $48 million for Chinese C–802 antiship cruise missiles. During the November visit by China's defense minister, discussions were held on the joint missile production.

Under the terms of the 2005 Sino-Filipino MOU, China offered to provide U.S. $1.2 million worth of military engineering equipment to the Philippines.[61] In 2007, China offered the Philippines an additional $1.8 million in military assistance and $6.6 million in grant aid for the purchase of military equipment.

In July 2004, Malaysia and China signed a technology transfer agreement. According to Defense Minister Najib Razak, Malaysia agreed in principle to purchase medium-range missiles from China, which would transfer short-range air defense technology to Malaysia.[62] In furtherance of cooperation in defense technology, the deputy political commissar of the general armaments department visited Malaysia in late 2007.

Security and defense cooperation between China and Indonesia only became possible with the collapse of the New Order in 1998. Diplomatic relations between Jakarta and Beijing, which were severed in 1967, were not restored until 1990. In 2002, Indonesia's defense minister announced he was considering buying military equipment from China. In September of the following year, the secretary general of Indonesia's defense department met with senior Chinese defense technology officials to discuss the sale of military equipment and future cooperation in research and production. Later, Defense Minister Juwono Sudarsono revealed that China initiated an assessment of Indonesia's defense-industrial enterprises at that time, but Indonesia resisted China's request for access to documentation on defense capability development.[63]

In May 2005, Indonesia's state minister for research and technology, Kusmayanto Kadiman, revealed that China and Indonesia would sign an agreement on the development of short-, medium- and long-range missiles during President Yudhoyono's visit to China in mid-2005. According to Kusmayanto, "We are a maritime country, so state defense should start from there. . . . the long-range missile for example could be stationed on small islands or vessels."[64] The minister also indicated that cooperation would take the form of technology transfer under which China would provide one of its missiles for research and study in Indonesia.

In July 2005, during the course of President Yudhoyono's state visit to Beijing, China and Indonesia signed a bilateral MOU on defense technology cooperation. China agreed to provide technical assistance to Indonesia's aircraft and ship-building defense industries and engage in co-production of ammunition, arms, and locally produced missiles with a range of up to 150 kilometers.[65] Cooperation in defense technology was discussed at the first China-Indonesia defense and security consultations in May 2006.

In April 2007, just after China and Indonesia initialed their draft defense cooperation agreement, Chinese ambassador to Indonesia Lan Lijun declared that "China is ready to offer Indonesia military hardware without any political strings."[66] Later that year, China's state-owned armed supplier, NORINCO, and Indonesia's PT Pindad signed an agreement to jointly develop rocket launchers and rockets. After the signing of the China-Indonesia defense cooperation agreement, China's defense minister visited Jakarta in January 2008 and agreed to cooperate in the joint production of military aircraft and transport vehicles. The political commissar of the general armaments department visited Indonesia to move cooperation forward, and a formal agreement was reached in April 2009.

In 2005, Indonesia placed an order valued at U.S. $11 million with China's National Precision Machinery Import and Export Corporation for a small number of YJ–82/C–802 antiship cruise missiles.[67] In 2008, these reportedly were fitted on one of Indonesia's fast patrol boats and successfully test-fired. Late the following year, Indonesia announced that it would place a major order for C–802 antiship missiles for its fast patrol boats and frigates and that a purchase of the smaller C–705 antiship missiles was under negotiation.[68] In January 2010, a Chinese delegation came to Jakarta to discuss further cooperation between their respective national defense industries.

In October 2005, the Chinese and Vietnamese defense ministers tentatively discussed cooperation between their national defense industries. Media reports suggest that NORINCO had provided Vietnam with ammunition for small arms and artillery and military vehicles and assisted in coproduction of ammunition and heavy machine guns.[69]

Timor-Leste, which gained independence in 2002, is not yet a member of ASEAN.[70] In the 2 years following independence, China supplied U.S. $1 million in military assistance including uniforms, tents, and transport vehicles and a further U.S. $6 million for the construction of barracks and officers' quarters. China also funded the participation of member of the Timor-Leste armed forces to undertake professional military educational and training courses in China.

In 2007, defense relations were raised with the signing of Timor-Leste's first major defense contract, which went to a Chinese company to supply eight jeeps mounted with machineguns. In April 2008, Timor-Leste signed a defense contract valued at U.S. $25 million with China's Poly Technologies for the purchase of two modified 175-ton Shanghai class patrol boats, the construction of a landing dock, and training for up to 40 crew members.

China's "Peaceful Development" and Southeast Asia

This chapter has reviewed the enlargement of China's zone of interaction with Southeast Asia since the end of the Cold War. During this period, China has continually engaged with regional states on a bilateral basis through the framework of long-term cooperative agreements. China has avidly worked to promote bilateral security and defense cooperation through a variety of traditional mechanisms including defense MOUs, high-level exchanges, naval ship visits, training programs, modest weapons and technology sales, and regular security consultations. China's "peaceful development" also has been accompanied by a complete turnaround in its view of and participation in regional multilateral organizations. Initially, China was skeptical and suspicious that multilateral institutions would impinge on national sovereignty. Within the space of a few years, China became a strong supporter of the multilateral process and began to play a proactive role.

Sino-ASEAN and Sino-ARF multilateral relations offer China an opportunity to expand its political influence and ability to reshape regional order. In 2003, China consolidated its position with ASEAN by becoming not only the first external power to accede to the Treaty of Amity and Cooperation but also ASEAN's first strategic partner. In late 2004, China hosted the first ARF security policy conference as an alternative to the U.S.-dominated Shangri-La Dialogue.[71] China has been a strong proponent of the ASEAN + 3 grouping over the larger East Asian summit processes that includes India and Australia.[72] China's position was reinforced by the decision of the 16th ASEAN summit held in Hanoi in April 2010 to invite both the United States and Russia to consider joining the East Asian summit.

China's economic growth will continue to provide a firm foundation for its defense modernization.[73] There are two main drivers of this process: the perceived intermediate and long-term challenge posed by the United States and the desire to project power into the western Pacific. Specifically, China's objective of reasserting control over Taiwan has resulted in extraordinary efforts by the PLA to purchase and develop weapons systems to deter the United States from intervening in a Taiwan contingency.[74] China's new defense capabilities will inevitably extend China's military reach into the South China Sea, the Malacca Strait, Southeast Asia, and the Indian Ocean. It is clear that China's growing military muscle has raised anxieties about how China will use its new power to influence Southeast Asia.[75]

Notes

¹ Zhang Xuegang, "Southeast Asia and Energy: Gateway to Stability," *China Security* 3, no. 2 (2007), 18–35, and Zha Daojiong, "China's Energy Security: Domestic and International Issues," *Survival* 48, no. 1 (Spring 2006), 179–190.

² U.S. National Intelligence Council, *Mapping the Global Future: Report of the National Intelligence Council's 2020 Project* (Washington, DC: U.S. Government Printing Office, December 2004), 47–64, and Keith Crane et al., *Modernizing China's Military: Opportunities and Constraints* (Santa Monica: RAND Project Air Force, 2005), xvii–xviii.

³ William H. Overholt, "China and Globalization," testimony presented to the U.S.-China Economic and Security Review Commission (Santa Monica: The RAND Corporation, May 19, 2005). For analyses of the complexity of economic relations, consult Leong and Ku, *China and Southeast Asia: Global Challenges and Regional Challenges*; Chen Wen and Liao Shaolian, *China-ASEAN Trade Relations* (Singapore: Institute of Southeast Asian Studies, 2005); Sheng Lijun, "China in Southeast Asia: The Limits of Power" *Japan Focus*, August 4, 2006; John Ravenhill, "Is China an Economic Threat to Southeast Asia?" *Asian Survey* 46, no. 5 (2006), 653–674; and Saw Swee-Hock, ed., *ASEAN-China Economic Relations* (Singapore: Institute of Southeast Asian Studies, 2007).

⁴ Martin Stuart-Fox, *A Short History of China and Southeast Asia: Tribute, Trade, and Influence* (Sydney: Allen and Unwin, 2003), 73–94. See also David C. Kang, "Getting Asia Wrong: The Need for New Analytic Frameworks," *International Security* 27, no. 4 (2003), 57–85, and David C. Kang, "Hierarchy, Balancing, and Empirical Puzzles in Asian International Relations," *International Security* 28, no. 3 (2003–2004), 165–180.

⁵ Herbert Yee and Ian Storey, eds., *The China Threat: Perceptions, Myths, and Reality* (London: RoutledgeCurzon, 2002).

⁶ For background, see Avery Goldstein, *Rising to the Challenge: China's Grand Strategy and International Security* (Stanford: Stanford University Press, 2005); Frank Frost, "Directions in China's Foreign Relations—Implications for East Asia and Australia," Research Brief, Department of Parliamentary Services (Canberra: Parliament of Australia, December 2005); Milton Osborne, *The Paramount Power: China and the Countries of Southeast Asia*, Lowy Institute Paper 11 (Sydney: Lowy Institute for International Policy, 2006), available at <www.lowyinstitute.org/Publication.asp?pid=370>; and Bronson Percival, *The Dragon Looks South: China and Southeast Asia in the New Century* (Westport, CT: Praeger Security International, 2007).

⁷ Wu Baiyi, "The Chinese Security Concept and its Historical Evolution," *Journal of Contemporary China* 10, no. 27 (2001), 278. Wu is Deputy Director of the Research Department, China Foundation for International and Strategic Studies. See also Michael Yahuda, "Chinese Dilemmas in Thinking about Regional Security Architecture," *The Pacific Review* 16, no. 2 (2003), 189–206.

⁸ Carlyle A. Thayer, "China's 'New Security Concept' and ASEAN," *Comparative Connections: An E-Journal on East Asian Bilateral Relations* 2, no. 3 (2000), 65–75, available at <csis.org/files/media/csis/pubs/0003qchina_seasia.pdf>. For a substantial elaboration, see Bates Gill, *Rising Star: China's New Security Diplomacy* (Washington, DC: Brookings Institution, 2007).

⁹ Carlyle A. Thayer, "China's 'New Security Concept' and Southeast Asia," in *Asia-Pacific Security: Policy Challenges*, ed. David W. Lovell (Singapore: Institute of Southeast Asian Studies, 2003), 90–91.

¹⁰ People's Republic of China, State Council, Information Office, *China's National Defense*, "Full Text of the White Paper on China's National Defense," Xinhua News Agency, July 27, 1998, available at <www.fas.org/nuke/guide/china/doctrine/cnd9807/index.html>. China issued its first white paper on arms control in 1995.

¹¹ The Council for Security Cooperation in Asia and the Pacific is a so-called Track 2 or nongovernmental organization that includes academics from leading regional think tanks and government officials "in their private capacity."

[12] Xinhua News Agency, September 3, 1999, quoted in Thayer, "China's 'New Security Concept' and ASEAN," 92.

[13] Ibid., 91.

[14] Mark Mitchell and Michael Vatikiotis, "China Steps in Where U.S. Fails," *Far Eastern Economic Review* (November 23, 2000), 20–22.

[15] Lyall Breckon, "Beijing Pushes 'Asia for the Asians,'" *Comparative Connections: An E-Journal on East Asian Bilateral Relations* 4, no. 3 (2002), available at <http://csis.org/files/media/csis/pubs/0203qchina_seasia.pdf>.

[16] Sujian Guo, "Challenges and Opportunities for China's 'Peaceful Rise,'" in *China's Peaceful Rise in the 21ˢᵗ Century*, ed. Sujian Guo (London: Ashgate Publishing, 2006), 1–14; People's Republic of China, State Council, *China's Peaceful Development Road*, December 22, 2005, available at <www.chinadaily.com.cn/english/doc/2005-12/22/content_505678.htm>; Bates Gill and Yanzhong Huang, "Sources and Limits of Chinese 'Soft Power,'" *Survival* 48, no. 2 (Summer 2006), 17–36; Jian Zhang, "Building 'a Harmonious World'? Chinese Perceptions of Regional Order and Implication for Australia," *Strategic Insights* no. 35 (June 2007), available at <www.aspi.org.au/publications/publicationlist.aspx?pubtype=6>; and Joshua Kurlantzick, *Charm Offensive: How China's Soft Power Is Transforming the World* (New Haven: Yale University Press, 2007). In the late 1980s, China initially promoted a policy of "good neighborly relations"; see Steven F. Jackson, "China's Good Neighbor Policy: Relations with Vietnam and Indonesia in Comparative Context," paper presented to the 47ᵗʰ annual convention of the International Studies Association, San Diego, March 2006.

[17] Joint Press Release, "The First ASEAN-China Joint Cooperation Committee Meeting," Beijing, February 26–28, 1997, available at <www.aseansec.org/5880.htm>.

[18] In September 2004, China hosted the ASEAN Regional Forum (ARF) Workshop on Drug-substitute Alternative Development, and in March 2005, it hosted an ARF seminar on enhancing cooperation in the field of nontraditional security issues.

[19] "Joint Declaration of the Heads of State/Government of the Association of Southeast Asian Nations and the People's Republic of China on Strategic Partnership for Peace and Prosperity," October 8, 2003, available at <www.aseansec.org/15265.htm>. For an analysis, see Lyall Breckon, "A New Strategic Partnership is Declared," *Comparative Connections: An E-Journal on East Asian Bilateral Relations* 5, no. 4 (2003), available at <http://csis.org/files/media/csis/pubs/0304qchina_seasia.pdf>.

[20] "Plan of Action to Implement the Joint Declaration of ASEAN-China Strategic Partnership for Peace and Prosperity," October 8, 2003, available at <www.aseansec.org/16805.htm>.

[21] Ronald N. Montaperto, "Smoothing the Wrinkles," *Comparative Connections: An E-Journal on East Asian Bilateral Relations* 6, no. 2 (2004), available at <http://csis.org/files/media/csis/pubs/0402qchina_seasia.pdf>.

[22] "Tripartite Agreement on Joint Survey of Seismic Activity in East Sea Signed," Vietnam News Agency, March 14, 2005; Ma. Theresa Torres and Niel Villegas Mugas, "RP, China, Vietnam to Explore Spratlys," *The Manila Times*, March 16, 2005; "China, Vietnam Agree to Joint Exploration of Disputed Areas," Xinhua, Beijing, July 4, 2005; and "China, Philippines, Vietnam Work on Disputed South China Sea Area," Xinhua, August 27, 2005.

[23] Xinhuanet, Beijing, July 19, 2005 in *People's Liberation Army Daily*, July 20, 2005.

[24] Agence France-Presse, "Philippines, China, Vietnam to Cooperate in Spratlys Security," Channelnewsasia.com, May 19, 2006.

[25] Robert Sutter and Chin-Hao Huang, "Chinese Diplomacy and Optimism about ASEAN," *Comparative Connections: An E-Journal on East Asian Bilateral Relations* 8, no. 3 (2006), available at <http://csis.org/files/media/csis/pubs/0603qchina_seasia.pdf>.

[26] Alice D. Ba, "Who's Socializing Whom? Complex Engagement in Sino-ASEAN Relations," *The Pacific Review* 19, no. 2 (June 2006), 157–179.

[27] Xinhua News Agency, September 6, 2000, quoted in Thayer, "China's 'New Security Concept' and ASEAN," 93.

[28] People's Republic of China, State Council, Information Office, *China's National Defense in 2000*, text of White Paper on National Defense in 2000, Xinhua Domestic Service, Beijing, October 16, 2001, available at <www.china.org.cn/e-white/2000/index.htm>.

[29] Ronald N. Montaperto, "Thinking Globally, Acting Regionally," *Comparative Connections: An E-Journal on East Asian Bilateral Relations* 6, no. 4 (2004), available at <http://csis.org/files/media/csis/pubs/0404qchina_seasia.pdf>.

[30] Lyall Breckon, "SARS and a New Security Initiative from China," *Comparative Connections: An E-Journal on East Asian Bilateral Relations* 5, no. 2 (2003), available at <http://csis.org/files/media/csis/pubs/0302qchina_seasia.pdf>.

[31] Dana R. Dillon and John J. Tkacik, Jr., "China and ASEAN: Endangered American Primacy in Southeast Asia," The Heritage Foundation Backgrounder No. 1886, October 19, 2005, 3. The second ARF Security Policy Conference was held in Vientiane in May 2005.

[32] People's Republic of China, State Council, *China's National Defense in 2004* (Beijing: Information Office, December 27, 2004), available at <www.china.org.cn/e-white/20041227/index.htm>.

[33] Ibid.

[34] People's Republic of China, State Council, *China's National Defense in 2008* (Beijing: Information Office, January 2009), available at <http://english.gov.cn/official/2009-01/20/content_1210227.htm>.

[35] These arrangements were variously titled *framework agreement, framework document, joint statement*, and *joint declaration*. For a detailed analysis, consult Thayer, "China's 'New Security Concept' and Southeast Asia," 92–95. For a general overview of China's bilateral relations with Southeast Asia, see Jürgen Haacke, "The Significance of Beijing's Bilateral Relations: Looking 'Below' the Regional Level in China-ASEAN Ties," in *China and Southeast Asia: Global Changes and Regional Challenges*, ed. Ho Khai Leong and Samuel C.Y. Ku (Singapore: Institute of Southeast Asian Studies, 2005), 118–140.

[36] Ronald N. Montaperto, "Dancing with China," *Comparative Connections: An E-Journal on East Asian Bilateral Relations* 7, no. 2 (2005), available at <http://csis.org/files/media/csis/pubs/0502qchina_seasia.pdf>.

[37] Robert Sutter, "Emphasizing the Positive; Continued Wariness," *Comparative Connections: An E-Journal on East Asian Bilateral Relations* 7, no. 4 (2005), available at <http://csis.org/files/media/csis/pubs/0504qchina_seasia.pdf>.

[38] Xinhua, "China, Indonesia to Expand Cooperation," *People's Daily Online*, June 30, 2007, available at <http://id.china-embassy.org/eng/zgyyn/sbwl/t328570.htm>.

[39] "Joint Statement of the People's Republic of China and the Kingdom of Thailand on a Plan of Action for the 21st Century," Xinhua News Agency, February 5, 1999.

[40] Xinhua, "China Helps Thailand Train Landmine Clearance Personnel," *People's Daily Online*, September 8, 2005, available at <www.highbeam.com/doc/1P2-15938272.html>.

[41] "Joint Statement on Framework for Future Bilateral Cooperation between the People's Republic of China and Malaysia," Xinhua News Agency, May 31, 1999.

[42] "Joint Statement on Bilateral Cooperation between the People's Republic of China and the Republic of Singapore," Xinhua News Agency, April 11, 2000.

[43] "Joint Statement Between the Government of the People's Republic of China and the Government of the Republic of the Philippines on the Framework of Bilateral Cooperation in the 21st Century," Xinhua News Agency, May 16, 2000.

[44] Quoted in Ranato Cruz De Castro, "China, Philippines, and U.S. Influence in Asia," American Enterprise Institute for Public Policy Research, July 8, 2007, available at <www.aei.org/outlook/26450>.

[45] "Joint Communiqué between the People's Republic of China and Brunei Darussalam," Xinhua News Agency, August 23, 1999.

[46] "Joint Statement on Bilateral Cooperation between the People's Republic of China and the Lao People's Democratic Republic," Xinhua Domestic Service, November 12, 2000.

[47] Lyall Breckon, "On the Inside Track," *Comparative Connections: An E-Journal on East Asian Bilateral Relations* 5, no. 3 (2003), available at <http://csis.org/files/media/csis/pubs/0303qchina_seasia.pdf>.

[48] "Joint Statement on the Framework of Bilateral Cooperation between the People's Republic of China and the Kingdom of Cambodia," Xinhua News Agency, November 13, 2000.

[49] Xinhua, "China, Thailand Stage Combined Training of Special Troops," *People's Daily Online*, July 16, 2007, available at <www.gov.cn/misc/2007-07/16/content_686577.htm>.

[50] "China-Vietnam Joint Communiqué," Beijing, August 24, 2006.

[51] Robert Karniol, "China Seeks Joint Military Exercise with ASEAN Countries," *Jane's Defence Weekly*, April 25, 2007.

[52] "China to Work with Singapore and Region to Fight Terror and Sea Piracy," Channel News Asia, October 25, 2005.

[53] Sutter, "Emphasizing the Positive; Continued Wariness."

[54] "China, RI look into Joint Maritime Ops," *The Jakarta Post*, July 28, 2007, available at <https://www.thejakartapost.com/taxonomy/term/633?page=127>.

[55] "Chinese Missile Aid for Indonesia," *IISS Strategic Comments* 11, no. 6 (August 2006), 1–2.

[56] Press Trust of India, "China Pledges Military Aid to Cambodia," May 3, 2010.

[57] Rommel C. Banlaoi, "Philippines-China Defense and Military Cooperation: Problems and Prospects," paper presented to the International Conference on the Thirty Years of Philippines-China Relations, Manila, October 22, 2005.

[58] Bruce Vaughn and Mayne M. Morrison, *China-Southeast Asia Relations: Trends, Issues, and Implications for the United States* (Washington, DC: Congressional Research Service, Report for Congress, April 4, 2006), 23–24. China has not established military bases in Burma; see Andrew Selth, *Chinese Military Bases in Burma: The Explosion of a Myth*, Regional Outlook Paper no. 10 (Brisbane: Griffith Asia Institute, 2007).

[59] Thai News Agency, "Military Equipment Barter Deal Bears Fruit," December 14, 2004.

[60] Montaperto, "Dancing with China."

[61] Rommel C. Banlaoi, "Philippines-China Defense and Military Cooperation."

[62] Ronald N. Montaperto, "Find New Friends, Reward Old Ones, but Keep All in Line," *Comparative Connections: An E-Journal on East Asian Bilateral Relations* 6, no. 3 (2004), available at <http://csis.org/files/media/csis/pubs/0403qchina_seasia.pdf>.

[63] "Chinese Missile Aid for Indonesia: How Strategic a Partnership?" *IISS Strategic Comments* 11, no. 6 (August 2005), 1–2.

[64] Antara, "RI, China to Cooperate in Rocket Development," *The Jakarta Post*, May 17, 2005.

[65] Ian Storey, "Progress and Remaining Obstacles in Sino-Indonesian Relations," *China Brief* #5, no. 18 (August 16, 2005), available at <www.jamestown.org/programs/chinabrief/single/?tx_ttnews%5Btt_news%5D=3887&tx_ttnews%5BbackPid%5D=195&no_cache=1>. Some analysts saw this development as Jakarta's response to Australia's decision to acquire long-range air-to-ground missiles; see "Chinese Missile Aid for Indonesia."

[66] Quoted in "China Offers to Open Door to Military Cooperation," *The Jakarta Post*, April 20, 2007, online edition.

[67] Jon Grevatt, "Indonesia Fits Chinese ASM but with an Eye to the West," *Jane's Navy International*, April 22, 2008, and Jon Grevatt, "Indonesia Seeks to Buy Chinese Made Anti-ship Missiles," *Jane's Defence Weekly*, December 23, 2009.

[68] Jon Grevatt, "Indonesia Strengthens Defence Co-operations with China and Malaysia," *Jane's Defence Industry*, January 25, 2010.

[69] *Jane's Defence Weekly*, January 4, 2006.

[70] Data on Timor-Leste was taken from Ian Storey, "China and East Timor: Good, but Not Best Friends," *China Brief* 6, no. 14 (May 2, 2007), available at <http://jamestown.nvmserver.com/122/?tx_ttnews%5Btt_news%5D=3961&tx_ttnews%5BbackPid%5D=196&no_cache=1>

and Ian Storey, "China's Inroads into East Timor," *China Brief* 9, no. 6 (March 19, 2009), available at <www.jamestown.org/programs/chinabrief/single/?tx_ttnews%5Btt_news%5D=34724&tx_ttnews%5BbackPid%5D=459&no_cache=1>.

[71] Chinese attitudes toward participation in the Shangri-La Dialogue changed in June 2007 when China upgraded its representation to the People's Liberation Army deputy chief of staff.

[72] See the emphasis given to these organizations in People's Republic of China, State Council, *China's National Defense 2006* (Beijing: Information Office, December 29, 2006), section one, available at <www.china.org.cn/english/features/book/194421.htm>.

[73] Crane et al.

[74] Office of the Secretary of Defense, *Annual Report to Congress: Military Power of the People's Republic of China 2007* (Washington, DC: Department of Defense, 2006), 30–42; and Ronald O'Rourke, *China Naval Modernization: Implications for U.S. Navy Capabilities—Background and Issues for Congress* (Washington, DC: Congressional Research Service, May 29, 2007), 28–49.

[75] Chien-peng Chung, "Southeast Asia-China Relations: Dialectics of 'Hedging' and 'Counter-hedging,'" in *Southeast Asian Affairs 2004*, ed. Daljit Singh and Chin Kin Wah (Singapore: Institute of Southeast Asian Studies, 2004), 35–53; Denny Roy, "Southeast Asia and China: Balancing or Bandwagoning," *Contemporary Southeast Asia* 27, no. 2 (2005), 305–322; Michael A. Glosny, "Heading towards a Win-Win Future? Recent Developments in China's Policy toward Southeast Asia," *Asian Security* 2, no. 1 (2006), 24–57; and Australian Government, *Defending Australia in the Asia Pacific Century: Force 2030*, Defence White Paper 2009 (Canberra: Department of Defence, 2009).

About the Contributors

Editors

James Clad is Senior Advisor for Asia at the Center for Naval Analyses. From 2007 to 2009, he served as U.S. Deputy Assistant Secretary of Defense for Asia Pacific Security Affairs, prior to which he taught at the National Defense University in Washington, DC, and was Professor of South and Southeast Asian Studies at Georgetown University. His previous career includes positions in Cambridge Energy Research Associates, the New Zealand diplomatic service, the Far East Economic Review, St. Antony's College, Oxford, the Carnegie Endowment for International Peace, and Harvard University. Clad is the author/coauthor of three books.

Sean M. McDonald is an Associate Professor of Geography at Bentley University. Previously, he was an International Trade Specialist with the United States Department of Commerce and Director of the Consortium of American Business Programs in Eastern Europe and the Former Soviet Union. McDonald was a Visiting Professor at Lancaster University, UK, and has guest lectured at numerous other institutions. McDonald is a founding partner of The Additional Group, which trains and advises numerous public and private sector organizations in economic impact assessment and evaluation. He holds a doctorate in geography from Scotland's Glasgow University.

Bruce Vaughn is a Specialist in Asian Affairs with the Congressional Research Service where he works on South Asia, Southeast Asia, and Australasia. He has taught as Adjunct Associate Professor for the Asian Studies Department and the Center for Australian and New Zealand Studies at Georgetown University. Vaughn worked as Senior Defence Analyst at the Embassy of Australia in Washington after completing his Ph.D. at the Australian National University. Vaughn has published articles in *Contemporary Southeast Asia, Geopolitics, Intelligence and National Security, Central Asian Survey, Indian Ocean Review*, and *Strategic Analysis* and is the editor of *The Unraveling of Island Asia? Governmental, Communal, and Regional Instability* (Praeger, 2005).

Contributing Authors

Zachary Abuza is a Professor of Southeast Asian politics and security issues at the National War College. He is a visiting guest lecturer at the Foreign Service Institute, U.S. Department of State, and the Department of Defense Joint Special Operations University. Previously, he was a professor of political science at Simmons College, Boston, and a Senior Fellow at the United States Institute of Peace. He is the author of *Conspiracy of Silence: The Insurgency in Southern Thailand and its Implications for Southeast Asian Security* (U.S. Institute of Peace, 2009); *Muslims, Politics, and Violence in Indonesia* (Routledge, 2006); *Militant Islam in Southeast Asia* (Lynne Rienner, 2003); and *Renovating Politics in Contemporary Vietnam* (Lynne Rienner, 2001). He is a graduate of Trinity College and received his Master of Arts in Law and Diplomacy and Ph.D. from the Fletcher School of Law and Diplomacy, Tufts University.

Richard P. Cronin is a Senior Associate of the Henry L. Stimson Center in Washington, DC. Cronin joined the Stimson Center in July 2005 following a long career as an Asian affairs specialist with the Congressional Research Service. Cronin was a visiting professor of comparative political economy of Asia at the Johns Hopkins University from 1996 to 2002, and he taught comparative economic policy of East and Southeast Asia to government officials in Vietnam and Laos in early 2005. Cronin earned a Ph.D. in modern South Asian history/studies from Syracuse University.

David Lee is Director of the Historical Publications and Information Section of the Australian Department of Foreign Affairs and Trade. He is the General Editor of the *Documents on Australian Foreign Policy* series and has edited volumes on Australia's relations with Indonesia in 1948 and 1949 and on its policy toward the People's Republic of China from 1949 to 1972. He researches on Australian foreign policy in the twentieth century, and his most recent publication is *Stanley Melbourne Bruce: Australian Internationalist* (London: Continuum, 2010).

Rhoda Margesson is a Specialist in International Humanitarian Policy in the Foreign Affairs, Defense, and Trade Division at the Congressional Research Service. Dr. Margesson conducts research and policy analysis on international organizations and global issues, with a focus on humanitarian assistance and intervention, disaster relief, refugees and migration, and some aspects of human rights. Previously, she was an Associate with Harvard's Program on International Conflict Analysis and Resolution and worked in the conflict resolution field on both domestic and international projects. She also held research and teaching fellow positions at the Fletcher School of Law and Diplomacy at Tufts University and Harvard's Kennedy School of Government. Dr. Margesson earned a Master of Arts in Law and Diplomacy and a Ph.D. from the Fletcher School.

Dick K. Nanto is a Specialist in Industry and Trade (senior level) and former head of both the International Trade and Finance Section and the Asia Section at the Congressional Research Service. He works primarily on U.S. international trade and finance and on U.S. economic relations with Asia. He received a Master of Arts and a Ph.D. in economics from Harvard University and a Master of Science degree in national security studies from the National War College.

Patricia O'Brien has been Visiting Associate Professor at the Center for Australian and New Zealand Studies in the Edmund A. Walsh School of Foreign Service at Georgetown University since 2001. Her publications include *The Pacific Muse: Exotic Femininity and the Colonial Pacific* (University of Washington Press, 2006) and the co-authored collection of papers *Amongst Friends: Australian and New Zealand Voices from America* (Otago University Press, 2005). She has written on gender and Pacific empire in various other publications, and her recent work explores Australian colonialism in Papua before World War II and the history of mining in Melanesia. She is a graduate of the University of Sydney.

David Rosenberg is Professor of Political Science at Middlebury College, Vermont, and Visiting Fellow in the Department of Political and Social Change in the Research School of Pacific and Asian Studies at the Australian National University in Canberra. He is also the regional editor for the South China Sea in the WWW Virtual Library of Asian Studies. His recent authored, coauthored, and edited publications include "Piracy and Maritime Crime: Historical and Modern Case Studies," U.S. Naval War College Newport Paper 35 (January 2010); "The Political Economy of Piracy in the South China Sea," *Naval War*

College Review 62, no. 3 (Summer 2009); and "Fisheries Management in the South China Sea," in *Security and International Politics in the South China Sea: Towards a Co-operative Management Regime*, ed. Sam Bateman and Ralf Emmers (Routledge, 2009).

Carlyle A. Thayer is Professor of Politics, School of Humanities and Social Sciences, The University of New South Wales at the Australian Defence Force Academy in Canberra. Professor Thayer has written widely on the domestic politics and international relations of Southeast Asia with a particular focus on Vietnam. He is the author of *The Vietnam People's Army Under Doi Moi* (Diane Publishing, 1994) and *War by Other Means: National Liberation and Revolution in Vietnam* (Harry Ransom Humanities Research Center, 1991), coauthor of *Soviet Relations with India and Vietnam* (Palgrave Macmillan, 1992), and coeditor of *Vietnamese Foreign Policy in Transition* (Palgrave Macmillan, 2000).

Michael Wood is a faculty member in the Humanities Department of Dawson College. He has recently taught courses on the politics of Southeast Asia and on Asia-Pacific foreign policy at McGill University. His research interests include Indonesian nationalism, the use and misuse of historical themes and symbols for purposes of nation-building and regime legitimization, and the place of Islam in Indonesian politics. His publications include *Official History in Modern Indonesia: New Order Perceptions and Counterviews* (Brill, 2005) and "Indonesian Nationalism," in *Nations and Nationalism in Global Perspective: An Encyclopedia of Origins, Development and Contemporary Transitions* (ABC-CLIO, 2008). He holds a Ph.D. from the McGill Institute of Islamic Studies.

www.ingramcontent.com/pod-product-compliance
Lightning Source LLC
Chambersburg PA
CBHW071016280326
41935CB00011B/1380